UNBROKEN BONDS OF BATTLE

★ ★ ★

UNBROKEN BONDS OF BATTLE

★ ★ ★

A MODERN WARRIORS BOOK OF HEROISM, PATRIOTISM, AND FRIENDSHIP

JOHNNY JOEY JONES

UNBROKEN BONDS OF BATTLE. Copyright © 2023 by Fox News Network, LLC. All rights reserved. Printed in the United States of America. No part of this book may be used or reproduced in any manner whatsoever without written permission except in the case of brief quotations embodied in critical articles and reviews. For information, address HarperCollins Publishers, 195 Broadway, New York, NY 10007.

HarperCollins books may be purchased for educational, business, or sales promotional use. For information, please email the Special Markets Department at SPsales@harpercollins.com.

Broadside Books™ and the Broadside logo are trademarks of HarperCollins Publishers.

Image credits: pp. ii–iii © iamseki/shutterstock; pp iv–v © Meysam Azarneshin/stock.adobe.com; pp vi–vii, 159 © Tom Wang/shutterstock; p. viii © New Africa/stock.adobe.com; pp. xii, 97 © subin pumsom/shutterstock; pp. 7, 8 © APChanel/shutterstock; p. 98 © hamara/stock.adobe.com; p. 160 © vladimirfloyd/stock.adobe.com

Photo insert: All images courtesy of individual service members unless otherwise noted.

Endpapers: © hamara/stock.adobe.com

FIRST EDITION

Designed by Nancy Singer

Library of Congress Cataloging-in-Publication Data has been applied for.

ISBN 978-0-06-322608-1

23 24 25 26 27 LBC 5 4 3 2 1

The price of freedom has a name, and a story. Daniel Greer, EJ Pate, Adam Benjamin, Chris McDonald, Jeff McDonald, and so many others perished while defending or after defending our freedom. I dedicate this work and the message it reveals to these eternal sentinels, to whom we are forever indebted. This book isn't just an imperfect memorial for those men but also our best attempt to show what lies ahead—how their legacy lives on through the new lives touched and love given, those who forged unbroken bonds with the best we left behind.

"Son, anything worth your time and sweat is worth doing right. Take the time to do it right the first time. You don't always get a second chance."

—Joseph Edgar Jones, my daddy

CONTENTS

— ★ ★ ★ —

UNBROKEN
BONDS OF
BATTLE

———— ★ ★ ★ ————

INTRODUCTION

Bonds are forged in many ways, much like how battlefields can take many forms. Yes, the deserts of Iraq and the poppy fields of Afghanistan were littered with IEDs and bullets whizzing by, but the land mines laid by our mistakes and choices in life are just as dangerous and come with less training. You might not expect that coming from a guy who actually stepped on an IED, but I believe it.

"Growing up," for me, was a time of learning absurdly simple, yet invaluable lessons. Growing up poor. Growing up in the South. Growing up the son of a brick mason and a house cleaner. Perhaps most importantly, growing up in a big, close family. I learned early to appreciate things, as we couldn't afford many luxuries and had to make what we did have last. We lived in a 1966 single-wide with one 220-volt plug-in. Meaning in the summertime, when the temps neared 100 degrees and humidity made the air feel heavy, we could either use a window-unit AC or have the clothes drying . . . so yeah, my clothes usually dried on a line, and through June often turned yellow from pollen. I learned to love the heat. If the modesty of our homestead didn't force me to learn that, laying brick and block in the July Georgia sun was something you either grew to enjoy or you just lived a tortured existence.

We didn't have the time or money to call a repairman, so you learned to make it, fix it, or have a friend who could. Living poor is a hands-on lifestyle. My dad, the oldest of three sons, was stoic in some ways, and a complete cutup in others. He stood at five feet eight on a good day and his dad, brothers, and I, his teenage son, were all well over six feet tall. Yet he commanded respect from all of us. We all lived next to each other. Worked together, ate meals together, vacationed together, and got through the tough times together, as a family. Above all, we respected him because he had the intellect and patience to learn any skill necessary. He was a mason by trade. Having "graduated" in the eighth grade, he could do long division in his head, but not on paper. He could figure square footage or degrees of slope seemingly by instinct. He could add and subtract in the standard measuring system as easily as units of ten. But we respected him most because of how much he valued two things: hard work and relationships.

My dad had a talent for spouting sage wisdom in extremely simple terms. He once told me, "Son, don't complain about the rain . . . complain about its timing." He had a lot to say about work, too:

"Anything worth doing is worth doing right."

"Take the time to do it right the first time. That's faster than having to redo it."

But his best advice was about people. For all the discipline and perfection that he expected from himself, he taught me the value of having grace and acceptance for others. He once told me, when I was upset that a buddy was avoiding paying me back some money I'd loaned him, "Never loan a friend more money than your friendship is worth." Then, when I told him the excessively high amount of money I'd loaned, he just chuckled and said, "Well, son, as long as someone owes you, you'll never go broke."

He even had such wisdom when it came to dating. My youngest

uncle raced dirt-track late models semiprofessionally, so I spent most weekends at a racetrack helping our family-owned race team successfully compete against teams with much more money. Another driver had three daughters, all close to my age. Going into high school all three had a crush on me and let me know about it.

In my immaturity, I was rude to them collectively. When my dad heard about it, he decided the best course of action was to take me for one of his infamous "loaferin'" rides, which were generally hours longer than advertised and consisted of mostly country roads and silent window-gazing. As a toddler, this was how he got me to sleep when I was pitching a bad fit; as a teenager, it was the only way he knew to start a conversation with me. While we were riding down a dirt road he started abruptly, "Son, be kind to those girls. Even if you don't like them. To have the affection of woman is a gift. You don't have to like them back, but respect that they chose you and that should mean something." I didn't have much to say back; at that early age I was piecing together what it meant to be a man, and he'd just dropped a big dose of wisdom on me. Something I knew was important and could put into practice easily enough, but would take years to truly understand.

His overall outlook on people, relationships, and the eventual bond we share with those in our lives was one of hard-earned perspective and surprising optimism. In simple southern terms he was usually described by those who knew him as the kind of man who would "give a stranger in need the shirt off his back." He knew from a life of manual labor and struggle what I myself would learn as a Marine: the bond we share with those who choose to be in our lives can be one of lifelong commitment to one another. Such a bond can't be forced, but it is worth the effort. Or in my dad's words, "Nothing worth your effort comes easy, and anything worth doing is worth doing right."

These days, it seems we live in a society that's lost touch with itself. We socialize online, we date through cattle-car apps, making huge determinations of a person's worth with a glance and swipe. We order food to be delivered, attend church in our living rooms, and "working from home" is an ever more popular occupation. As a populace we've traded necessary human bonds for efficiency and convenience. Likewise, when veterans returned home from the last long war, Vietnam, their goals were simple but huge. Marry the homecoming queen, take over Dad's hardware store, buy that house on Main Street and start a family. To most veterans coming home from our war, those goals are too small, yet that big, beautiful world we're accessing online leaves little more than detachment and loneliness in our lives.

However, for many people in this book, the military provided a lifeline out of that loneliness. Choosing to serve offers people a path to a chosen family, an interwoven network of brothers and sisters who will have your back in adversity. Not the family one is born into, but blood brothers nonetheless. Not because they have the same blood in their veins, but because they've spilt blood on faraway battlefields for the same purpose. It's a family that's one phone call away for the rest of your life. The military offers an escape from an alienated society to one built on lifelong bonds.

When Amos Benjamin's older brother was killed in action, he found his brother's friends coming around him for support, rallied by their commanding officer, Greg Wrubluski. Greg himself had found a family in the Marines when his own relatives didn't bother showing up.

That same give-and-take is true of so many stories in this book. Lacy Gunnoe discovered how ennobling it could be to teach young people to have the self-belief he didn't possess growing up in a small town in West Virginia.

I don't know that he'd have put it that way, but that was the way my dad thought about people. He knew bonds weren't something you forged lightly or threw away cheaply.

As a Marine, those bonds became more than merely shared circumstance or convenience. The bonds we make on the battlefield can remain unbroken if we let them. I left home a lost, naïve-to-the-world, and relatively inexperienced eighteen-year-old. It was only through the unselfish efforts and genuine concern of friends who became family that I was able to survive all the adversity war and life threw at me. And it was with their faith and mentorship I learned to thrive after it. What constitutes a bond comes in many forms. Some, like my two high school best friends, Chris and Keith, who also joined the Marine Corps and Army, respectively, are obvious. But others were nameless faces who, in a moment, remind us how small the universe is and how significant we are in it. Like the nurse at the US Army hospital in Landstuhl, Germany, in 2010 who looked at me without hesitation as I awoke from sedation to see that my legs had been amputated and arms mangled and said firmly, "Don't worry, hon, you'll walk again." Her words, showing blind faith, motivate me to this day.

In the following chapters, I offer the sometimes tragic, often inexplicable, and consistently heroic stories and shared experiences of some of those who have left a permanent mark on my own life. These are the warriors, heroes, and humble Americans who have learned firsthand the powerful nature of those "unbroken bonds of the battlefield," and it is my honor to share them with you.

BAND OF BROTHERS

Not that I want to there to be situations where people are struggling and dying, but to be in a place where you feel like everything you do matters, and it does, is special. We were fighting for those who can't fight for themselves. So to share that experience with others, that's a very rare thing.

—*Nate Boyer*

It said a lot to me that all these people in boot camp were willing to set aside their differences and unite themselves for a common cause.

—*Greg Wrubluski*

I made a deal with God. All I ask is that you don't take me in front of my brothers.

—*Jacob Schick*

The Burden of Command

MAJOR, COMPANY COMMANDER (RET.) GREG WRUBLUSKI

★ United States Marine Corps ★

"I don't know if they know
it. They're like sons to me.
They're like brothers to
me. That's my family."

I think it's summed up in two words: I care. I care about my Marines. And I'm sure they do, too. There are a lot of Marine officers. You know, I'm not disparaging other people. But no, I fucking care about all of these guys. Like, I don't care about what happens to me, I don't care about my career, I don't care about anything as much as I care about these guys. That's it.

The ironic thing is, I didn't want to lead an EOD Company. I didn't want to be a company commander. I had a great job already. I had the best job in the Marine Corps, Explosive Ordnance Disposal, you could possibly have. I was with the 2nd Marine Special Operations Battalion. I had eight guys working with me. I had all the money I could ever want to buy whatever they needed. I couldn't have had a better job. And I got a phone call from someone saying to me, "Hey, they really need help at Second EOD Company."

I was thinking, You're out of your mind. I'm not going there.

But he was persistent and said, "They really need help. You sleep on it."

So, I said, "Yeah? I'm gonna make some phone calls then."

He added, "They got some really good guys over there, but they're about to leave for new assignments and they need leadership."

I did what I said I would do. I made some phone calls. I thought about it. I thought about the reason why I became an officer to begin with. It came down to this: "Hey, this is what you did this whole thing for. And now you're gonna turn around on that because you have this cushy job over at MARSOC [Marine Forces Special Operations Command] and not step up? This is why you are here. This is why you went through all the things you did. Put up or shut up." That's how I ended up over there.

I called back the next day and said, "I'll take the company."

★★

I first met Greg at Walter Reed National Military Medical Center in Bethesda, Maryland, in 2011. I was freshly recovering from my injuries a year earlier and he was just back from Afghanistan, and was at the Navy hospital in Bethesda visiting the Marine EOD techs injured under his command. Greg was their commanding officer, their leader, and they had just endured one of the deadliest deployments in Marine EOD history. I quickly learned that Greg was the kind of leader who would only ask of his Marines what he himself had done and was willing to do. Good leaders know their subordinates well, but great leaders have walked in their shoes. The community of Marine EOD or bomb technicians is a small and very specific group made up of Marines who all have certain things in common. Every EOD tech comes into the field having already enlisted (no commissioned officers are allowed in) as some other job and has spent years in the Corps doing it; they are either single or have written permission from their spouse to partake in such a dangerous job; and most importantly, they have chosen this job for themselves. No Marine is forced to do it. In short, every Marine who becomes an EOD tech did so because they wanted to and worked hard to earn it. The underlying culture of bomb disposal is one of mandated humility. The goal is to weed out glory-seekers, because such motivations lead to reckless decisions, which in turn often lead to people getting hurt or killed. The men and women who earn this occupation within the Marine Corps first prove their selflessness and dedication before even their brazen courage or steady nerve. Major Greg Wrubluski (Ret.) is no exception to the rule.

Greg was born in North Carolina but raised in Jacksonville, Florida, as he'll often remind you by sending a "Duuuuvvallll" text (referring to Duval County, Florida) when something good happens in North Florida sports. One of the formative experiences in his life was when his parents divorced when he first started high school. The middle child, with an older brother who was off to college and moving in a new direction and a younger sister whom he didn't want to burden with his feelings, Greg did what a lot of intellectually smart and emotionally developing kids do—he chose to shut himself off in response. He didn't confide in teachers or coaches or friends. He just sucked it up and moved on. Getting out and getting away was the way forward for Greg. He figured if he could just isolate himself, then things would go his way.

That picture—of a man who shut himself off—is a far cry from the man who defines himself by how much he cares. Greg is that rare Marine who rose through the ranks from an enlisted man to officer, what we refer to as a "mustang." From parachute rigger to enlisted EOD technician to EOD officer to Special Operations Command and then that crucial period as the commander of an EOD until wearing the rank of Major is a steep climb. What makes Greg special is that while his rank changed from black chevrons to gold oak leaves, the type of man and Marine he is didn't.

The price you pay for leading, and caring and staying true to who you are and what you believe about yourself can sometimes be high. But because you did all those things and you are all those things, other people step up and try to follow the example you set and let you know that they care, not just about you but also about the way you do the job.

We have inherent bonds and responsibilities as Marines and EOD techs. We accept and live true to the idea that our job is to take the risk and potentially sacrifice ourselves for the oftentimes nameless and faceless men and women around us, be they Marines we're supporting, the local population, or the brothers and sisters we work alongside. The commitment to sacrifice is consistent. However, when you're defending brothers downrange, people you've spent years getting to know and love and work with, that's the kind of bond you can only earn on the battlefield, the kind that a peer-turned-commanding-officer like Greg feels for a lifetime.

★★★★★★★★★★★★★★★★★★★★★★★★★★★★★★★★★★★★★

CALL OF DUTY

Middle school into high school were pretty rough years. I was basically on my own. My mom was doing the best she could and my dad was pretty much nonexistent. I was doing a kind of fend-for-yourself kind of thing. I was going to high school, playing football, and trying to help out at home by working until two or three in the morning unloading trucks at a grocery store as a sixteen-year-old. I was fortunate that I was a pretty good football player because that earned me a chance to play at a prestigious private school in Jacksonville. The Bolles School was an athletic powerhouse; their swimming and diving program won national championships, and their football team won about thirteen state titles.

As a private school, they could kind of "recruit" students, and I was among a couple of the rednecks they brought in along with a few African American kids. There's nothing wrong with how Bolles or other private schools are, but I just didn't fit in at first as a public school kid who'd never seen a high school parking lot filled with expensive cars—and they weren't driven by the faculty. But at least the few of us on the football team who couldn't afford those kinds of cars stuck together and hung out the entire time we were there. It took some getting used to, being in that environment. At one point the school had been a military academy. They'd dropped that affiliation, but they kept some remnants of it. We had to wear dress shirts and ties. I got mine at Marshalls and the rest of them wore rep ties they got from . . . This shows you how different we were in some ways. I can't even name a high-end department store where they might have shopped.

But there were some guys who welcomed us, too. It just took a while for those relationships to develop. I do remember once we started going to house parties hearing some people saying to whoever was hosting it, "Hey, aren't you afraid that one of them is going to steal something?" I heard that and thought, Can you be serious? Steal something from you?

In a way, it was kind of like being in a teen comedy movie about rich kids and kids from the other side of the tracks. But I didn't resent the fact that any of them had a lot of money and didn't have to work like I did or seemingly had it easy.

One of the things that stuck with the school in its transition from military academy to private school was the demerit system. You got points deducted for being tardy, talking, and more serious offenses. If during any particular week, let's say the limit was seven demerits, then you had to go to Saturday school. Usually by midday Monday, my plans for Saturday were set for me. So, going to school six days a week became my routine. I wasn't doing anything really serious to get in trouble, just general goofing off. Having that group of guys who were outsiders like me made it all bearable.

Eventually I graduated. But I was pretty directionless. I had wanted to continue to play football, and I got a few scholarship offers from some small schools, but I realized that I was a small guy. I was five ten or so and weighed 170 pounds, so I was realistic about my chances of playing even at that level. I had liked playing football, defense in particular, because I took out some of my aggression in hitting people, but that wasn't going to get me to the NFL or anything like that. So I tried college for a while, but that didn't last.

I got a job framing houses. It was a paycheck, a steady one, but I came to a crossroads after a while. I didn't have much else going on in my life. The work was okay, but if it rained and we couldn't do the job, I didn't get paid. If the guy who ran the crew got drunk the night before and didn't show up, we didn't get paid for that lost time, either. One night I was sitting on a roof drinking a few beers and my brother called me up. He was still up in Valdosta, Georgia, going to college. He started telling me about his roommate who worked as a Marine Corps recruiter. He said that maybe I should join the Marines. I said, "Fuck off. Are you out of your mind?" He kept saying that I should and giving me reasons why, but I kept thinking that if I didn't fit in at Bolles and got demerits all the time because I didn't like following rules and resented authority figures, what was going to happen once I joined the Marines?

I told my brother again that he was out of his mind and hung up. I told my buddies about the call and they were like, "You can't do that. That's stupid. Don't do it."

Then I guess the contrarian in me started thinking that maybe I should. What the hell? It's four years. So, I did a real deep analysis of my situation. Actually, I just fell asleep, but the next morning, I called my brother and then talked to the recruiter. I told him I was in. He said great and then asked me when. I told him right now. This was in November 1993. The day after Thanksgiving I was on a bus to Parris Island in South Carolina for boot camp.

I had no idea what to expect. I didn't talk to anybody about what life in the military was like. I had a grandfather who'd been in the Navy, but he died when I was pretty young, and we never talked about his service. I went into this whole thing blind. Zero preparation. Zero expectations. But I do remember going with the recruiter back to

Bolles School to get my transcripts. The women in the office had this look on their faces, kind of like, it's about time someone is going to whip this boy into shape.

I guess my being completely unprepared isn't strictly true. I had been given some pamphlets when I enlisted. I read those. And when I was younger, I was an avid reader and I'd read a bunch of books back then about Marines in Vietnam and in World War II in the Pacific Theater, island hopping. But that was reading. That wasn't living it, and on that bus was really when I started living it.

Things hit home for me on that ride to Parris Island. At one point we stopped in Hardeeville, South Carolina. The bus driver pulled up in front of a Hardee's restaurant and said, "You might want to take advantage of this. This is your last chance for a decent meal."

That's when it hit me that there was no turning back. We're doing this thing. I spent my last eight bucks and bought a fried chicken dinner. I think I might have eaten a bite or two. I was too nervous. The anticipation of it was too much. I knew enough about the Marines to understand what Parris Island was all about. Only I didn't. The first few moments and hours were kind of chaotic and then for the first few days I was thinking, What have I done? I've got four years of this shit? Are you nuts?

And then I started thinking, Well, okay, you've got a roof over your head. You don't get to sleep a whole lot? You're getting yelled at all the time. You're getting knocked around a little bit. Who cares? I was in decent shape because framing houses is physical labor. I'd even started to run a bit.

My life up to that point had been pretty chaotic and I'd responded to that with rebellion. But instead of rebelling against the regular and regimented nature of things at Parris Island, I just went with it. I wasn't fully aware of the whole "we'll break you down and create a new you" kind of thing. But some of what was being stressed has stuck with me to this day, little things like I still make my bed every morning in the way that I learned to do it in the Marine Corps. As much as anything else, I felt more at home there than I did back when I was in high school.

We were all stripped down and given the same clothes and had the same haircut. So everybody was looking at everybody else and nobody knew who came from what and if the guy next to you had a million dollars or a penny in his pocket. And it didn't matter where you came from or how much you had or didn't have, because you were going to be treated just the same as everyone else. You were going to rise or fall based on what you did, how you performed. The other big thing early on was that every single one of us was going to go through a miserable time. We were going to do it together, and whatever other barriers there might be, what other differences there were among us, those things were basically gone.

It said a lot to me that all these people in boot camp were willing to set aside their differences and unite themselves for a common cause. Along the way, I met guys like Sangki Oak, who was a Duke University graduate and Silicon Valley software engineer when he quit to enlist. We're in the middle of Afghanistan getting hammered by machine-gun fire. And I'm thinking, What's this guy doing here? He could potentially lose his life. And that guy could be doing anything else with his life, but he chose to be there. And he's out there serving next to people like me. And that started at boot camp at Parris Island and continued throughout my time in the military. People from all kinds of backgrounds came together to serve. Sangki's a surgeon now.

While I didn't form lasting friendships, boot camp did mean I forged a real deep and lasting bond with the institution. After boot camp, we scattered to the winds. The first four years of my enlistment, I'd occasionally come across someone I knew from one period or assignment or another, but not regularly. The percentage of people that stay in longer than four years is pretty small. At the time my choices about what to do were limited by the number of spaces available in any one area.

The next thing I did came along after an unexpected conversation. After basic, I did infantry training, and someone came in the room one day and said, "Hey, does anybody want to jump out of airplanes?" Nobody raised their hands. Then they said, "It pays an extra $110 a month." I thought that was a good deal, so I took it. There was no this-is-a-dream-of-mine-that-I-have-to-fulfill mentality for me. I was still thinking about just getting to that four-year deadline, and if I could pocket more money along the way than I thought initially, so be it. Plus I had a daughter on the way, and I wanted to support my family as best I could.

So that's the inspirational story of how I became a parachute rigger. I was a parachute rigger for two years. I'd done one year in Okinawa, Japan, and then I was back in the US at Camp Pendleton, in Southern California. It was okay, but after a while I started to feel like I had to do something else. I was two years into my four-year commitment. One night we were doing jumps. Along with jumping out, we packed for some guest jumpers. We had some staff sergeants there who were jumping with us to keep their qualifications. Afterward, we were all sitting around drinking beers, and I was saying to everyone that I really needed to find something else to do. I had to change jobs. One of the staff sergeants said that I should come over and join EOD. I didn't know what that meant. He explained that it was Explosive Ordnance Disposal. Okay, so what does that mean? What do you guys do?

They told me that they disarm bombs.

Okay. Sounds good.

I went to their shop the next day for an interview. The next thing I knew they were getting my package ready so that I'd have all the paperwork done to transfer over. (A Lateral Move Package is a comprehensive paper record of you and your career performance that is sent to United States Marine Corps headquarters for them to approve or deny a Marine switching from one job to another within the USMC.) One night I didn't even know what EOD was, and the next I'm interviewing and on my way. I don't think that I was alone in the Marines or in the general public in my ignorance about EOD teams. This was in 1998, well before we all heard about improvised explosive devices (IEDs) and hurt lockers. What struck me was that the guys in the unit all seemed to get along well. They all seemed to be having fun, too. So that interview was a very positive experience, and I did my EOD technician training and was stationed at Camp Lejeune, North Carolina.

In my first couple of years with the EOD guys, I developed some good friendships. It was different from my first assignment because of the nature of the work. You can be in garrison or you can be downrange in combat. Ordnance is ordnance and it's live no matter where you're at. We all knew that our lives were in one another's hands. As a result, we put a special premium on the times we had together. That was important to us, and even though we might not have expressed any of those sentiments out loud, we understood that. Each of us knew that, hey, when it's time to go do our jobs, it's serious—life-or-death serious. For the time in between deployment, we need to practice and prepare. I took the job seriously and I committed to going beyond my original four years.

In September 2001, I was deployed with the 24th Marine Expeditionary Unit and I was listed with the 2nd Force Recon Company Direct Action Platoon. We were in Kosovo as part of a peacekeeping force of the North Atlantic Treaty Organization (NATO). I don't remember all the code and lingo associated with the message we got, but it was essentially this: The sky has fallen. Stop everything. Get back to base. We walked back to camp a few miles away and were then told what had happened. Two planes had crashed into the World Trade Center.

That was definitely a paradigm shift for all of us.

LEADERSHIP THAT CARES

It's funny what motivates you and how your life can turn on a dime. I enlisted quickly. I committed to EOD quickly. I was a pretty good Marine, but I remember one thing happening to me that really got to me and made me want to be better. I once had an officer put in a fitness report on me. A fitness report is one of the primary ways that leadership can evaluate whether a Marine should be promoted. There was an error in it, marking me low in a performance category. I knew that was impossible, because I had received some minor commendation during the observation period. So I caught it. I went into his office to point this error out. If I let it stand and it was on my record, there could be consequences down the line. It would have set me behind my peers in relation to promotion to the next rank (staff sergeant at the time).

But he told me that it wasn't an error. He did it on purpose. He wanted to be sure that I read the report on me. I was thinking, What kind of leader does something like that? Does he believe that I don't have enough respect for myself and my future that I wouldn't even read the thing?

I wondered about that kind of leadership, where he played tricks and mind games. At the time, this unit I was with wasn't in the best shape. We didn't have any of the equipment we really needed to do our training. I thought that was a function of this person in command, who didn't do everything he could to make sure that this unit excelled. It seemed to me that he didn't care enough. I decided that

I could be assigned to a unit like that, that I could be made to serve under a leader like that, but I didn't have to *be* like that. I decided I was going to really throw myself into this job. I was not going to just sit around and bitch about how bad things were; I was going to do what it took to make things better. I wasn't going to be among the guys who were drinking beer and playing volleyball at 11 a.m. because we didn't have the right things we needed to train properly.

I was a lance corporal for forty-two months. People used to joke around about that a lot. That's an eternity to be a lance corporal, a whipping boy in the Marine Corps. Forty-two months of being treated like absolute shit. That incident over the fitness report was when I decided that I was going to become an officer. I was going to buckle down, bust my ass, and, even more important, when I became an officer, I was never going to treat a Marine the way I'd been treated by that officer. There were some other officers who looked down on enlisted men. I wasn't ever going to do that.

It wasn't like I was a bad Marine and that kept me from getting promoted. There just weren't enough openings. Because I'd spent so long being a whipping boy, I wanted to become the voice of the little guy like me. I was going to scream that to the high heavens. I didn't care if what I said or did would affect my ability to advance my career. I didn't care about myself; I cared about the other Marines. I didn't care about awards or citations or medals. I didn't care about Marine protocols. Period. I didn't care about all that and I was going to say what was on my mind and speak the truth. I will say anything to any-body to ensure that my Marines get taken care of and we have what we need to do the best job possible. I'm going to stand up for the people who don't have a voice and not be so concerned about chain-of-command factors that I put chains on my guys that drag them down, make their jobs more difficult, and put anyone in harm's way to a greater degree than what they choose to do themselves. When I became an officer, I told myself, I was going to be a lance corporal in an officer uniform.

That's what I did. It wasn't always easy going for me, but by 2004 I was an EOD officer and in 2006 I was deployed as such in Iraq.

★★★★★★★★★★★★★★★★★★★★★★★★★★★★★★★★★★★★★

Greg had also deployed in 2002 in support of a government agency to an undisclosed location for Operation Enduring Freedom and in support of 3rd Battalion 6th Marines to Afghanistan in 2003. In the first case because of the nature of the assignment, he's not at liberty to discuss what took place.

★★★★★★★★★★★★★★★★★★★★★★★★★★★★★★★★★★★★★

STAYING TRUE TO MY ROOTS

Something that's unique to Marine EOD is that all officers are prior enlisted EOD guys. We're all grown from within. When I came to EOD, I was working with a bunch of enlisted Marines just like me, who had been my friends. So the transition to officer and being in charge of guys you're friends with is a tricky one. You have to walk a fine line, and I think that everyone understood that there were rules and regulations that had to be adhered to. That's understandable. So, one day I'm an enlisted guy like them and the next I'm an officer. But that doesn't evaporate the friendships that you have and the bonds that you've built.

Also, for me at least, it was important to remember my roots as an enlisted man. When I got promoted to major, a formation was held. A bunch of people from the battalion all show up for the ceremony where you get your leaves pinned on you or whatever. You're also given the opportunity to say a few words to this pretty large assemblage of people, including quite a few of the higher-ups. My entire EOD company was there to support me, and I decided that I needed, and wanted, to send a message to them. During my very brief remarks I said, "Chalk one up for the lance corporals of the World." I heard a lot of hooting and hollering at that. I also got an earful later from command, saying that I had exhibited behavior that wasn't very becoming of an officer. I had crossed a line, but I didn't care. All the regular Marines loved it and that mattered more to me than the fact that a lot of the regular officers were infuriated. I had to be true to myself.

One of my good friends was an outstanding Marine named Adam Benjamin. He was also an outstanding human being. Master Sergeant Benjamin operated out of Camp Lejeune and was killed in action while serving as an EOD tech in Afghanistan's Helmand Province in August 2009. His loss was devastating to his family and to our close-knit EOD community. At the time, I also knew his younger brother Amos, who was just beginning his career in the Marines and is covered in another chapter of this book.

Adam was being a good older brother and bringing Amos around to the EOD shop. On the day I learned of Adam's death, I thought, We have to take care of Amos now. His brother's gone, but he's got all of us. He's still welcome here. He's one of us even if he is still a grunt. The kid needs a place where he can go and hang out and get away or find a place where he belongs. That was true in 2009, and it's true now in 2023. Amos is one of a group of guys with whom I'm still in regular contact. It's not that he needs to rely on the others and me all the time; he provides support and kicks in the ass to others as needed. Like I said, there are lines between us when we serve, but we get to decide just how thick they are and how much they separate us. When needed, we erase those lines completely. When it comes to dealing with grief, with loss, with frustration, with injury, with mental health issues, there's no distinction between enlisted and officers. There are just people who need help and people who want to help. A lot of the time, you're both things simultaneously.

One of my very close friends, though, was among that group I'd grown up with in EOD. Ralph "EJ" Pate and I had been friends for quite a while. He was the ultimate wild man, a fun sumbitch to go out and about in town with. I was in a bad marriage at the time and needed to get out, get time away from it all, and he was always ready to assist with that task. It helped that he was also really easy to talk to and funny as hell. He could help you get your mind off things or listen to you until you got your own head out your ass. Whatever you needed, he was there. It didn't matter what time or what the circumstances were: if he saw something that needed to be done, he'd do it. And he cared about people. He cared about Marines.

I'll tell you a story about that. On one deployment together we were out working in support of a group of Marines. We were taking a break while out on patrol one day. We were tired, just wanted a break. But there was a new guy with us. His brand-new, shiny metal detector was about as clean as his freshly creased uniform was. And this young guy was walking around with the metal detector practicing with it. Neither bore a speck of dirt. EJ turned to me and said, "That replacement is not working that thing right." My buddy got up and walked over to the young kid and asked him how things were going.

"Pretty good. Pretty good."

"Well, we need to get you from pretty good to excellent real quick."

For the next twenty minutes, instead of taking a break, drinking some water, downing some food, or just resting, EJ gave that kid a class on metal detecting that would hopefully keep a lot of guys safe and their legs intact. And let me tell you, humping all that gear and working that metal detector wasn't the easiest lifting in the world. But

THE BURDEN OF COMMAND

he knew what needed to be done, and rest be damned, he was going to do the right thing. That's the kind of guy he was.

I have a hard time still, more than a decade later, using the past tense in talking about him.

★★★★★★★★★★★★★★★★★★★★★★★★★★★★★★★★★★★★★★★

In that unit Greg commanded were several of my close friends I'd gone through EOD school with. My closest friend, Danny Ridgeway, and our buddy Johnny Morris were among them, just to name a few. That deployment didn't leave them unscathed. Danny went through protocols for a traumatic brain injury and Johnny Mo lost a foot to an IED. As the years passed I lost touch with Greg, but I stayed in close contact with many of our shared friends. I heard rumors that Greg had struggled getting past the loss of his Marines, had unceremoniously retired, which was strange for such a storied career, and wasn't in a great place.

In 2018 I was working in Georgia at Camp Southern Ground and recruiting veterans to participate in a pilot program I'd helped design. The program sought to help post-service veterans in their transition. I got Greg's number and gave him a call. Two hours later I knew more about him and the responsibility of true leadership than I'd known in all the years previous. For the next few years Greg and I grew closer. I invited him on hunting trips with our shared friends and we had more phone calls sharing more personal details about what we both struggled with after war and even some things we struggled with growing up. When my dad died suddenly in my arms in late 2019, Greg was quick to remind me how lucky I was to have had him for thirty-three years of my life and that I was there to hold his hand and say goodbye. It was something perhaps only Greg could point out to me given his absent father and the fact he met too many Gold Star families who didn't get that chance to say goodbye. I took his words to heart, and it helped me grieve.

On his last deployment, in Afghanistan as commanding officer of 2nd EOD company, Greg had a hard job. He had a daily average of 154 total Marines and 4 Navy corpsmen for a total company of 158. This swelled at times to a total of 170. Of these, 124 were EOD technicians and officers. But those techs were scattered in two- and three-man teams at fifty-four locations and some other special positions throughout the 22,000 square miles of Helmand Province for which they were responsible. So he was both working as a team leader himself, taking IEDs apart, but also as the higher-level boss for all the other teams while all were getting hit by IEDs regularly. That required a huge amount of commitment and composure.

★★

PROJECTING CALM UNDER FIRE

In the late spring of 2011, shortly after I decided to leave my job at Marine Forces Special Operations Command (MARSOC) to take over the 2nd EOD Company, we got word that we were being deployed to Afghanistan. About six weeks before we were scheduled to deploy, I decided to hold a meeting for the entire unit, including wives and significant others. I'd been fielding a lot of phone calls from spouses and other family members because word had it that we were going into Afghanistan again. They all had seen the news about how intense things were back then. They didn't know where we were going exactly, but they could put the pieces of the puzzle together. Their concerns were heightened, and were justified. They also figured out that a deployment was coming up because their family member wasn't around at home as much as usual when we were garrisoned. We had to work very hard in preparation, and for those family members for whom this wasn't their first rodeo, they figured things out.

So I arranged it so that entire company could be there. We had food, drinks, and things for everybody. After that, I stood up and told them that I couldn't lie to them. You know what's going on. You know what's at stake. So, I'm going to promise you this: I'm going to do everything I can to bring every Marine home. But if something happens to any one of you, you have my word that I will stay by their side, if I'm able, from the time they're injured until the time they get flown out to Germany. I will do everything I can to keep in touch with you and keep you updated on what's going on. I will not leave your side. I will not leave their side. I will not leave anyone alone. You have my word on that.

In 2011, we were gone for seven months. I made good on that promise. That was one of the most dangerous deployments we'd been through together. I spent more than twenty nights at field hospitals. I stood by the bedsides of men with gunshot wounds, some with catastrophic wounds from ordnance. It didn't matter what, didn't matter if they were conscious, asleep, awake, or if they knew I was there and acknowledged it or not. I kept my promise. I sat there by their bedside with a satellite phone in my pocket, and I'd get up every now and then, go outside the room, the unit, and call their wives to let them know what was going on.

I had their backs, just like they had the backs of every other guy in those units. I would have done that for any group, but for 2nd EOD Company, it was a way of acknowledging the extraordinary bonds that they had developed with one another. The level of camaraderie, the chemistry, the caring that they'd shown for one another was off the charts. This was a special group of guys. That's why I had no apprehension whatsoever in those weeks before we deployed to get them all together with one another and with one another's families. We all had to trust one another, and regardless of the potential consequences or how anyone else might have handled that situation, I had to stay true to myself and show how much I cared. I really believe in and tried to live out that we're Marines. Together, not above you, alongside you.

I had put myself in their shoes. I sensed that morale was getting a bit low. I knew that everyone was apprehensive. I had to acknowledge the reality of what we were facing. That's one of the key things that bonds us, builds unity. Let's not bullshit anybody. We don't have to openly discuss our fears, but we can. Just like we have to face reality, acknowledge the possible consequences, and then go do it. I noticed a difference in our approach after we had that meeting and I made that promise.

I pushed all my chips to the middle of the table that night. I let everyone know the extent of my responsibility to them. I was going to do everything in my power to make sure that every one of those Marines came back alive. I was going to be by the side of everyone who got injured and who died. Even though I'm intelligent enough to understand that I can't be everywhere, and that as company commander I had fifty-four different teams scattered around Helmand Province, Afghanistan, I took full responsibility for every one of those under my command.

On one extremely hard day in June 2011, I was out on patrol with my team. The guy in front of me stepped on an IED and lost both legs. EJ was killed by an IED just a few minutes later, and shortly after we had gathered up him and his things, one of the Afghans with us lost his leg to another detonation.

With EJ, I had to deal with that crossing-lines thing again, balancing my natural instincts and my duty. It was just devastating to witness what we did. To see EJ lying on the bank of that canal and the condition he was in. My thoughts immediately went in two directions—first to his family.

I couldn't then, and I can't now, put into words the devastation I felt. It would be an insult to his parents and to so many parents who have lost their sons to pretend that the loss I experienced was as profound as what they lost. But it's got to be pretty damn close because I know it hurts every day. And I'm feeling like I failed. I had said that I would do everything I could to make sure that your husband, your son, the father of your child or grandchild, is going to get back home. And I failed. I failed in a big way.

The second place my mind went was to the rest of the men in that unit and on that deployment. I knew that they were looking at me and expecting to see leadership and guidance. How I handled that loss in the immediate was important. How I set the tone was crucial for all of us to get through that horrific scenario. Here I am feeling all of this shock and I've still got about 170 other Marines that I have to think about. I'm the damn company commander. And the most experienced guy out there just got blown up. I knew that those younger guys were thinking that if it could happen to him, then it could happen to them. What do you do when you have all those men looking at you to see how you're going to react, because we've still got a job to do. What's on their minds, besides that loss and those casualties, is the question of what our leadership is going to look like. I had to hold it together for them.

There's no textbook for this, for how to work through it. The military doesn't give you anything. Absolutely nothing. When I got back, we all sat down with psychiatrists, and I got one who was still a student. I literally hadn't even gotten to talking about that deployment and she started crying and left. Some other lady came in and apologized and said the other one was having problems processing all of that. And I just thought, Isn't she the therapist? I'm the one having problems here. That's the kind of support you got when you got back.

I keep in regular communication with EJ's family. Memorial Day, Veterans Day, the anniversary of his death. Random days. I keep it together with them, much like I did with the rest of my team. But as soon as I hang up that phone with his mom and dad, I'm an emotional wreck. It's that devastating. I still cannot believe it to this day. That man is not here. And every day I think about him.

★★

I think I was a unique friend for Greg. I had a bond with several of his subordinates, but I wasn't one he'd taken to war. I had the unique experiences that only Marine EOD techs can have, but I wasn't personally one of "his guys." I was assigned to a sister unit on the opposite coast after EOD school, while most of my friends were sent straight to his unit. I deployed with 1st EOD Company to Afghanistan eight months before Greg's unit.

I was someone who could understand, but not one of the guys he felt responsible for. Greg's story is not unlike many officers who take units of sometimes hundreds or even thousands of Marines to war and have a handful they don't bring back. The difference for Greg is twofold. First, his unit was smaller, less than a hundred, and the number of killed and catastrophically injured was more than two dozen. That meant he didn't just know their faces and names; he knew their wives and children, their smiles and scowls, their hobbies and insecurities.

Second, as a prior enlisted Marine, he had truly walked in their shoes, he could see himself in all of them. The bonds he has to this day with the Marines he lost, and those he brought back, many of whom are our shared closest friends, aren't just unbroken, but forever adhered to his soul. He shares in their pain, and in their joy. He's the brother they chose, the friend they admire, and the voice they respect. That's our bond.

★★★★★★★★★★★★★★★★★★★★★★★★★★★★★★★★★★★★★★

RESPONSIBILITY

You're sent out to do a job. There's missions and patrols and they come with all these orders and things that you're supposed to accomplish while you're out there. But overarching that is a pretty simple concept: take these Marines, go to Afghanistan, and bring them home. Pretty simple.

I also understand the reality that in war not everyone is going to get to come home alive. I can't be everywhere and I can't protect everyone from everything. But that is also my job. Here's where leadership or command pulls a double standard on you. If we're back at camp or not in combat someplace, and one of my Marines goes out and gets in a fight in a bar, who gets held responsible for that? I do. Now, if I'm in combat and one of my Marines gets killed, people try to tell me that I'm not responsible? It's not my fault? Well, hang on. How come that doesn't apply back home but it does here?

I don't buy that. If I'm responsible in one set of circumstances, then I'm responsible in the other. I don't buy that split. I can understand that duality intellectually. It does make sense, but it doesn't feel right. I've felt that way for a long time and I still do. I've got a lot of people who tell me that I shouldn't feel that way. I understand them doing that. They're trying to help me, and I get it, but I don't, and I won't ever.

The good news is that I've been through some really rough patches in trying to deal with my responsibility. Fortunately, there have been people who've been here for me. Not my family. I've been through eleven deployments and they never showed up when I got back. But I'm on a group text with about fifteen friends and we regularly text with each other. I'm not gonna lie to you: If I hadn't gotten on that thing, at one point in my life, I'd be dead. I would have killed myself. That's a fact. I don't know if they know it. They're like sons to me. They're like brothers to me. That's my family. As odd as it sounds, that's the truth.

I already mentioned Amos. We really made a point to make sure he knew he could come hang out with us when Adam died. Amos has been through some rough patches. I cannot imagine having to go through what he's been through. Johnny Morris. The whole bunch of those guys. Justin Heflin, Gage CoDuto, Clifford Farmer, James Whidden, Jon Key, Greg "Gummy Snake" Palmere, Mike Disla, Jerry Slattum, Lukas "Spoonman" Vincent, Rich Stahurski, and Esteban "Doc Rod" Rodriguez. Danny Ridgeway is another EOD guy and a good friend.

Because of the bonds that we've formed, we don't just text, but we've got a kind of sixth sense about one another's states of mind. If a text doesn't get responded to—and I have to admit that a lot of what we do in texting is bust one another's balls—we pick up on things. Same as if we call somebody. You know them well enough that a little change in inflection gives you a big clue.

Sometimes things aren't so subtle. Amos and Joey and Danny and a bunch of the other guys are still trying to convince me that I shouldn't feel responsible for all the losses in that deployment. They were all great friends with him, too. And they all absolutely believe that I'm stupid and that it's dumb for me to feel the way I do.

Despite that difference in perspective, we have been through so much together and separately that nothing can break us apart. Danny Ridgeway is an awesome guy. A redneck but human gold. Danny and I have taken epic road trips together and the man will only stay in a

Red Roof Inn and eat at a Waffle House. We've gone from Florida to Texas together. We've been all over Alabama and North Carolina together. He lives in Maryland, and I drove up there to spend time with him and do some hunting. I have a hard time forgiving Danny and a few other guys for not including me in a couple of elk-hunting adventures they had together! I also wish I could have been there when Danny took down a massive red stag in New Zealand.

I've got plenty of time on my hands. I got medically retired in 2016 due to multiple blast explosion exposures. I'm 100 percent disabled according to the US Department of Veterans Affairs. But you don't ever retire from those relationships that you have. And I don't want to forget what I experienced. There was a time when I would get kind of down, and I would think about just getting a job working at a grocery store and living my life like none of that happened. Just start over. But then I would think—and unlike other times in my life when I made snap decisions about jobs and things, I didn't start bagging groceries—and realize that I wouldn't be who I am today without those experiences. I wouldn't be who I am if it weren't for those people I met and the friendships I have. I gained so much from all of that. It's hard to balance that against all the pain and suffering we witnessed and felt, and that the families endured. Still, I don't have any regrets. I wouldn't change my life. As crazy as it sounds, if somebody said "here's the reset button" and pushed the device across the table, I wouldn't do it.

Life outside the military has its bumps in the road as well. My wife and I just bought a condo in Englewood, Florida. We stayed in it two nights before a hurricane came along and leveled it.

And you know what? As soon as I was able to get back on my phone, there were a bunch of voice mails and messages from the guys offering to come down and do whatever they could to help us out. I appreciate that, but I appreciate even more the fact that guys who were under my command and who were my friends learned a lot by being in the Marines. In the Corps, we always had to identify problems and do what we could to fix them and to make things better for ourselves and our unit. Now, since they've gotten out of the service and gotten on with their lives, I see them overcoming more obstacles and taking on more challenges. I've gotten to see them growing their families and moving into different professions and becoming successful in all kinds of endeavors. They're winning. That's incredibly rewarding to see, and I'm glad that I'm around for it. It's an honor and a privilege to know that after all these years they still want to include me in their lives. I'll always be grateful for that and humbled by it.

Unexpected Guardians

SERGEANT AMOS BENJAMIN

★ United States Marine Corps ★

"You can't push away the people
who care about you. And if
you're one of those people being
pushed, dig in your heels."

★★★

College football is big in the South, where I grew up. I'm known to spout my love for the University of Georgia Bulldogs from time to time on social media, or on-air, or in a group text or . . . even in a book about my amazing friends. But in the military your college football team really becomes part of your identity no matter where you're from. I think most obviously, it's because most colleges have the state right there in the name, so it helps identify who that person is and where they are from, but also, it's one of the positive reinforcements for the competitive spirit embraced in military culture. We're always learning new skills, employing new tactics, pushing our physical abilities, and being graded on and ranked by our performance in each. But we do this by pushing each other and supporting each other.

Amos Benjamin stands a head taller than most folks, weighs 250 pounds, and if I didn't know he was a Marine, I'd probably think he was a pro football player when I finally met him in person. Amos was an infantry Marine, or grunt, but his older brother Adam served with me and many of my friends in the EOD community. After retiring from the Marine Corps, Amos found himself working as a strength and conditioning coach for the Florida State University Seminoles football team. I knew about Amos through our mutual friends who'd served with his brother and one day I got one of those calls where someone takes you completely off guard and leaves you speechless. Amos and I had never met, but he knew I lived near Atlanta. Amos had left the staff at FSU but was coming to town with the team for the season kickoff game against top-ranked Alabama and had an opportunity to bring along a friend, me. When he invited me, he said, "I knew you lived close and thought you might want to watch two of the teams UGA might play up close and personal." A few hours later I was decked out in FSU gear on the sideline of the biggest game of the year, cheering for his Seminoles. That's what a brotherhood is: you share a bond with folks you've never met, sometimes through tragedy, sometimes through triumph, and sometimes through watching eighteen-to-twenty-two-year-olds don colorful tights and hit each over a ball made of pigskin. Amos's life has been exceptional for all those reasons, and I'm proud to share his story of triumph and perseverance.

★★★★★★★★★★★★★★★★★★★★★★★★★★★★★★★★★★★★★

AMOS

I come from a family of twelve children and I'm one of the middle ones. By the time I came along, my brother Adam, the oldest of us, was thirteen years old. Five years later, he had enlisted and gone into the Marine Corps. So, when I was in kindergarten, or first grade, Adam was this human being who would just suddenly show up. He'd be gone for seven, eight, nine months at a time and then, all of a sudden, he'd be home for a week. It was a pretty chaotic household most of the time, but when he came back, things settled down a lot. Then he was gone again. Then he'd pop back up. We'd get phone calls and things from him, but he was always this larger-than-life figure to me. I knew he was my brother and all, but he was this guy who showed up all decked out in his uniform and with medals and ribbons. And, you know, he was out saving the world. He'd tell me stories about being in Malta, the Mediterranean, Kosovo, and Iraq. As a kid I was thinking, *I want to be just like him.*

BROTHERS

I grew up in northeast Ohio in a family that had a history of family service. That was why first Adam and then I gravitated toward military service. I had an uncle who served in the Army; before him, my grandfather was in the Marines. Of course, my grandfather didn't talk much about what he'd done in the war. I now have all of his military records, but I haven't gone through all of them yet. All I really remember as a kid is seeing that whenever we went to Grandpa and Grandma's house the two of them had their own bedrooms. That wasn't what it was like at my house or anybody else's house I ever visited. I thought it was strange then and never really understood why. Only later did I put it together that it was post-traumatic stress. I lost my grandfather when I was a freshman in high school, just about the time I might have been able to ask him more about what his life had been like. I did know that he'd been wounded overseas, and I suspect that he had post-traumatic stress disorder. I imagine that what he went through must have been pretty traumatic.

As a kid, though, I didn't think about that part of the war experience. I had GI Joes and played with them. Adam would come home on leave and he'd show me how GI Joe should really be played. We'd make forts and foxholes out of couch cushions, and Adam, even though he was thirteen years older than me, would join in with us when we shot at each other with Nerf guns. We also had plastic toy armor and we'd dress up and battle like knights. I haven't thought about these things in years, because, you know, when you lose somebody close you don't like to think about it. But I remember how, playing war with Adam and making those couch forts and things, he'd shoot me in the leg with one of those Nerf bullets and I'd yell, "Oh man, my leg!" Then five seconds later it would be all healed up and I'd be running again. "I'm back!" And Adam would say, "You can't come back! I just blew your leg off!"

At that age, you don't understand. I didn't understand what Adam's life was really like. What war is really like. Later on, of course, when I was thinking about joining the military and wondering what it was like, I would go to him. There were so many instances when Adam helped me understand the reality of life. But back when I was a kid, I was like, "You can't use those rules in this children's game." It was just not that serious. We were making couch forts!

★★★

I met Amos through my fellow EOD techs who served with his brother Adam with 2nd EOD Company out of Camp Lejeune, North Carolina. Danny Ridgeway was my roommate and best friend in EOD school, and when we graduated, I went to 1st Company on the west coast and Danny went to 2nd Company on the east coast. Through Danny I met some amazing techs, like his commanding officer Greg Wrubluski. Although I never had the honor of meeting Gunnery Sergeant Adam Benjamin, I knew of him. It's a small community and a tech with his résumé, operating for fourteen years—deploying twice to Iraq, in 2007 and 2008—gets to be known by all. However, shortly before Danny and I checked into our new EOD units in 2009, Adam Benjamin, on his third deployment in as many years, was killed in action while conducting EOD operations, by an explosive device, in Afghanistan. His legacy lives on within our community of professionals, but also in the humble eyes of his very big little brother Amos.

★★★

THE WORDS I NEEDED TO HEAR

When I was graduating from boot camp in 2007, my brother got home from Ramadi, Iraq, just three days before the ceremony. I'd been talking to him while he was in Ramadi, and he kept saying, "I don't know if I'll be back in time. Don't count on it."

I have a traumatic brain injury, or TBI, and lose my car key and phone forty times a day, but I can remember that day in 2007 so clearly. I can still picture him. He was wearing khaki shorts, a blue T-shirt, black leather flip-flops, a silver watch with a black face, and these black sunglasses that he always wore.

I was walking out on the parade deck to graduate and I spotted him. We locked eyes, and I'm like, Holy smokes, he's here! That meant a ton to me. Afterward, he said that I had made the best decision I'd ever made in my life.

I needed to hear that then. You know, boot camp is no fun. I don't care what anybody says. Nobody enjoys going and getting locked down on an island that is humid and full of bugs. You can't leave. You're getting screamed at all the time. I think he could tell that I was feeling a little discouraged. He sensed that those three months had been awful, because he'd been through it, too. So he knew just what to say.

To have this guy say that I'd made the best decision when I was questioning it meant so much to me. I began to see things differently. I mean, I knew that on the outside I was different than before boot camp. I was standing straighter. I was making eye contact with people. And that was hard. I was always socially awkward and more of an introvert than he was, so engaging people fully didn't come easy to me. Adam helped me see that I could be not just a good Marine, but an outstanding Marine. That began with wearing my uniform proudly and went on from there. During wartime, regulations sometimes get a little lax. Guys are in and out of country a lot, and so wearing faded camos or whatever gets overlooked a bit. But Adam told me that after boot camp, I was a Marine now. I had standards to live up to. I didn't want to be on the same base with him and him looking all badass and me looking like I just didn't take any of this seriously. I could never be lazy about anything. I carried that with me throughout my career. I wanted to make him proud, so that afterward we could say to each other, man, we had a good ride.

So, when he came back from his deployment in 2007 and I was going through my whole workup prior to deploying to Iraq, we spent a lot of time together. It all came down the pipe and I found out where I was going: it was to Ramadi. That was great because I could pick his brain and prepare myself better for something I knew nothing about. What's the temperature like? What do I need to be aware of that we're not told to be aware of? He really helped me get squared away in a way that I couldn't have done on my own.

★★★★★★★★★★★★★★★★★★★★★★★★★★★★★★★★★★★★★★

Amos's first deployment to Ramadi, Iraq, in 2008 was in the wake of the 2006 Battle of Ramadi, a fierce conflict for control of the capital of the Al Anbar Province. It lasted eight months, from March to November 2006, and resulted in a coalition victory. The victory came at a cost of ninety-four American lives and more than two hundred wounded in action. In response to the reenergized insurgency in Al Anbar, then president George W. Bush deployed another twenty thousand troops to Iraq under the command of Army General David Petraeus. This strategy was coined "The Surge" and sent ripples throughout the Marine Corps. I also deployed to Al Anbar in the spring of 2007 as part of this major surge. By March 2008, Ramadi had become a much safer city thanks to our efforts. Unfortunately for Amos, IED explosions were a common fixture in combat operations and the concussive effect of being too close meant a high risk of an internal injury, the kind that can be hard to detect or diagnose until long after exposure. The cumulative effect of being too close to too many explosions would eventually lead to his traumatic brain injury and result in retirement from the Marine Corps in 2013, after his third deployment. As harrowing as his experience was downrange that first time, the worst was yet to come.

Amos was fortunate that he had his brother looking out for him in lots of ways.

★★★★★★★★★★★★★★★★★★★★★★★★★★★★★★★★★★★★★★

A SELFLESS ACT

Everybody knew I was Adam's younger brother. There was no mistaking that. And it felt normal to me after a while to be a private first class and then a lance corporal and hanging out with these staff sergeants and gunnery sergeants. I knew there were lines I couldn't and shouldn't cross, and I didn't cross. These guys were friendly but also, they were above me. When Adam was on a deployment, he told them to look out for me, to keep an eye on me. He told me that I had better keep up with my discipline because he instructed those guys to let him know if I was messing up at all. Maybe this was against regulations, but sometimes when I hadn't heard from Adam for a while, I'd go down to the EOD shop and check in with them to find out if they'd heard from him and how things were going. A few times, they let me use their satellite linkups so that I could talk to Adam directly. They had given me this all-access pass to my brother and that helped me a lot.

Also, when Adam was around, he was my GPS as to how the

military operated. When he was deployed and later, after he was killed, the other EOD guys would help me out, asking if I needed any gear, anything at all. I was still making the transition from civilian life to military life, and they eased that for me.

The thing about war and military life is that you experience some of the ultimate highs and lows of your life. That can be all in the same day, too. That's how it was for me when I found out that Adam was killed in action. First, it was a great day for me in the Marine Corps. That morning, we ran the combat endurance course. It takes you through deep mud bogs and you're out there with your team struggling through it. At the end, everybody's so caked with mud that there's a fire hose out there so you can rinse off. We had a good run through the woods that day. We were all motivated because we'd been out in the field that week doing other training so we were being cut loose early that day. So the sooner we got back to the barracks, the sooner we could start our long weekend.

I got back to the barracks, and Adam called me from Afghanistan. He sounded really tired, more tired than I could ever remember hearing him. That was the first time that I thought about the fact that my brother is human. The funny thing is, at that point he didn't really have to be in Helmand Province on that deployment. But he did the kind of superhuman thing, made a bigger sacrifice than normal that had him there. My brother had a friend named Chris who was a Marine EOD also. The other bond that Adam had was that Chris had married this girl who was from our hometown in Ohio, and she and Adam had been best friends growing up. In July 2009, Brandy was nine months pregnant and Chris had learned that he was being sent to Afghanistan as a combat replacement. Adam was supposed to be deployed in January 2010, but he didn't want Chris to miss the birth of his child. So Adam volunteered to take Chris's slot.

For the time that Adam and I had been in the military together, whenever we were on the same base together, we never mixed. I didn't really see him during the day and we tried to keep things as professional as possible. But the last week in June 2009, I got a phone call from him in the middle of the day. He told me that we had to meet that night. He wanted to talk to me about some stuff. That's when he told me about Chris and that he was going to take his place on that deployment. I was totally caught off guard. I had been looking forward to him being home for a long stretch. I was coming off my Iraq deployment and the two of us had talked about all the hunting and fishing and other things that we'd do together. I was kind of selfish, thinking, No, man, I don't want you to go. But when he explained why he was doing it, I thought that was the most selfless thing I'd ever heard. He was going to put himself in danger to help a friend. That was who Adam was. Also, the funny thing is, Adam had decided that as long as he was in the military, he wasn't going to get married. He didn't want to put a woman in a stressful spot. He didn't want the distraction, didn't want to be thinking about how he was affecting someone else's life like that.

THE WORST DAY

I remember that whenever Adam came home or called home when he was serving and I wasn't yet in the Marines, he would tell everybody that he was fine. That things were fine. Come to think of it, he was kind of like my grandpa was. He didn't talk about it much. It wasn't until after my first deployment that I really understood what "fine" meant. I had done what he'd done when calling home and talking with family after returning. We never wanted to say anything that would get anybody worried. Don't stress them. That kind of thing. That was good and what we needed to do.

So hearing him sound so exhausted the morning before we did our Combat Endurance Course, it seemed like he wasn't hiding anything from me. He didn't go into much detail, said he just wanted to check in. I hadn't heard from him for the first weeks he was in Helmand. I understood how things were when you were first in-country. There's some lag time at first and then things pick up and you relocate. So, I figured that was what he was calling to tell me. But that wasn't it. He didn't say much verbally, but that sound in his voice had my head going, Nothing feels right about this. I wish I could do something for him.

But I had another voice in my head saying, Man, I have a long, fun weekend ahead of me at Myrtle Beach, South Carolina. But my brother's being run ragged over there. I felt like crap for feeling so good.

We finished up our phone call, and after we got cut loose late that afternoon, I tore off my uniform and put on a pair of board shorts. In my mind, I was thinking, Myrtle Beach, here I come. I'm ready to drink beers and hang out.

One of the squad leaders in my platoon popped his head into my room and said, "Lance Corporal Benjamin, get your camos back on. You have to go see the colonel." In the Marine Corps, as a low-level infantryman, if you have to go see the colonel that means you really screwed up. I panicked. What did I do? I knew I was a well-behaved kid. I knew that I hadn't done anything wrong. So I was like, "C'mon, man. Not today! I just got cut loose. I'm trying to go to the beach!" There was a lot going on in my unit at the time. We had a change-of-command shift. I figured I was being reassigned to go somewhere else. After getting dressed again, I drove up to the squad leader, irritated. We had all morning for this meeting. Why now? After this, I'm going to get stuck in traffic and I start having a bitch fit in my head. Immature twenty-year-old stuff.

I had to wait twenty to twenty-five minutes in the company office. It was basically empty, so I was like, What the hell is going on?

Finally, our company gunnery sergeant came in and told me that the colonel was ready to see me now. I got up, and as I look back on it, I'm not proud of how I walked in there with this pissed-off attitude. I should have conducted myself better. When I walked in, I locked eyes with Adam's friend Chris. He was wearing his service alphas—his green coat and trousers, a khaki shirt, and tie. I knew that something had happened, but I didn't know what. My whole chain of command was there. The colonel didn't say a word to me. Chris stepped forward and handed me some papers that he was clenching pretty tightly and said, "I didn't want you to hear this from anyone else." He handed me the papers. Then he said, "Your brother was killed this afternoon."

I just hit the floor. I didn't really know what to do, what to say. I just collapsed.

I don't think I ever cried that hard a day in my life before this. I don't think I've ever cried that hard any day since. A lot of things started to move really, really fast but at that point, I wanted nothing to do with the Marine Corps, ever. I thought, Now what? I'm from a small town in Ohio. I came down to this massive military installation and it felt like home because my brother was here and I was following in his footsteps. But now . . .

I knew that the Marine Corps was exactly where I was supposed to be in life. It meant everything to me and still does to this day. I had dreams of one day being the sergeant major of the Marine Corps, the senior enlisted Marine of the entire Corps. But while the Corps had felt like home, now my brother was dead. The minute I knew that I'd never see my brother alive again, everything about the military just flipped over for me. At eighteen you don't realize how impressionable you are; that only comes later in life.

I made it back to the barracks, and everybody was gone except my roommate who I was supposed to be going to Myrtle Beach with. He didn't know what happened. I sat down on my bed, rolled over, and just lost it again. He read the papers I'd been given and he then knew.

After that, I had to start to make arrangements to go to Dover Air Force Base in Delaware to do the dignified transfer to take Adam home.

You know, I love Chris and Brandy to death. I do. Brandy knew Adam from the time they were toddlers. But I have to be honest: while Chris did everything he could to step in and help me, at the time I hated him. And it was for the most selfish reasons. I was sitting there like, If you would have left, he would still be here. I did all the childish crap. I started to place blame. I didn't know what to do with all these feelings. I'm feeling crushed. I'm feeling angry. I'm in this high-stress infantry job at this base that once felt like the greatest home I'd ever been a part of and now I want to run as fast and as far away from it as I can. Absolute belonging and absolute rejection at the same time.

Then, and down the line, I'd see Chris's wife and her baby. I knew how close she and Adam were, and I knew how she was feeling. After a while when we were together it started to feel like sitting in a windowless room that was on fire. At first it was just flame and then it got hotter and hotter and there was no escape. I was wondering how I was going to deal with all of this. It wasn't just Chris and his wife; it was my family. My mother, our dad, brothers and sisters, cousins. I was supposed to be deploying soon. All these things were happening at the same time. I couldn't balance that. So I just started to cut things out. Part of that was Chris. As I said, I love Chris to death. But it was so hard for me to be around them, because I was so angry at him. It wasn't even anything that you should be angry for, but at that age, with all that happening and weighing on me, it just about broke me.

I'm so happy Chris is still here and can be a parent to those two kids and a husband to his wife. When my brother passed, he didn't have a wife and kids left behind. So there are some good things that came out of a tragedy. I felt caught in the middle. Like, I miss my brother to death. And he could still be here if Chris wasn't here. I'm almost grateful that this happened to my brother, because Chris doesn't have to leave a widow and two kids. But I also have to go home and deal with my family. So Chris became a focal point of my anger because I didn't know how to deal with anything. He was the easy target, which was not fair and one of my biggest regrets to this day.

★★

Those feelings Amos calls "selfish" are quite understandable. He'd lost his rock, his mentor, his flesh and blood. With an enemy so difficult to understand or even identify, he directed his anger at what he thought was the one person who could've been in Adam's place, instead of toward those faceless, nameless cowards who actually killed him. That's grief, an emotional roller coaster that often hits us without warning or reason. Thankfully Amos can look back and see clearly that with any loss considered a "sacrifice," there has to be those who benefit from it. Chris's kids are Adam's legacy in that way. And that's something to honor, not resent. Leaving little time to grieve, Amos was set to deploy very soon. But he didn't have to deploy so quickly after his brother was killed in action. Understanding the sacrifice his family had just paid, and the immense emotional weight of losing a brother, the Marine Corps offered Amos the choice to stay stateside while his unit deployed. But Amos felt he knew what Adam would have done: Adam would've gone to war with his unit. His other brothers. Amos struggled to make that decision, a decision about whether to honor his brother and his unit, or to respect his own grief and stay here, safe with his family.

He had felt isolated and alone in the first days following his brother's death, and many reached out to him, most meaningfully, members of Adam's unit 2nd EOD Company, those who knew Amos as Adam's little brother when he brought him around to their shop. Encouraged by 2nd Company Commander Greg Wrubluski, the Marines' simple gestures brought Amos back into the fold again. My own best friend, Danny Ridgeway, was one of those Marines who reached out to Amos, as was another well-respected tech, EJ Pate. They all knew that Amos was in a vulnerable state, and they were grieving the loss of one of our own as well. They acted as a sounding board and a return to normalcy for Amos, letting him know that he was welcome to be back there as one of the guys just as he had when his brother was alive and bringing him by. They also talked with Amos about his dream to try to dissuade him from following in Adam's footsteps and becoming an EOD tech. Given the high-risk nature of the work and the real possibility that his family could suffer another loss, Amos agreed that setting aside his plan to make a lateral move to join us was the right thing to do. Ultimately, Amos needed to make the right decision for himself, not simply walk in Adam's footsteps. If he joined EOD, would he be doing it because EOD was his dream, or simply because he was following his brother? Amos chose his own path, in honor of Adam, but not in his shadow. Adam was gone but the bond he helped forge between Amos and the Marines Adam served with remained firmly in place. Regardless of Amos's decision, if he chose to pursue a career in EOD, or to continue his own path as a Marine infantryman on the ensuing deployment, whatever Amos decided, he had a forever bond with the Marines of 2nd EOD Company.

★★

DEPLOYING TO ESCAPE

When my brother died, there wasn't a day that I didn't see Gunnery Sergeant Ralph "EJ" Pate. He became the big brother to me that Adam had been. He'd give me a call and say, "We're going to Raleigh," and we'd go have dinner or whatever. I also met Danny Ridgeway, who was one of my brother's mentees. Adam had mentored Danny as an EOD tech, which in turn brought us a lot closer than many even understood from the outside looking in. I was around these guys when I didn't even know how badly I needed them. I was trying to figure out so many things, including going on that scheduled deployment.

Because of how I was being treated by the EOD guys, I felt even more of a responsibility to the guys that I was training with. I mean, you eat, sleep, breathe the same air as these guys 24/7 and they're counting on me to be there. Even so, I had teammates that were like, "Don't do this. Go home." I was also approached by a Marine Corps commander who told me that if I didn't want to do this after what happened to Adam, I wouldn't have to go. I could be discharged and they'd assist me in making that happen. I understood all that, and I was dealing with lots of different factors and input and opinions from people, and all the emotions and stresses were getting to me. The most toxic part of the chaos was the ability to learn to compartmentalize trauma versus dealing with it. I should have stayed and received professional help but again I chose to do it my way. I never wanted anyone to know I was hurting, but what I didn't know was that I was doing an awful job hiding it.

Ultimately, I realized that the only thing that you have to do on deployment is focus on one thing—staying alive with your tribe. You don't have the stress of paying bills. You don't have to worry about your car insurance payment. I didn't have to think about being a support for somebody else. Being deployed, I could totally disconnect from the reality I was living in. For me, that was perfect. So I took all the anger, all the hate, all the rage, all the guilt, and bottled them up, put a cap on it, and I was like, This is going to be the jar of fuel that gets me through this next deployment so I can escape all this stuff. When I come back, it will all have blown over and life will go on. So that's what I did.

I thought I just needed to get out from underneath this cloud. I needed to really learn to love being a Marine. I needed that deployment to help me as well as to serve. I also needed to get away, to not have a cell phone and not have people constantly checking in on me or trying to control my every move. I didn't want people to be thinking about the fact that I'd lost my brother and needed people to be all sensitive around me. I was trying to just come back to work and not be treated differently. I didn't want anybody treating me like was a frickin' charity case. That's not who I am. I knew that if the situation was reversed and something had happened to me, Adam wouldn't have quit. There's no way he would have gone home. There were two things I 100 percent knew about my brother: he loved being a Marine, especially an EOD tech, and he knew exactly who he was.

★★★★★★★★★★★★★★★★★★★★★★★★★★★★★★★★★★★

I can understand and maybe even empathize with what Amos was thinking and feeling. He found comfort in the familiarity of simply being a Marine, and being around the other men he called "brothers," men he'd grown to trust and shared a bond with. Amos also struggled with the knowledge that if he was distracted at all, if he couldn't be at his best while on that deployment, he could possibly put one of his fellow Marines at risk. Recognizing that possibility, he said he struggled the most with that factor. Ultimately, he vowed to not let that happen. He was determined to be the kind of Marine that Adam had told him he needed to be. There was a lot riding on him rising to the occasion. Amos met that challenge and knew that once he chose to deploy, there was no turning back.

★★★★★★★★★★★★★★★★★★★★★★★★★★★★★★★★★★★★★★

GUARDIAN ANGELS

Once, on that deployment after Adam was killed, I was in Afghanistan and I hadn't really seen or heard from anybody back home. I got a radio call from a Staff Sergeant Collins. I didn't know who he was, but he was an EOD tech who knew my brother. He was just checking in on me because he knew my brother and knew I was in-country like he was. It was as if I had a guardian angel looking out for me wherever I went.

So, after I did that first deployment after Adam died, I had two months back in garrison. I didn't even want to go home to Ohio, so I didn't. I stayed at Camp Lejeune. I was there for a month, and then deployed again. That's not how it usually went in the Marines. Normally, you'd be back for an extended period of time. I had reenlisted at this point, and I had a buddy from my hometown who was in the 6th Marines. We knew each other our whole lives. He enlisted a year after I did. I found out he was deploying in a few weeks, so I went to the career planner and asked if he could get me transferred there. I knew that I could stay disconnected from some of the things at home that were too painful for me. I felt like I'd healed and was getting back to normal as a Marine. I worried that if I stayed back in the States, I'd fall back into some emotional traps. I needed to stay disconnected from all that I had run away from.

Thing was, I couldn't run away from everything. During that time in 2011, EJ was out in Helmand Province. We connected over the sat radio one day, and I let him know that I'd be heading his way in a few weeks with 1st Battalion, 6th Marines. He told me that we'd be sure to link up. We never got the chance. On June 26, he got killed by an IED that detonated while he was working on it. Instead of seeing him in Afghanistan, I attended his funeral, days before going downrange. EJ and I had gotten so close, and now I'd lost another guy who had been like a brother to me. Just like before, deploying and seeing combat felt kind of like the thing I needed to do to keep from stuff getting to me too bad. Even though I'd lost Adam and EJ, the web of connections I had with the EOD community through them wasn't severed completely.

When I got to Afghanistan, we were temporarily staying at Camp Dwyer before we headed to the Sangin Valley, and I went to the EOD shop there just to check in. At this point a lot of the techs that I knew in the field had been banged up pretty badly. One of the master sergeants looked at me and said, "Didn't you just go home?" I told him yes, but I just came back with 1st Battalion, 6th Marine Regiment.

He took me outside and put his arm around me. His tone was completely different and he said, "What are you thinking coming back here?"

It was one of those talks where he told me I was playing with fire. He didn't really understand what I was going through, but I appreciated him talking with me and looking out for me. He did get that I was playing with fire, but he didn't understand that this fire was hot enough that I never had to feel cold from behind me. So if I stay close enough to this fire, everything back home that brings me down and puts me in those cold, dark places—I get to stay away from it. But then he talked to me about selflessness and being selfish. Well, he said, what about your parents? What about the people back home who love you? This was one of those reality checks that I got from that EOD community of being big brothers. They reminded me: I needed to cool it; I needed to really be careful in this deployment and go home safe.

SAFE BUT NOT SOUND

Safe but not sound, I guess is the way you could put it. We were operating in Sangin Valley doing a clearing operation. We had helicopter support and they hit this house with an air strike that we were taking fire from. This was right outside our patrol base. After that first strike, we were going to hit the house twice more to take down a rock wall that enclosed the compound where we hoped to take out the guys who were shooting at us and then conduct a Battle Damage Assessment. Once the wall was breached, our team was to make entry and take out the high-value targets (HVTs) inside if they'd survived the air strike. This was a night operation and our team ended up getting too close to that wall. The detonation of those two rockets knocked me out. When I came to, my shoulder hurt a bit from some shrapnel, but everything else was very, very different after that. I was heavily concussed.

The two corpsmen who worked on me told me that I needed to be medevaced out of there for treatment. Even though I was in a fog, I had clarity about one thing. If I got flown out of there, I wasn't ever going to be allowed back in. I told them that. It was eighteen months since I lost my brother, and I still wanted to be there. We discussed our options as a unit, and finally decided that the medevac wasn't necessary. I wound up going to the company position and got seen by the battalion corpsman and medical officer the next day. I was with it enough that I could convince them that all was well. I got sent back to my platoon. In hindsight, that was a bad decision, indeed probably one of the worst decisions I have ever made.

I could barely sleep, maybe at best two to three hours a night. Then things started to get even worse. I could tell that something wasn't right at all. I couldn't taste. I couldn't smell. I started to get really, really angry. I was struggling to remember things, and that wasn't good from a performance or leadership perspective. My teammates began to notice how I was deteriorating and kept checking in with me. I had the best teammates, though, and I knew that I could convince them I was fine and so have their support. And I did. They trusted me, and I appreciated that.

I did manage to get home safe, but unfortunately that wasn't the case for a lot of others. And while I physically appeared to be okay, after that deployment, the wheels really started to come off for me. That period was incredibly perilous for the Marine EOD community. Greg Wrubluski was in command of all the teams positioned around. He was out in the field, too, doing the same job as the men who were under his command. There were about 124 EOD techs and many died or were catastrophically injured. I wasn't counted among that number.

When you're deployed, you're riding this giant adrenaline high. I was, essentially, in combat for fifteen straight months and my adrenal glands were just pumping out the stuff every day. I couldn't shut that off for a while. I developed sensitivity to light. I had debilitating migraine headaches. I still wasn't sleeping. I had the good sense to go to our team corpsman at Camp Lejeune and tell him that something was wrong with me. He said that it was time for me to take a break and not deploy for a while so that I could get evaluated and treated. That was the first time I felt like I could do that. I couldn't keep running away and using the war as an escape. On top of that, deployments were starting to slow down. I surrendered to that because there wasn't anything I could do to cover it anymore. There wasn't the thought process to keep pushing. I was absolutely broken mentally, physically, emotionally, and spiritually; just broken and exhausted.

Tests revealed that I had some brain swelling. So they sent me to Florida for hyperbaric oxygen therapy for four months. I chose that over some more serious options that were presented to me, and the thought of which didn't sit too well with me. The oxygen therapy had proven fairly successful. The second I got down there, I knew it was going to be a very rocky four months. This was the first time I was isolated. I didn't have any teammates around me. I was in Florida. I was going to a medical appointment every morning, then returning to my hotel room, and I pretty much felt like crap all the time. I had gone from a high-functioning, physically fit go-getter to a dang hospital patient. My body was killing me, my head was constantly pounding, and all these emotions were starting to come out of me that I couldn't control.

For the first two and a half months I was in Florida, I turned to alcohol to get me through. I was down on the Gulf Coast, with white sandy beaches and nothing much to do except the two hours a day it took to get to and receive hyperbaric treatments and then go home. I did that every single day. I still couldn't sleep, so thought, I'll drink enough and eventually I'll pass out. My motor was running so high that when I'd check in at clinic they'd tell me that my resting heart rate was 140. They told me that I needed to calm down, but I couldn't do that on my own, so I turned to alcohol again. It wasn't just the physical stuff. I still didn't know what to do with all the emotions I was feeling. When you run at a high op tempo for a long period of time, and then you have to be still, it really messes with you. Especially psychologically. When you are in isolation you can end up entangled in thoughts and emotions that you haven't had, felt, or thought about in a long time. When that collides with a brain that doesn't function properly, it's a recipe for suffering.

I kept hearing that I was screwed-up, and I wondered what was next for me. What does a screwed-up person do for the rest of their life? I didn't have an answer. I didn't have anyone around me in Florida who could help me find the answer. I was absolutely stuck. For the first time in my life, I was just stuck.

Then I met this young lady, Courteney, while I was down there. For whatever reason, when I was around her something about her just calmed me down. I wasn't "cured." I was still dealing with all the physical stuff, but at least I had some peace and felt some emotional connection. For the rest of the time I was there, we got closer.

But then I had to return to Camp Lejeune after the treatments were over. I was looking forward to being back with the guys on my team, in familiar surroundings, and getting back to doing what I'd done before. Being able to serve and have a purpose and a focus seemed like the answer to how I could get unstuck.

That's when I got hit in the face by reality.

REENTRY

I was told that I couldn't do what I'd done before. They answered my question about what steps I was going to take next in my life. I was going to have to step aside and report to Wounded Warrior Battalion–East. That was located right there at Camp Lejeune, but it was, in lots of ways, a world away from where I'd been and what I'd been doing before. Its motto is *Etiam in Pugna*, Still in the Fight, and that's true for some. It's dedicated to the nonmedical care of Marines who are either wounded, sick, or injured. Some who go there will be returned to duty and some are being prepared to transition out of the military and into civilian life.

Again, I felt isolated. None of my teammates were there. All my buddies were in the field and training for the next workup. I was sitting there wondering, What's next? I didn't have long to wait to find out. I was told that I was being retired out of the Marines. Due to my brain injury, I wasn't physically capable to do the job.

That was hard to hear. I'd always considered myself to be a strong physical specimen, and now I was told that I wasn't. I couldn't. I'd been all about "I can" and "I will" for so long. And especially from the time of my brother's death until I was sent to Florida, I had some stability. Something I could count on where I belonged, where I had teammates. I went from ultimate stability to having to figure out what I was going to do next in four months.

I don't know what would have happened to me if it weren't for Danny and Greg and the rest of the EOD community. They were straight up with me. This is the reality you're going to have to deal with, so accept it. It helped that Danny and some of the other EOD techs were in the same situation I was in as MiTTs—Military Transition Team members. Simply put, we were all on the way out to getting medically retired.

We were all just emotionally wrecked at that point. We had had all these plans of what we were going to do, visions of our future, and now that was shut down. I'd thought about that future in terms of who I was going to do some of those things with, and a few of those people were gone. I knew that I couldn't go home to northeast Ohio. I'd worked so hard to leave my childhood home. I'd worked to elevate myself to do great things and to build a life that I was proud of. That life was in North Carolina in the military. But that life was slowly unraveling. So, as I was driving out those gates for the last time, I felt like I went from having everything to having nothing. I think in the service we take for granted the food, water, shelter, community, purpose, identity, health care . . . until we blink and it's gone, and we have to find it ourselves. In my right mind I never saw myself out of the service. At least not this soon.

On top of that, when you have a traumatic brain injury, how you process information, how you interact with other people, how you behave, how you assess the environment in a room of people, how you deal with your anger, is all messed up to one degree or another. There is a lot of paranoia, hypervigilance, and awareness you develop because of what you go through during your time in service, and that is all amplified with brain injury.

Through that mixed-up muddle of thoughts, I thought I was leaving a place and a life where I was making the ultimate kind of sacrifice and service by fighting a war to—what? Sit in a microeconomics class? I felt like nobody cared about anybody else out in the civilian world. The military was a very "we, not me" mentality, the polar opposite of how the real world worked. All my friends now lived all over the country, versus having them live in the same building with me.

I still couldn't bring myself to go home. I felt like there was nothing there for me. I mean, I had a good relationship with my father, but I wasn't that close with all my siblings. After a death in the military, some families grow closer. That didn't happen for us. Everyone was angry. There was already substance abuse in my family—that didn't get better. I don't blame them; everybody has to try to cope with things as best they can and sometimes you make unhealthy choices.

I felt like, if I went home, I would be doomed.

WHO AM I NOW?

I was so lucky that the woman I met in Florida, Courteney, was still in my life. She suggested that I come down to Florida again and she'd help me out and get me into college. I had no idea how to go about using the GI Bill for school, but I always knew from the time I met her that I could count on her.

So I did that, but bounced in and out of school for a few years.

With my brain injury and the emotional instability it caused, on top of the burden I was carrying from service, I was going berserk. I was going through the culture shock of being a civilian. Being a Marine had been not just my identity, but how other people identified me. It gave them an easy in to talk with me when I came home. "How are you doing? Where are you training? When are you going to deploy next? It's so good to see you." And after you're out, people still say it's good to see you, but that's about it. No one is interested in what you've got going on. Life went back to what it was. I knew no one owed me anything. My service was voluntary, and I did it because I love our country. But it was still a change I wasn't expecting.

It must be what athletes go through when they retire. When you're playing, people are all about you and your career and how you're doing. After that, when you leave the game, a lot of people just aren't as interested as they once were. Nobody cares when you're not on the field anymore. I kind of felt that way about how I was being looked at and in seeing how other vets were treated.

I had to adjust to a different world of people and their attitudes. I started hearing people talking about racial issues. In the military, that really wasn't even a thing as far as I experienced. No one cared if you were Black, Hispanic, or Estonian or whatever because we were all on the same team. We were a tribe. But we were fighting for this country where everyone was divided. I just thought, Are you people out of your minds? I remember sitting in a college class one time and hearing kids say, "I don't believe in the military." It created a lot of anger. There I was sitting in class, a hidden mess, having to listen to people who had no idea what I had been through say things like that. But that is also what makes America so great. The ability to believe what you want to. For me, still, it was tough to hear.

I felt like my life was coming apart. That factored into my troubles with school and in keeping focused on that. So many different things were coming at me at once. Finding the right information and treatment for brain injuries was really hard. Medical experts were still trying to figure out this new category of war wounds. A lot of the Veterans Affairs hospitals at that time didn't even have neurology clinics. I experienced that personally when I moved to Pensacola, Florida. I was here a few months ago getting hyperbaric treatments, so why can't I continue with those? Well, they said, because you're not active duty anymore. We don't have that as an option for veterans. I kept hitting obstacle after obstacle and in a matter of months I went from Ultimate Warrior to just pounding my lights out.

THE PEOPLE WHO SUPPORTED ME

I was so blessed to have Courteney in my corner through every bit of it. Both of her grandfathers served in the Navy, and she was very patriotic anyway. She cared about me on top of that and told me, "Hey, anything you need, I'm here." She wanted to help me and to help us build a life together. At the time, I didn't think that was possible. I felt like I was broken. Building something? I didn't have what it took to build a new life because I so busy and so exhausted trying to piece the one I once had back together. I couldn't think about a life with a big wedding, kids, family vacations, and all of that. But she stuck with me, and she still does, going on about eleven years now. It wasn't so much that I felt depressed, but I was bored. I couldn't get that adrenaline fix that I had chased and chased and chased all those years. But every step I took in a positive direction, it was because Courteney was there guiding me and leading me. Together we turned over every rock we could to get treatments for me. Still, I was coming further and further apart.

For some reason, I reached out to Joey Jones. I'd heard about him as an EOD tech, but I'd never met him. I contacted him through social media and we became friends that way. I invited him to a football game in Atlanta. I knew about his injuries and things. One day he called me and said that he'd been invited to an elk hunt in Wyoming that was set up for wounded veterans. Joey told me that he couldn't go, and wondered if I would like to. I said to him, "What do you mean you can't go? What, don't you have any legs?" Joey laughed.

To hunt elk up there, I knew we'd have to hike up and down mountains and that would be tough on a guy using prosthetics. But I got him to agree to go and meet me there. I ended up piggybacking him for a part of the hiking. Then Joey bagged an elk and we definitely bonded over that experience! When you are hiking half a human on your back, up and down mountains in Wyoming for a week, you become very close. I say half a human because Joey doesn't have legs and we joked about it throughout the hunt. Someone might be missing legs but that doesn't mean they are lightweight!

But it came with a price. That was my reintroduction to the outdoors. After Adam died, I couldn't hunt or fish. It just crushed me to do it by myself. Every time I was in the woods, it was like he was there with me but he wasn't really. That was just too much, too many memories. Joey saw on that trip that I was really, really having a hard time. He recognized that and I recognized that. But at least we had that bonding experience, but once that was over, it was over, and I spiraled down a bit lower. I was at the point when I thought I was so defeated I was going to become just another statistic.

ON THE BRINK

Then, around Thanksgiving time, I got an invitation to another hunt, this one down in Texas for deer. I wasn't too crazy about the idea. I don't like hunting with people I don't know or haven't shot with before.

I don't want to be around strangers and have rounds flying through the air, even if it is on a hunt. Reluctantly I did go down to San Angelo, Texas. While I was down there, my sister called me. I didn't answer even though I hadn't heard from her in years. I didn't feel like dealing with any family stuff, especially not on that trip. We were more or less estranged at that point anyway because I had isolated myself from home. I knew that my dad wasn't doing well, though. I know what it's like to lose a brother, friend, but not a child. I can't imagine the pain that causes anyone who has to go through it, whether it's war related or not. But I watched it dismantle him slowly from the time it happened.

My sister kept calling and calling. Finally, one of the hunting guides I was with said, "Bro, just take the call." I did answer and I barely recognized the voice. Then she said that I needed to come home. I almost laughed. No chance of that. Then she said that my dad had taken his own life.

At that point in my life, I was done. I was sitting in a deer blind with a bolt-action rifle in my hands and I was saying, I quit. I think that was the first time in my life I thought that way. I had nothing left to give. I was totally defeated. I thought: I can just put the barrel of this gun in my mouth. I can pull the trigger. I'll be out of here. I sat staring at the rifle. It was just like one of those moments from a movie and my whole life flashed before my eyes. I made a conscious decision that I would grab that gun, put it in my mouth, and pull the trigger so I wouldn't have to feel that way anymore. I had lost the Marine Corps, my friends, my brother, I was slowly deteriorating mentally and physically, and now my father was gone. You couldn't take anything else from me at that point. This was it.

Scenes from childhood, middle school, high school, my military years all passed before my eyes in a few moments. I felt tears running down my cheeks. I was not a very religious person. I grew up going to church, youth group, and stuff like that, but I never invested in it.

After experiencing Iraq and Afghanistan and extreme religious terrorism, it messed me up. I would think to myself, *These people will legitimately die for their God right now, but will I? Was it real? Was any religion real?* It really screwed me up.

But before I raised the gun, I sat there and silently said to God, if you are real, and have something more for me, then you had better do something right now because I'm about to see you in five seconds. After that, everything went kind of numb and blank. I'd never experienced this in my life before. I didn't feel any pain. I didn't feel any emotion—happy, sad, nothing. I was in this totally blank space, floating.

Something changed in me in that moment. Something happened, but I can't explain it. The heaviest burdens lifted off me in that deer blind. I felt that somewhere in this there is hope because what I am feeling cannot be mistaken.

I turned and looked at one of the hunting guides. He was already crying. He had overheard the phone call. He knew what was going on. He said, "Hey, man, let's go ahead and just leave that rifle there. Let's get on up to the lodge. Let's get you home."

And at the word, *home,* I just melted down. Get home? I'm in San Angelo, Texas. My wife is in East Hartford, Connecticut. My family is in Ohio. And I quit. And that good feeling had just happened and it was the biggest God moment in my life. But now . . . I had to get a plane ticket. I was going to have to deal with lines, with TSA. I didn't have the energy to do it. But with that guide's help I got back to the lodge. Standing there was a guy I knew had to be the ranch owner, Danny Knox. I immediately felt like a burden. My dad had killed himself. I'm just this burden to everybody I come in contact with. Especially to this man who opened his ranch to me to heal.

But this man put his hands on my shoulders and said, "Son, don't worry about anything. I have a jet. It's going to take you to

Connecticut to get your wife and then the two of you are going to go on to Ohio for the funeral. I've already paid for two weeks at a hotel there. You'll have access to a car and to a driver. If you need anything between now and then, you just call me. Just go and relax in your room. Have some time to yourself and you'll leave in the morning."

I was thinking, You have a jet? Who says those kinds of things? I was about to blow my freaking brains out in a deer blind and now this guy has come in and is going to take care of all these things for me? You have a jet?

But he did. Everything he said he would do, he did. And I really, really needed that then. Courteney had had about enough of me at that point and I really did not think that we would make it. She had been so great to me for so long, but I was being so destructive that I didn't think that I'd be able to come out of it, even before learning about my dad's suicide. She stuck with me, though, and if it wasn't for her in my life, there is no telling what would have happened.

A DIAGNOSIS THAT WOULD CHANGE EVERYTHING

A couple of weeks after my father's funeral I get a call. It was Joey. He had heard through the grapevine what happened and he thought that I needed to bust up out of there to get away and get some relief. He said, "Do you want to go on a deer hunt in Texas." I'm thinking, This isn't any time for jokes. (I also didn't want to be around guns because of my headspace and because the feeling I felt in the deer blind was still dwelling inside me.) But Joey wasn't joking. He also wouldn't take no for an answer. He's one persistent human being. Every day for two weeks he called me. "We're going. We're going." Sure enough, two weeks later I was down in Fort Worth, Texas. It was just Joey and me and we headed out to another ranch. This one was owned by a man named Randy Cupp. Randy looked like he just fell out of a Clint Eastwood western. He was one tough old cowboy, and at first I didn't like him very much. We stayed a couple of nights and did some hunting. I was still not in a good place, deciding between living and dying. I didn't have gas enough in the tank to keep going on.

We finished up the hunting days and were getting ready to leave. Keep in mind that Randy hadn't said a whole lot to me the entire time. We were out in the driveway and he walked up and put his arm around me and said, "I'm really proud of you." I felt like a rattlesnake had bitten me. In that state of mind, the last thing I needed to hear was that someone was proud of me. I wasn't proud of myself. And this guy is proud of me? I wanted to punch him out. I just wanted to get the hell out of there. And we did. A few weeks later, Courteney and I were in Chicago together so that she could interview for a potential position at Northwestern University. My phone buzzed and I looked at it and it was Randy Cupp. I immediately went into badass mode, thinking, I'm going to tear into this guy. I hate you, Randy Cupp. But I went ahead and answered it anyway, feeling all defensive and pissed-off.

He asked me how I was doing.

How do you think I'm doing? I was getting ready to unload on him.

He asked me if I'd be willing to take a phone call from someone. He had noticed while I was down there that I was dealing with some stuff. He thought he could help me. I thought that this redneck rancher couldn't do anything to help me. Nobody really could. I said okay to the phone call if it was kept short. I hung up on him. A moment later another Texas number showed up on my phone's display. I jabbed at the green phone icon hard enough to put my finger through the screen. The next thing I knew, I felt that same sensation take over my body as the one that had in that deer blind. Blissful. This crazy thing. The sweetest voice I ever heard introduced itself as belonging to

Kara Williams at the Brain Treatment Foundation. She told me that they had a relationship with a doctor in Boston who could really help me. I was living in East Hartford, Connecticut, at the time so Boston was not far at all. "I don't think so," I said. "There aren't a lot of people who have the baggage I do."

Kara told me it was worth my time to try this out. I did not have many options at that point. Thinking about what my dad had done, in a sick way, gave me the confidence to do it, too. I thought if he could do it, I could. I told myself, If this doctor doesn't work, well, sayonara. I went to see this doctor and I had a four-hour appointment, which had me antsy and angry. They did a big blood draw and told me that I'd hear from them in a week. I wasn't sure I'd last that long, but God had other plans.

When I showed up for the next appointment, the doctor told me she was going to fix me. I thought, Yeah right. But basically, she said, as a result of my TBI, my brain was not functioning properly, so my body was all out of whack chemically, molecularly, hormonally. She started pumping all kinds of fluids into me to get my body to start regulating itself properly.

It changed everything. I couldn't believe how good I was progressively starting to feel, and over the next few months I started to make leaps and bounds in a positive direction. For the first time in years, I had hope for the future. I've been undergoing these treatments for two years now, and they've totally turned my life around. A lot of the guys that I connected with through all these tragedies and have been injured themselves are getting the same treatments and doing well with them.

It all happened because Joey had been persistent. He put me in touch with Randy, who put me in touch with Kara, who put me in touch with Dr. Kathleen. That bond we have, with Danny and others as well, has had a huge ripple effect. And I have a strong bond with

God now. In that deer blind, I turned to Him, and He put all those pieces in place and made all those connections. I now go to church regularly and belong to a men's group there, where I find a strong connection and sense of belonging with them. My life is back on track. Courteney and I are still together, and happily married. We have a six-month-old, and things have really turned around for me. I even finished college. Courteney has been one of the biggest blessings of my life, along with our child.

It's been a heck of a ride, and even through all the hard spots I'm grateful for how things went. I spend a lot of time traveling around the country telling my story and encouraging veterans, anyone who is struggling to not give up. You've got to be resilient. You never know the road map your struggles can be for others who are in a place that you once were, but that map cannot be used if you quit and remove yourself. You can't push away the people who care about you. If you're one of those people being pushed, dig in your heels. I know that guys like Joey, Danny, and Greg are super special, but there are other people out there like them in most people's lives. The great thing about them was that they didn't just ask me what I needed: they were proactive and did things for me and kept after me. I can honestly say that, though I still miss Adam every single day, and I know that I caused a lot of people in my life stress and anxiety and worry, I'm proud of myself and proud of the relationships that sustained me then and now.

I'm grateful for God's love, grace, and mercy through all my struggles. I remember one of the first church services I attended through my struggles while trying to find healing. The pastor said, "If you are struggling with God, why don't you look up the meaning of your name? God put your name in your parents' head because of the plan He had for your life, and there is a reason why you are named what you are." So I looked mine up. "Amos" biblically means "able to carry." It made everything so clear and has helped me to lean on God more and more as I go through life. We don't have to carry everything alone. We have Him, and those He surrounds us with.

★★★★★★★★★★★★★★★★★★★★★★★★★★★★★★★★

I don't think Amos knew it, but I wasn't just inviting him on a deer hunt. I was asking him to come have a big, uncomfortable conversation over a few days and watch God's creations just live their simple but necessary lives. But not a conversation with me, or my friend Randy Cupp: a conversation with himself. Amos had been through more than anyone should have to endure. He'd seen more loss than any man his age should have to. But he had been blessed, too. He had a beautiful loving wife, he'd escaped the worst of war mostly intact, and he had so many people who loved him and needed him in their lives. He just needed to see it, and respond to it. I'm a firm believer that a deer blind and a plain-spoken Texan can shake a lot of sense into someone like us hardheaded Marines. Amos found something that weekend that Randy and I saw even before he did. He left knowing he was going to have to get through this and live his life and maybe even learn to be happy again. That kind of feeling can be uncomfortable, but it's also the kind of feeling that reminds us of the bonds we have, the responsibilities we have to those we love. Amos stepped up to the plate, took action, and started the journey we all seek, the journey to happiness.

★★★★★★★★★★★★★★★★★★★★★★★★★★★★★★★★

Blood Brothers

STAFF SERGEANT (RET.) DANIEL W. RIDGEWAY

★ United States Marine Corps ★

"I was trained by the best and
simply performed as expected
in the environment I was
placed in. With that said, as
an EOD technician it was my
responsibility to protect the
incredibly brave 1st Battalion,
5th Marines on the battlefield
from the complex IED ambushes
of Sangin, Afghanistan."

★★★★★★★★★★★★★★★★★★★★★★★★★★★★★★★★★★★★★★★

Some people ease into your life. You slowly get to know each other and maybe, eventually, you become friends. Others, well, they barrel in, elbows up and with a grin that says, "Boy, you're stuck with me whether you like it or not." It was in that fashion I met Danny Ridgeway. Danny and I met in EOD school down near Destin, Florida. We both needed a roommate to share a house with, we both talked like sweet tea and banjos, we both loved college football, working out, hunting, fishing, drinking cold beer, and, well . . . chasing women.

I'm from Dalton, Georgia, in the northwest corner of the state, and Danny is from Gadsden, Alabama, in the northeast corner of his state. If you folded the states together like a book, our two hometowns would touch. When people would ask us where we're from I'd say, "I'm from top left Georgia, he's from top right Alabama." We hit it off quick and man, did we have fun. We were in one of the most highly secured schools in the military, which meant we couldn't take any material, notes, or conversations home. Five days a week we were training to be bomb techs for twelve hours a day, and the other twelve hours were ours to do with as we saw fit. For me and Danny that meant trips to fine establishments like Harry T's, where a cover band sang songs like "Mustang Sally" while we drank blue-colored Long Island Iced Teas from quart jars.

The average age of their patrons was fifty-five, then there was me and Danny in our early twenties. We dated the entire weekend shift at the Destin Hooters—yes, you read that right. And took part-time jobs as floor models at the Abercrombie & Fitch clothing store.

On the weekends we hosted other Marine EOD students at our house for beer pong or just beer. Saturdays we were at the beach, then the nightclubs, and on Sundays we'd sober up by drinking Sparks (an alcoholic energy drink) and playing volleyball at Whale's Tale beach. We had a lot of fun together. But that year of training was hard. The stress is intense under the constant cloud of "double tap and you're out," meaning if we failed the same test twice, we were gone from EOD school, back to our old jobs. With top secret security clearances needed to be there, we couldn't have any alcohol-related incidents even if it wasn't our fault, or else we'd lose our clearance. We also dealt with personal struggles. My grandfather passed away while I was in the middle of school and it was the first real loss I'd experienced. Danny was there for me through it all. My Rammer-Jammer-Yella-Hammer, Bama-lovin' partner in crime. We knew the war was ramping up, IEDs were becoming more effective and harder to find or disarm, and within a year of graduating this difficult school in the heart of a country boy's paradise, we'd both be in Afghanistan doing the "long walk" ourselves.

★★★★★★★★★★★★★★★★★★★★★★★★★★★★★★★★★★★★★★

DANNY

About three years ago, I got a text from Amos Benjamin. He wanted me to come up to Pennsylvania to meet him. He and his wife were living in Connecticut at the time. She was getting her PhD and he was getting an undergraduate degree. I asked him what was up and he texted back telling me that he had something for me. I thought, Well, then, okay.

"When?" I texted back.

"Tomorrow."

I let him know that I could take a couple of days off work.

I now live in Southern Maryland and we met somewhere in Pennsylvania near the interstate. I got out of my truck and then Amos got out of his. He ducked back inside for a second and then when he turned around I could see he had something bundled up in his arms. Turned out it was an English spaniel puppy. I was in a text group with a bunch of guys like Amos, and Joey, and Greg, and a few others. I'd told them that my dog Leeroy had died last Christmas. I'd had Leeroy since I was still in the Marine Corps. When I wasn't deployed, Leeroy and I spent all our time together. He slept in the bed with me, even. Christmas Eve, I went to sleep and Leeroy was right there. I woke up Christmas morning and thought, Where's Leeroy? I got up and found him on the floor. It was like he just lay down and went to sleep and passed away.

So, Amos found out about me losing Leeroy, and he decided that I needed another dog. He took time out from his studies and flew down to Tallahassee, Florida, where he picked up a female English spaniel for me, got her all her shots so she would be good to go, then took her back to Connecticut with him until he had the time to meet with me. I named her Miss Daisy Marie, and she's got champion bird-dog bloodlines in her. The first night I had her as a pup, I wondered if she'd retrieve. I threw a ball. She ran after it and brought it right back. I was like, "Wow! Check her out!" When I got her home, I took her out in the yard. She just started zigging and zagging, flushing the whole area. Then she saw something that got her interest and she started pointing, lifting her paw up and so on. I didn't have to teach her any of that. Amazing!

★★★★★★★★★★★★★★★★★★★★★★★★★★★★★★★★★★★★★

When Danny and I lived together in EOD school, one of our Marine instructors gave us an old female English bulldog named Sadie Mae. Danny fell in love with her, which was ironic considering I'm the Georgia fan and he's an Alabama fan. He kept her when we moved to our units and later got Leeroy, to keep her company. After going through so much in those first years after EOD school, those dogs were his family. Unfortunately for Danny, and most of us, loss was a common experience by the time Leeroy passed away, but we also knew how to help each other through it. That's why we had a group text, that's how we deal with our emotions and stay connected to the only men in the world who know what we are going through and how it feels.

The group text is mostly Marine EOD techs who all deployed together. I went to the sister unit on the west coast, but I went to EOD school with all those guys in the group so I'm closer to them than most of the guys I deployed with. Second EOD Company took some hard hits when they replaced us and held Afghanistan in 2011. Along with losing some of the best techs in the Corps to IED strikes, they performed heroically. Danny was awarded the third-highest combat valor award, the Silver Star, for his actions. At the time he was presented with it at Camp Lejeune in December 2013, he was one of only forty-three Marines who had received the Silver Star for their actions in Iraq and Afghanistan since the beginning of the Global War on Terrorism.

In 2011, Danny was serving with 1st Battalion, 5th Marine Regiment in Sangin, Afghanistan, when the routine heroism of risking his life by rendering safe an IED turned into crawling on his hands and knees clearing several IEDs on a path to reach his teammate who'd been injured by an IED himself. When he finally reached his brother, Danny treated his wounds, escorted the corpsman to his teammate to continue treatment, and then cleared a hundred-meter by hundred-meter landing zone so his brother could be evacuated by helicopter. After that, they came under fire, and Danny kept at it, clearing more of the area for the Marines he was supporting, disarming even more IEDs there and three more on another patrol that afternoon.

How rare were Danny's heroic actions? As Major General Michael C. Dana, the commanding general of the 2nd Logistics Group while Danny was deployed, said, "What he did for the Marine Corps, his fellow Marines, was absolutely selfless. His actions reflect the best that EOD brings to the fight."*

Just as would be expected from one of our ranks, when he was presented with the Silver Star, he spoke of the bond that he had with another Marine in particular, his mentor, Gunnery Sergeant Ralph "EJ" Pate. EJ was Danny's mentor and was killed in action in 2011. For Danny, and several others in Danny's unit, losing EJ was extremely difficult to take. Losing a friend, losing a mentor, is difficult enough. When you endure heavy losses in a relatively short period of time, the pain isn't just hard to handle—it's soul crushing and life changing.

Just as our new friends will never replace the ones we lost in battle, Daisy isn't meant to replace Leeroy, but she is there to remind him that life goes on, and there's a bond and love to share if we keep ourselves willing. As Danny said in an interview following his Silver Star presentation, "It's about how hard you can get hit and keep moving forward." That's a quote from the movie *Rocky Balboa*. Honestly, I don't think there's a more perfect example of just how pure and country and simple but genuine Danny Ridgeway is than quoting a Rocky movie at his Silver Star ceremony. And just

---

* https://www.dvidshub.net/news/106250/humble-hero-alabama -marine-receives-silver-star-medal

like the celebrated movie character, Danny has kept getting back up. Despite sustaining multiple traumatic brain injuries from the concussive blasts doing his job in Afghanistan, Danny keeps looking and moving ahead. And like a good hunting dog, we're still here by his side, ready for the next adventure.

★★

INSPIRATION TO SERVE

My grandfathers and my uncle Mike were the reason I joined the military, them and my dad. My grandpa Wayne was an MP in the Army. Grandpa Ralph was a Tin Can Sailor and Uncle Mike was a gunner's mate in the Navy then retired as a Colorado State Trooper. My dad didn't serve in the Marines, but he always held them in high regard. It seemed like a lot of people I knew felt the same way. My baseball coach, Brandon Johnson, had a friend who was a Marine, and he brought a lot of that military discipline to our squad, including having to have our baseball cleats at a high polish for every game. We couldn't wear them in our clubhouse or locker room, either. All of that stuck with me and added to my interest.

As a high school kid, I kind of lost my way for a bit. I ended up wanting to be a wild young man more than anything, and by the time my senior year came around, I quit baseball so that I could take a second-shift job. I gave my buddy who was my backup on the team my glove. I figured I should because we were friends and it was on his grandpa's property that I went hunting for the first time. Hunting is kind of an individual thing, but I enjoyed being with a group. I was good friends with Matt and Marc Powell. Along with them and their father, Larry, I was a part of the Greene County Hunt Club down past Tuscaloosa, Alabama.

My biological mom and dad had divorced when I was very young, and I still got on pretty well with my stepmom and dad, but that experience with the Powells and the rest of the men at the hunt club was really good for me and I learned a lot. There were about twelve to fifteen men and young men in it. Come Labor Day and early September, we would have a workday. This was cool because it was different from anything I'd experienced in Gadsden, where we had a family printing business. So, before the opening of rifle hunting season, all these men would bring different pieces of their farming equipment down to the hunt club. They'd bring whatever they had and plow up the fields and plant rye, winter wheat, chicory, and various types of clover to be food for deer. They'd call them green fields because, quite simply, they were about the only green vegetation around during the winter and early spring months. After that we'd put up our deer stands. It was a lot of work, but I saw how if a bunch of people got together, you could get a big job knocked out all in one day. Also, you'd know where all the stands were on that property so when hunting season came along we'd know the land better. Finally, we'd sit around a fire and eat hot dogs and talk. There was the camaraderie of all that. I had learned to hunt and fire a gun on my own, and got pretty good at it. But I got a lot better in the Marine Corps. I had instructors and other guys to talk to about technique and other things.

★★★★★★★★★★★★★★★★★★★★★★★★★★★★★★★★★★

That camaraderie Danny speaks of with his hunting mentors and buddies is commonplace growing up in the South. Maybe it's the hot summers, or the slower pace, or simply the fact most of us are poor, but growing up down here means you share a tight bond with the men you work and hunt with. Those experiences pay off well for us when we join the Marine Corps and become absolutely necessary in EOD. Like most of us, Danny learned of EOD from working with EOD techs in-country.

Before becoming an EOD tech, Danny served in the Marines as a communication repair technician and eventually as an augmented machine gunner in the turret of an armored vehicle. Ironically, or perhaps through the touch of fate, I, too, started my Marine Corps career as a radio repairman and also deployed as an augmented machine gunner in a turret in Iraq. Which meant we literally covered the same ground and had the same experiences that led us to find EOD. While on deployment, he spotted something in the road ahead. He recognized it was a Meals, Ready to Eat (MRE) package. The enemy was known to use them to disguise IEDs. Having trained with and learned from the EOD teams in his area, Danny knew exactly what to do. After spotting it, and confirming it was indicative of a possible IED, Danny's team called in EOD to inspect and potentially render safe the IED. This is the exact way of working with and learning from others that Danny experienced with his hunting club. Men with different jobs and different levels of experience working together to accomplish a mission and achieve collective success.

★★★★★★★★★★★★★★★★★★★★★★★★★★★★★★★★★★★★★★

FINDING A PURPOSE

I didn't realize it then, but after going through EOD school and then doing similar work, I knew that techs want to speak directly with the person who spotted the suspected device. They want to know what tipped me off. What caught my eye about it? Every little thing that could help the EOD team piece the puzzle together. So, in this case, the EOD tech walked along the side of our convoy and was eventually told to talk with me. I was a lance corporal at the time. As a Marine I was used to strict discipline of following regulations and proper customs and courtesies. The EOD Marine came up alongside the truck I was in and introduced himself by his first name. Then he proceeded talking to me like I was just a normal guy and not a lance corporal. You've got to understand: any EOD tech is a sergeant (E5) and above, and this particular EOD Marine was an E7 gunnery sergeant. A lance corporal is an E3, many ranks lower. So a gunny talking to me so casually was quite surprising. I know now that he was attempting to make me feel comfortable with him so that I would accurately describe everything I saw regarding the suspected device.

Later, I went to my platoon gunny and asked him about how I could go do EOD work. I was coming up on the end of my enlistment and was trying to decide if I should get out of the Marine Corps or not. He told me that if I was thinking about it, I should just go to the EOD compound where those guys were set up at the forward operating base. As a result of that, I found something that I really, really wanted to do. Before joining the Marines, I had other things I wanted to do—I hoped to get a baseball scholarship, I wanted to join the pro bass fishing circuit. The first of those I didn't have the discipline for; the second I didn't have the money for all the gear I would need. I was a good student, in honors and Advanced Placement classes and all that, but let's just say that I started to like the girls a little too much. I had enough credits as a senior that I only had to go to classes for half the day. The other half of the day I worked at a hazardous waste plant and then eventually as a member of an Osmore Utilities crew that inspected power poles for Alabama Power and various other power companies. I did that right up until I joined the Marines in 2004, when things in my personal life were getting a little out of control. I certainly had to reassess my priorities and needed the discipline that the Marine Corps would teach me.

On March 14, 2004, I went to boot camp at Parris Island, South Carolina, and stepped on the yellow footprints. I knew there was change ahead but had no idea what I was actually getting myself into. I was naturally athletic and did well in the physical part, but I was having a hell of a hard time understanding what it was the drill instructors were saying! They talked so fast in this frogman kind of voice. Because of that, and my slow country bumpkin twang of an accent, I had a hard time understanding the drill instructors and made a lot of mistakes. At least I got the most important thing they were trying to teach us—teamwork. I understood that we were stronger together than separate. I'm not a patient guy, so it's probably a good thing I was deployed pretty quickly after boot camp. I'm also a quick learner, when there isn't a language barrier.

In August 2005, I set off on my first deployment. I stepped off a plane in Kuwait and got hit by a blast of heat like nothing I'd ever felt before. I recall feeling the soles of my boots softening on the asphalt runway. This wasn't Alabama heat. For example, I had been dipping Copenhagen Fine Cut for a few years by then, and after the first couple of days out in that heat, I had heartburn so bad I gave my three logs of Copenhagen away and that was it for that stuff. I was in communications and didn't see any kind of serious combat on that deployment. The highlight for me was being assigned to a security element at Baghdad International Airport. I was on a joint service team whose mission was to search, screen, and disperse Iraqis throughout the country to work election poll sites. We worked alongside the Army 10th Mountain at Camp Victory to select and search the hopeful Iraqis. Then we transported them back to a small compound outside Sather Air Base set up to screen them using fingerprint and retinal scans. Surprisingly enough, we did have a number of bad guys who tried to integrate into the masses of otherwise good citizens.

Once they were screened, we would transport the Iraqis over to the Air Force personnel who were waiting on the runway in their C130s to take the workers to poll sites. Once the elections were over, we would transport the workers to Camp Victory, where they would return to their daily lives. It was quite the adventure and helped me see clearly that communications was not what I was looking to do. Once I returned from that deployment, I was immediately placed into a provisional rifle squad whose purpose was base force protection as well as convoy security, and put on rotation to deploy back to Iraq. This was the deployment during which I began seeing the effects of IEDs and experiencing the incredible heroism of EOD techs.

I don't like to talk too much about some of the things from my EOD time. When I do, I get a cold, numb feeling all over my body. I often describe my time as an EOD tech in Sangin, Afghanistan, as the best yet worst time in my life. Beyond that, I don't feel like there's anything productive that can come from talking about it in detail. Some things I forget. Other things I can't forget.

I met Joey when I was in EOD school. He was in a different class than me, but his grandfather had passed away, and he was granted leave to go home. His class kept going, so he wasn't able to rejoin that one, and he was waiting for another class to reach the point where he'd left off. So, while waiting for that to happen, he was serving as the Marine Detachment platoon sergeant. We were in early morning formation and Joey was out front and center calling off names. As I heard him calling off the names, I thought, This guy has to be from northern Alabama with that accent. He got to me and I said, "Here" with as much accent as I could. He stopped and looked at me and then at the clipboard.

"Say that again."

I did.

"Where are you from?"

"Top right Alabama."

Most people haven't heard of Etowah County, Alabama, or Gadsden so I gave him those "coordinates."

He understood immediately and said, "Well, by God, I'm from top left Georgia. We need to have a talk!"

From that geographical connection, we wound up being roommates because someone had moved out of his place and he needed a replacement. In the end, we wound up being really good friends. That's saying a lot, considering he's from Georgia and is a Bulldogs fan. But we grew up the same way, and we had similar jobs in the Marine Corps before turning to EOD. It's crazy. I'm an Alabama fan. He's a Georgia guy, but I wouldn't be too sad if Alabama lost the national championship and Georgia won it. At least Joey would get to celebrate something. I'm not so big and stingy that I wouldn't want him to enjoy his team winning.

★★★★★★★★★★★★★★★★★★★★★★★★★★★★★★★★★★★★★★★

Danny conceding a smile for my Dawgs winning the 2021 national championship over his Tide is a really big deal and indicative of the bond we share. It may seem trivial to many, but as we say in the South, if "you ain't from 'round here," you just can't understand. Maybe it's because our universities have the state right up front in the name: University of Georgia, Alabama, Tennessee, Florida . . . Or maybe it's because we didn't have any major professional sports teams until the late 1960s, or maybe it's simply that growing up in the South is a "hands-on lifestyle" and football is about as hands-on a sport as there is. Whatever the reason, we're passionate about it.

It's not just combat that can create these relationships that surpass even our deepest passions and identities. Danny and I bonded over a similar past, we shared the experience of going through EOD school, and the promise of certain tragedy if we were "lucky" enough to graduate and join this fraternity of insane bomb techs we volunteered to be a part of. And that promise was kept. I, in 2010, and Danny, in 2011, saw good, courageous men fall on the battlefield, sacrificing their own tomorrows for others. Then comes the guilt, the sadness, and the grief. We miss them each in our own ways, but we never ever stop saying their names.

★★★★★★★★★★★★★★★★★★★★★★★★★★★★★★★★★★

MENTORS

On my first tour as an EOD tech, I went out on a team with Gunnery Sergeant EJ Pate. He was our section leader, and he doubled as my team leader. He was the most knowledgeable and skilled guy we had, as he had just returned from a very kinetic (kinetic is how we say "a lot of direct enemy activity") deployment to Marjah, Afghanistan. We were fortunate the first bit when we were there in Sangin. It was during the poppy harvest, and the Taliban didn't want to disrupt those operations too much. The sale of black-tar heroin produced from those poppies was a big part of how they funded their operations. We were out patrolling, mostly finding legacy IEDs—ones that had been planted a while ago. The combat engineers were sweeping for them and the infantry Marines would often spot as well. It wasn't a very kinetic situation at first, but toward the end of the poppy season, in early May or so, that changed.

EJ had trained me from day one as a team leader. Any time off we had during the day was spent doing "backyard training" with our metal detectors, identifying visual disturbances on the ground, and discussing previous IED scenarios. I did my best to pass on that training. One day we got a call at sunrise, way earlier than we'd ever been called before. An infantry squad had found a suspected IED. We got there and went to work. There were five IEDs in that one compound. Based on our examination, it was likely that they'd been placed the night before. That's when I realized that the heat had just turned up.

Over the next few weeks, EJ and I began working multiple IEDs daily in many areas across the battlespace. Then one of the teams to the north of our area of operations experienced mass casualty incidents due to complex IED ambushes. These ambushes consisted of multiple IEDs set up with land-mine warfare tactics. A number of enemy fighters would be in an L-shaped–style ambush with medium and light machine guns, and occasionally mortars, recoilless rifle systems, and various rocket platforms. Once the patrol made it through a canal and/or tree line and into a field, the enemy would open with small arms fire, with the intent to push the dismounted Marines through tree lines and into canals seeking cover. In the tree lines and on the edge of canals is where the IEDs would be waiting.

A platoon of Marines sustained so many casualties that they were deemed combat ineffective and had to cease patrols until they received replacements. The EOD team in that area was injured during these mass casualty incidents as well. That's when EJ and our command made the decision to promote me to team leader and send me north. They believed that I was ready to take on things without him watching over me.

I was assigned a new teammate and my team joined a platoon of Marines who had come in from elsewhere to patrol the area of operations around Patrol Base Fires until the injured platoon received their replacements. Based on the intense fighting and multiple IED strikes there just a few days before, we knew what was in store.

We were aware of where the enemy fighters were operating. I studied all the current intelligence reports and the ones from previous years. My team was embedded into the dismounted infantry patrols to remove IEDs and prevent another mass casualty incident. Essentially the goal was this: disarming the enemy and breaking their will to fight. Our first day there, the enemy opened up the L-shaped ambush on us in the middle of a flooded field. Luckily we were able to counter their attack and get out of the field without taking any casualties.

The next morning, we patrolled into the same area, fully expecting a fight. I had just made my way into the field when my teammate was on his way out of the canal . . . and that's when I experienced what felt like a power surge. I had no idea what had happened. At first I thought we'd been mortared. When I heard my teammate yelling, I realized he'd stepped on an IED. Knowing there would be more IEDs close by, I yelled for everyone in the patrol not to move as I walked the short distance back to assess his injuries and apply a tourniquet. I remembered all the teachings from my friends about working slowly and cautiously. However, I knew Marines were fully exposed in the open without cover, and I had to neutralize the IEDs and open an egress route. The rest of that day was written up for a Silver Star citation.

★★★★★★★★★★★★★★★★★★★★★★★★★★★★★★★★★

After Danny cleared a path to that teammate and put him on the helicopter, the enemy began shooting from multiple directions. During the engagement he searched for, found, and rendered safe five additional IEDs within close proximity of the initial strike. In this same time frame the squad leader was maneuvering his Marines, who were fighting in the open, against the enemy positions. They began to hear reports that the enemy had taken casualties. Once the IEDs were neutralized, the squad leader began removing his Marines from the kill zone in the field in order to return to base. Later that day, Danny requested to join the next patrol, due to the high probability that there would be more work to do. Sure enough, he soon found himself clearing another IED-saturated field to reach an injured lance corporal. He went crawling on his stomach through the dirt for forty meters, moving more quickly and less delicately than normal in his haste to reach the injured man.

He then swept another hundred-meter-square area to clear for the Marine's medical evacuation by helicopter. Throughout the day, Danny ended up using hands-on render-safe procedures to disarm eight IEDs.

He went back on patrol that day because he knew the Marines operating in that dangerous area needed EOD support. He was their best option.

To put it in top left Alabama terms, it was his job to take away the enemy's best weapon: IEDs.

★★★★★★★★★★★★★★★★★★★★★★★★★★★★★★★★★★★★

THE IMPORTANCE OF TRAINING

I did my job. I had gone into the EOD field because I knew that the number one weapon used by the enemy in the Global War on Terrorism was IEDs. EOD techs have the most extensive knowledge and training with these devices, so it seemed to me that EOD was the correct decision. I also felt that doing the job, in itself, is a very honorable and noble display of a person's character. And thanks to EJ training me, I was able to become pretty damn good at it. Not to be a cocky bastard, but I was pretty damn good. I was trained by the best and simply performed as expected in the environment I was placed in. With that said, as an EOD tech it was my responsibility to protect the incredibly brave Marines on the battlefield from the complex IED ambushes of Sangin. I knew that I belonged in EOD, just like I knew I belonged clearing that area so that we could get a helicopter in there and get the Marines who were providing security back to safety.

EJ was twenty-nine years old when I met him. That's a lifetime in the Marine Corps. I was twenty-five. EJ had done, I think, seven deployments and maybe five of them were in EOD. So, he'd seen how things had evolved from doing mounted operations—patrolling in a vehicle—to dismounted. In Sangin, we would patrol on foot down little goat paths, literally stepping in the boot prints of the Marine in front of you. Once, one of my buddies from EOD school was on his way home, and I asked him for advice. He said, "Every step is a conscious decision." I never let that out of my mind. I also heard catchy ironic phrases like "Welcome to Sangin, watch your step!" and "2011 Spring Break—Bangin' in Sangin!" This was dark Marine humor we used to cope, because a lot of Marines were losing legs and getting shot. The area was historically known for combat units sustaining very high casualties. Our EOD section nicknamed Sangin the "Epicenter of Evil." Every one of us wanted to be there. Working in Sangin as an EOD tech was comparable to playing in the Super Bowl.

I got to know EJ really well, and what can I tell you? He had a number of motorcycles and a black BMW car, and everywhere he went, he was going there fast. However, speed wasn't his thing when he was working. He was cool, calm, and collected. A bona fide "BDP." Use your imagination. It probably means what you think it means. He was as meticulous as could be, and as professional as could be. He was the team leader everyone wanted to be working with. I was the lucky boot tech who got to work with him. I owe being chosen to work with EJ to another friend of mine, Johnny Morris, who went to school with Joey and me. So, when the EOD guys make it back from deployment they get to pick from among the newly trained guys (boots) to have as a teammate. It's kind of like the Major League Baseball draft. EJ came back and Johnny told him that he should select me. It was mostly about the fact that EJ and I had similar interests, being hunting and fishing guys and all. It wasn't just that, but those activities require you to be a really good observer. Things like noticing patterns, ground signs, and any little detail that could prove to be the difference in success or failure, all of which comes in handy as an EOD tech.

I had a lot of respect for EJ and at first it was mostly about that. Later on, when we were deployed and there was downtime, we talked a lot more, worked out, had breakfast, lunch, and dinner together, and every now and then we would watch a movie or play a video game on his portable TV he had mounted in a Pelican storage case. After he was killed by an IED, we were all shocked. To me . . . I felt a very cold feeling rush over my body, which then turned into a numb feeling. If I could describe it, I would compare it to being stabbed in the spine with a frozen ice pick. We all agreed that he was one of the best. Even the best can do everything right and still end up having a bad day resulting in injury or death. That's the inherent risk that comes with EOD. Playing for keeps. No second chances. Everyone knows it and accepts it. I only knew him a short while if you measure it on a calendar, but when you know somebody under those circumstances, it kind of speeds things up.

I got to meet his mother, Erma, and his pop the night we were leaving for deployment. When I was awarded the Silver Star, I invited them to the ceremony. After the ceremony, we went back to the EOD shop. Greg—Major Wrubluski—was in charge of the company. He said, "All right, we're opening up the bar." Greg gave me the opportunity to say a few words and I presented Erma with the medal I had just been awarded. It was absolutely the right thing to do. I mean there was no question that was going to happen. Every one of us who got back alive, even the ones who were injured, agreed that it was because of what EJ taught us that we made it. He was the dude, you know. He was the guy.

Now for years since then, I'll go on my own or go with Greg to visit Erma and Pop. It's sad that their house burned down and the medal's gone. EJ's shadow box with his uniform and medals burned in the fire, too. We organized a fundraiser for her so that she could rebuild. Pop was gone by this time. She needed our help and we were glad to do what we could.

★★★★★★★★★★★★★★★★★★★★★★★★★★★★★★★★★★★★★

Danny, Johnny Mo, and I went to school together. I deployed first in early 2010, then Johnny, then Danny. All within a little over a year. We all knew that showing up at a new EOD unit was scary. The job field is small; you either know everyone or know "of" everyone. Each EOD tech has a reputation. This reputation is earned through good work, or bad decisions, and we all wanted to both earn a good reputation and work with those, like EJ and Greg, who'd earned theirs through tough deployments and good work.

EOD isn't just a job field, it's a community. We have a culture that exists solely within Marine EOD. The nature of the job is intense. Whether we are at war working IEDs or clearing bombing ranges on bases here at home of unexploded ordnance deployed during training, we can lose our lives any day of the week just doing our jobs. And since everyone makes honest mistakes on the job, when an EOD tech makes a mistake that might have ended in injury or death but doesn't, it's customary to "punish" them by charging them a case of beer that goes into a fridge at the shop. Then, when something happens worthy of celebration, or one of us is killed in action overseas, the unit commander "lights the beer lamp" and no matter what time of day, if we're at work, we stop and crack open a beer. Having lit the beer lamp too many times for good men lost in battle, Greg and all of 2nd EOD needed something to celebrate.

★★★★★★★★★★★★★★★★★★★★★★★★★★★★★★★★★★★★★

MEETING GREG

Greg's a great guy and a lot of officers wouldn't do the kind of things he does for the guys in his command or their parents. I know he took the loss of any of his men really seriously. He took his job in all kinds of ways very seriously. He came back to EOD to help whip us into shape. We had one guy who went out on a ride on his motorcycle with his girlfriend on the front naked. He hit a tree and that's when they called Greg in to straighten things out in the command. I remember the exact moment I met Greg. Because he was the commanding officer, he had a designated parking space. The rest of us had to find what we could find, but a lot of the time we let one of the more senior guys have the one next to the CO's spot. The day Greg assumed command, I got there super early and decided it was okay to take the spot next to Greg's empty one.

When he showed up that morning (he was a captain at the time), he walked in the front door shouting, "Whose piece-of-shit F-250 is that with the Alabama plates and the Roll Tide tag?"

"Sir, that's mine, sir," I told him.

"Well, I'm a Gators fan, and I'll tell you what, this year we're going to kick your ass!"

He was the first officer I met at his level that would bullshit about football in the manner he did. I loved it.

Greg was with EJ on the battlefield the day he died. He went out with EJ as his teammate per se, which isn't very common for a high-ranking officer to do. Over the years and ever since that deployment, he's always looked out for me, knowing how much EJ meant to me. Greg was a damned fine officer then and he still takes care of his guys to this day. I know he carries a lot of responsibility on his shoulders, and I talk with him, in one way or another, every day. There's a group of us that are real tight and look out for one another, most of whom worked with Greg or for him.

Sometimes we talk about what we went through that day and a lot of the time we just talk about what's going on in our lives or in the world. It's not like it's all talk therapy, but talking and sharing with people who understand what you've been through because they went through their version of it themselves helps a bunch.

★★★★★★★★★★★★★★★★★★★★★★★★★★★★★★★★★★★★

They say the men who came home from World War II were so successful, following such a brutal war, because they had to float on a ship for a month together to get back home. They spent that time talking, and listening, to one another. Now, decades later, we come home in a few days. We don't get that mandated soak time to get our minds right. We deal with the hidden injuries of war in different ways, and for Danny, Greg, myself, and many of our friends it's our annual hunting trips that allow us to retell our best days and sometimes solemnly remember our worst. Perhaps it's a Band-Aid fix to a tourniquet problem, but it definitely helps. Hunting trips are eerily similar to deployments in both aesthetics and atmosphere. We're in bare-bones and makeshift dwellings, in remote places, focused on a mission and "fighting" an enemy we rarely see. But those nights are when we sit around and have nothing else to do but talk. One postwar story gets told annually, especially if a new guy is hunting with us. It really explains all you need to know about Alabama's finest son, Danny Ridgeway.

★★★★★★★★★★★★★★★★★★★★★★★★★★★★★★★★★★★★

OUTFOXED

I ended up going to a TBI clinic two different times. I didn't have one catastrophic injury, but like a football player who got his bell rung too many times, the damage builds up. Eventually I was recommended to go to the National Intrepid Center of Excellence (NICOE). That's a Department of Defense organization that provides care and does research into TBIs and psychological health for military service members. It's in Bethesda, Maryland, right near Walter Reed National Military Medical Center. I would go in for treatment, but wasn't staying there full-time, so I was living in the Fisher House with my ex-wife and other service members and their people. My ex-wife and I had our own room, but there was a community kitchen and eight or so community refrigerators where you put your own food separate from everybody else's food.

Somewhere along the line, I was told that if there was anybody interested in hunting, there was an organization (I forget which) that was going to take wounded warriors on a trip the next weekend. I was like, "Heck yeah! I'll go out with them." So I went hunting and ended up getting a red fox. I wanted to get it full mounted because it was pretty big and a real beauty. I had a taxidermist in mind back home that could do the work. Along with those refrigerators, there were stand-up freezers. The deal with them was that if you put any food in there, you put your name and the date on the package so folks would know whose was whose. I'm from Gadsden, Alabama, and I've put game in a freezer a bunch of times. So I triple-bagged that fox and put my name on the package and added the date just like regulations required. In the freezer it went.

Then Thanksgiving came around and my ex-wife and I stayed in the area rather than go all the way down to Alabama to see my family or out to California to see hers. We spent the time with some of the other guys being treated there at one of the other clinics. After we got back to Fisher House, I decided to check on my fox. I opened the freezer door and it wasn't there. *What in the world?*

It had been in there with a bunch of turkeys that had been donated so that the families could have a bird for Thanksgiving dinner. I guess that the housekeepers were told to move the turkeys from one of the Fisher Houses to another. They loaded up all the frozen carcasses and transferred them. They must not have seen my name and date and whatnot on the bag, and grabbed my fox up and took it. Then they were wanting to thaw all those turkeys to cook them up. When they tore into my fox bag, those ladies freaked out. We're talking Bethesda, Maryland, here, and those ladies hadn't been in a country freezer before. They reported to their supervisor and then she contacted me. She was a hard-core, left-leaning type and told me that she was going to have to report this incident to the police. I was like, "What?" She went on to tell me that she put that police tape all around the freezer because anything in it might be contaminated with rabies.

She also said that she had contacted the emergency room medical officer over the phone and he had said that I was going to have to get rabies shots. In an attempt to negotiate, I told her I would go get checked for rabies, in hopes that would smooth things over. She agreed to it. I went over to the emergency room and the nurse started wheeling out a cart with a bunch of big long needles. I asked what they were for.

She said, "Honey, the only way to get checked for rabies is to saw the top of the skull off and examine the brain. You're getting rabies shots!"

I jumped up and said, "No, I'm not!" And walked out.

The medical officer at the emergency room was not happy I left. So she called the Navy master chief who was in charge of active duty enlisted personnel at NICOE. This was turning into a huge fiasco. Lucky for me, the master chief was from Texas and grew up around the hunting culture. I told him that I had observed the fox for a period of time and it never showed any signs of being rabid. It didn't bite me, I didn't kiss it, and I didn't drink its blood in some crazy ritual. Then I posed the question, do you mean to tell me that anybody who has ever harvested an animal or eaten wild game has had to get rabies shots? No. I wasn't going to subject myself to all those shots because this lady was upset that I went hunting and got a fox.

Still, that wasn't the end of it. Animal control got involved and took the fox to check it for rabies. A federal police officer had to investigate it all and interview me and take my statement. The whole thing had gotten way out of hand.

The fox came back testing negative for rabies. Of course, by that time someone in Bethesda had run a story, you know, "Marine Kills Fox" or something like that, but they never did report it was negative for rabies! All that when I could have called the game warden because somebody stole my fox that I'd legally harvested. I had a tag to hunt fox. I was doing everything legal. The game warden could have come and checked my license and that would've been the end of it. The whole thing was a real eye-opener and got all blown out of proportion. Some folks are living on a whole different planet.

After I was done at NICOE, I went back to EOD company. Greg was there and he wanted to check on me and to see how things had gone with my treatment and everything else. He was planning on going there himself. I told him it was pretty good, but I never said a word about the fox. About a month later, Greg reported to the same medical facility.

As soon as he walked in, they spotted his EOD badge and asked him if he knew Danny Ridgeway. He told them he did and they asked him if he knew what I had done. He didn't have a clue but wanted to know, thinking, Good Lord, what's another of my guys done? I told you the shape we were in when he took over.

It tells you the sort of guy that he is that Greg automatically saw the funny side of it. He wrote up the incident and had all the details and then passed them along with recommendation to General Dana. If Greg hadn't been so good with the details and all that paperwork, it's likely the Silver Star would have gotten busted down to a lesser one. I was flat-out blessed that it all worked out the way it did. A lot of other guys weren't as fortunate to receive the kind of recognition that I did, and some didn't get much credit at all for the things they did except within their tight little group. So I was lucky, Greg being a good storyteller and telling that fox story in a way that entertains everybody so much.

Of course that fox story got around, and I get grief for it, but that's okay. I kind of wish that they'd talk about the story of the red stag I harvested down in New Zealand instead. That red stag was freaking ginormous.

But I've got a lot of people who understand what I've been through with the TBI and PTSD. Sometimes it's not easy because there's no obvious physical sign that we're wounded warriors. People sometimes look at us differently because we may seem kind of weird or whatever and they wonder why we forget things all the time or struggle to find words. We've got a bond because that injury is different from other ones. So, it's like there's a circle within a circle, but none of those bonds are any stronger; they're just different.

★★★★★★★★★★★★★★★★★★★★★★★★★★★★★★★★★★

Not to be too cheesy, but there's no one I'd rather have in a foxhole with me than Danny Ridgeway. He's my brother. We don't share the same blood, but we've bled for the same cause, the same land, and the same people. Danny and I are brothers for life. We even fight like it, with passive aggressive texts from time to time. But we love each other just the same. When anything in life gets too much to handle, we know we're only a text away, or a last-minute flight if need be. Having earned a Silver Star in combat, Danny is a true war hero, but he was already a hero to me, having been there when I needed him in EOD school to get past the grief of losing my granddad, or "Papaw," and again at the hospital after losing my legs, and again by my side in the garden of the Commandant of the Marine Corps' residence in Washington, DC, on the day I said my marriage vows to my high school sweetheart. Danny has always been there for me—that's a bond even the horrors of a battlefield can't break.

★★

A HIGHER MISSION

A job is a thing you do. A "mission" is a life you choose and the actions you undertake to ensure that lives and ways of life are preserved.

—*Wesley Hunt*

Joining the military was like opening up a door to a whole new world.

—*Aaron Hale*

If I can play just a small part in helping someone believe that they can do something greater than they first thought, then that's the greatest currency I can ever possess. How much impact you have on the lives of others is how you measure success.

—*Lacy Gunnoe*

A Legacy of Service

CAPTAIN (RET.) WESLEY HUNT

★ United States Army ★

"Military service is literally
what my family has been all
about. We haven't just talked
it; we live it. We understand
that America, this country, this
experiment, has to be defended
every single generation. And if
not me, then who does step up?"

★★

I grew up poor, in the Deep South. Papaw was a moonshiner and my dad was a brick mason. Both dabbled in the gray areas of law, and if they performed any "service to the community," it was in an orange jumpsuit on Sunday because they had too much fun on Friday and Saturday. Military service, or even national patriotism, wasn't big in our family. It was respected, but not sought out. Papaw was born in the late 1930s and missed World War II. My dad was born in the late 1950s and missed Vietnam, although he did try to sign up with the army at age seventeen. But they were both strong and respected men.

Papaw grew up in Ellijay, Georgia, population "more than a few, less than a bunch." In the mid-1960s he fled his mountain town for the budding metropolis of Dalton, Georgia, partly because he wouldn't join or share his moonshine business with the local Ku Klux Klan. No, he wasn't a civil rights activist or anything, but he used to tell me, "Son, when you're as poor as we were, you don't have any business thinking you're better than a man working just as hard as you for less money, even if they look different than you do."

When they got to Dalton he turned his moonshine-running '55 Chevy into a dirt track race car and that became our family bond. My papaw would say, "As long as there are people on this earth there will be restaurants, funeral homes, and racetracks . . . We all have to eat, we're all gonna die, and you gotta have fun."

The first Black man I met was at the local racetrack. He went by the nickname "Pud'n" and he loved working on race cars. He and my papaw were quick friends. The first time I met him he introduced himself to me and reached his hand out to shake mine. I was probably four or five years old. I shook his hand and immediately looked at my palm. Seeing my reaction, and probably having seen it before, he smiled and said, "Don't worry, son, it don't come off." With grace and wit, he made a lasting impact on my life.

Wesley Hunt is one of the single most impressive individuals I've ever met. He talks in a way that nearly requires a dictionary and thesaurus but does it with such charm and such a big smile you just seem to understand what he's saying. Even if the words go over your head, you take them to heart.

Wesley and his siblings grew up with a father who was a veteran. Their dad made sure his children understood the value in hard work, education, and military service. A Black man who came of age during the civil rights movement, in the Deep South. You might think Wesley and I grew up very differently, and in some ways, I'm sure we did. But we quickly learned there are a lot of similarities growing up poor in the South. My family didn't have an education or serve in the military, but they understood grace, and had a patient love for people, much like Wesley and his family do. They didn't feel the brute force of racism on their shoulders, but they recognized its immorality and took risks to escape it in their own way. Ultimately, both our families raised their young men to simply work hard, love others, and be better, better educated, better prepared, and make better use of the opportunity this great country provides. Wesley Hunt stands as a testament to the idea that, in this country, you can come from anywhere and go anywhere. This is his story and I'm humbled to share it.

★★

A LEVEL PLAYING FIELD

I know that for a lot of young people from impoverished backgrounds, and even those who are of greater means, the military is seen as a way out. Well, my dad never looked at it solely that way. My dad grew up in poverty in New Orleans. He was a very talented young man and very smart. He graduated at the top of his class. My father is a retired lieutenant colonel in the Army. He was a Reserve Officers' Training Corps guy at Southern University in Baton Rouge, Louisiana. A public, historically Black land-grant university, Southern was established in 1880 and has provided many Black men and women with an opportunity to pursue a higher education that they may not otherwise have had. The ROTC program he was enrolled in was also critical to his success. He rose through the ranks and after twenty-three years in the Army, he retired as an adjutant general. In our family, we see the military as the closest thing to a meritocracy as you can get. You rise and fall based on your own skills and abilities. My father was born in 1949, and the Civil Rights Act wasn't passed until 1965, when he was sixteen years old.

He grew up in a very segregated South. He saw that the military was one of the few places that were integrated. Certainly the military had racial issues of its own, but he saw military service as an avenue to reach a level playing field that was hard to find in the 1960s. He managed well on that field, getting promoted very quickly since he was an excellent soldier. He chose to go on to serve in full-time active duty before transitioning into the reserves, where he remained until his retirement. I can't say for certain what percentage of my father's outlook and values were a product of him being in the military. All I know is that my father is a gentleman who never made excuses. He taught us—my older sister, D'Hania, my younger brother, Wrendon, and me—the same thing. My dad would always say things like, "You know, son, if you think it's difficult today being Black in America, you have to understand that you don't really have a hard time. I had it hard." Though he didn't talk about it much and didn't complain about it ever, I knew that he was right.

My father always had the ability to keep things in perspective. He let us know that even on its worst day, America remains a pretty good place to be. Even though he faced Jim Crow policies and laws and other aspects of institutionalized racism, and racism in more insidious forms, he always had a dream, not just for himself, but for his children. That dream was for each of us to be able to do more. And the way you do more is by serving your country, because life in the military and being of service cuts through race, religion, color, and creed. That's because service is service. It has no color. The bond is the bond among those who serve regardless of skin color or background. My father saw that the military was a place of equality and a means to make things better for the next generation.

I had, and still have, an excellent relationship with my father. I remember that we had a whiteboard in our house while growing up. Every day, my dad would list out our chores and tasks on it. On top of the whiteboard was a saying: "Jesus plus education equals success." I remember seeing that from the time I was three, four, and five years old. My dad would also always say, "You can't be as good as; you have to be better than." He also placed a huge emphasis on education. No one can ever take that away from you. Don't ever stop educating yourself. Always stay in school and reach the highest level of it that you can attain. He believed that education was the differentiating factor. My dad talked about the importance of serving in the military, but he also said that having an education, no matter your color or race, would make you stand out. So make sure you have both that military service and an education.

Military service is literally what my family has been all about.

We haven't just talked it; we live it. We understand that America, this country, this experiment, has to be defended in every single generation. And if not me, then who does step up? That's the kind of attitude I was brought up around and continue to espouse. With my dad serving, and then each of my two siblings and me following his lead, we've firmed up the bond between us. More important, we're links in a chain that will grow stronger over time and make this country an even better place for the next generation, the next links in the chain.

★★★

Fresh off a victory in November 2022, Wesley Hunt now serves in Congress. Exchanging his military uniform for civilian attire didn't mean that Wesley was done doing the right things to help keep America strong. Wesley is a lifelong conservative, and has been active in his community in the Houston, Texas, area. In addition to holding office, he serves on the board of trustees at St. John's School. Founded in 1946, its stated mission is to "[provide] the community with a school of exacting standards in the development of individual, spiritual, ethical, intellectual, social and physical growth." The school's website goes on to say that it places an emphasis on personal fulfillment and contribution to society and seeks to develop leaders. Wesley Hunt is embodiment of those principles and has more than met those exacting standards there and later at the US Military Academy at West Point.

While St. John's played a pivotal role in his development, I'm certain that even if Wesley hadn't attended, he would have attained great things. His mother and father, Willie and Diane, were central to his growth. Family bonds are among the tightest any of us develop in our lives. Parents who take their responsibilities seriously are essential to producing leaders like Wesley. They instill values in our young people and serve as role models beyond the confines of their own homes, out into the community. In some ways Wesley's family story isn't unique at all, and in other ways it is. But one thing is for sure: their story is as American as apple pie!

There was a time, perhaps too long ago, that politicians were viewed as servants to the public. I'm not sure most Americans feel that way anymore, but I do know that with every veteran who earns a seat in Congress, there comes with them a renewed understanding of service, sacrifice, and the value of freedom.

★★★

LEAD BY EXAMPLE

My dad served as leader by example and by words. He could be stern with us, but he was also what I would call a stand-up comedian. I could see that he knew that he had to lead by example. When I was coming up in middle school and in high school, we attended a private school that was about an hour away. We lived on the north side of Houston, and the school was closer to the downtown area. My dad would drive Wrendon and me to that school every day. Once, I think I was in the seventh grade and Wrendon was in fifth, we were driving along and my dad got pulled over by a highway patrolman. Back then there was still somewhat loose enforcement of the seat belt laws and my dad wasn't always so good about buckling up. So, when he saw the flashing lights behind him, my brother and I knew that it wasn't because he was speeding, so we said, "Dad! Dad! Your seat belt! Put it on!"

The officer approached the car. My dad had scrambled to get his seat belt on by this time. The officer peered into the car and said, "Sir, excuse me. I stopped you because I thought that you didn't have your seat belt on. I see that it is on."

My dad looked at me and then at Wrendon. Then he looked at the officer and said, "No, I did not have it on." Then he started laughing. He couldn't lie to that officer, especially not in front of us. That says a lot about his character and especially his integrity. I thought it was funny then, and still, almost twenty years later, that story still comes up and we still laugh about that incident. I think that seeing my dad in that situation and how he handled it brought us all closer together. So did going on those drives with him every school day.

My dad would talk a lot about not being a victim and not blaming anybody else. He didn't like the idea that often Black people were painted as victims or painted themselves as victims. Life doesn't happen to you, he would say; you make life happen. I was fortunate that I had two parents who both had college educations and who urged us in that direction. They insisted that we understand that the buck stops with us. I was also fortunate that they were willing and able to put up the bucks to give us the best education that they could afford. My dad was in the reserves and he was also a pretty shrewd businessman, and we were living a middle-class lifestyle, and my parents made a lot of sacrifices to pay for our private education. They invested in us at that early stage and it paid off for them down the line. They never had to pay a thing for our higher education and we all went on to earn advanced degrees.

I appreciate what they did for me, both then and now, but not always as much as I should have back then. St. John's was in one of the most affluent parts of Houston, River Rose. A lot of my classmates and friends lived right in the vicinity, while I had that hour-long commute each way. I think I was in ninth grade when I started thinking, This isn't fair. I came home one day and walked into my dad's office and told him just that. He pushed himself away from his desk and said, "Now, you can either choose to go to the best school in Texas, and live here, or we can live closer to town, but not go to that school. We can't afford both. I know those may not be the optimal choices for you, but that's what you got. Fortunately for you, I've already made the choice for you. And I've busted my behind to send you to that school, and do you really mean to complain to me about an hour drive? That's not a me problem; that's a you problem."

With that, he turned away and resumed working at his desk. I walked out of his office and the subject of the commute never came up again. He taught me a very valuable lesson there. You don't get anything without hard work and sacrifice. Somebody always has to pay for something. Somebody has to go above and beyond. He didn't want to hear about me having to get up an hour earlier than my friends. He let us know that doing that made us work harder and that was a good thing.

My sister is one of my role models. She is ten years older than me, and at the age of seventeen, she earned her way into the US Military Academy at West Point. I have such vivid memories of taking her there for the start of her first year. Seeing your sister go to West Point changes your life, especially when you're an impressionable seven-year-old. Then, four years later, when my sister had hung in there, we went back to attend her graduation. Bill Clinton, the president of the United States, gave the commencement address. I remember thinking to myself, I want to go to the kind of school where the president of the United States speaks at graduation!

★★★★★★★★★★★★★★★★★★★★★★★★★★★★★★★★★★★

That first impression of West Point stuck with Wesley. After completing his high school education at St. John's, where he played football and excelled academically, Wes qualified to become a member of the West Point Class of 2004, joining roughly one thousand other cadets that year. He also was a part of the football program as a running back. The bonding experiences with the larger team—the entire corps of cadets—and the smaller—the football team—began immediately after high school graduation. Two weeks after finishing up at St. John's, Wes was on the campus at West Point, New York. He was there to take part in what is formally known as Cadet Basic Training, but which is more popularly known among the cadets as "Beast Barracks." He was about to begin a two-month program designed, like most other military initial training programs, to simultaneously break individuals down while building them up. The attrition rate at West Point is somewhere between 5 and 10 percent each year during CBT. That may not sound like a lot, but when you take into account the admissions process, that often requires a nod from your member of Congress, among other things. That's one out of every ten of our very best high school graduates who can't take the regimented and disciplined life required to be a cadet. For those who remain, those who survive the 5:20 a.m. reveille and the 6:00 a.m. start of physical training and endure being constantly scrutinized and called out if they fall short of exacting standards, those initial days forge bonds that last throughout their four years and remain intact throughout their career and post-service life. More than just recalling that they had only four options when spoken to—"Yes, sir," "No, sir," "I do not understand, sir," "No excuse, sir"—they remember the shared suffering and the satisfaction of having risen to the challenge. In the simplest terms, when life is miserable, you trust most those beside you. At the very least, they've proved they can hack it when others can't.

★★★

JOINING THE WEST POINT FAMILY

I was there with a young woman, Sarah Penn, who was in my first squad. Later, the day before the election, I got a text from her wishing me good luck. We went through that twenty-two years ago. I haven't seen her in a decade. But the bonds we forged then, at the very start, they're completely unbreakable. But that's what happens there. I don't even know Sarah's political affiliation, but she wanted to wish me the best. That's a very special thing. That bond is still there.

The terrorist attacks of September 11, 2001, happened at the beginning of my second year at West Point. Here I must explain that you can go to West Point for two years and pay nothing and owe nothing. After two years, if you decide to continue, you're what's called "locked in." That means that if you choose to leave you have financial obligations that you have to repay. So, when 9/11 happened, and the reality that we were likely to have to go to war upon graduation was right there in front of us, the vast majority of us decided to stay. And as is true in combat when your concern is for the person to the right of you and to the left of you, that's how we felt then. It wasn't the financial obligation or the consequences that was on our minds. It was that down the line, literally and figuratively, we wanted to be there for one another. Ultimately, we lost fourteen classmates. One of them was a good friend of mine, David Fraser. We were actually deployed together in Baghdad at one point. He passed away on his last mission.

Those bonds are infused in us both formally and informally at West Point. It begins with the discipline and having to do things like get up every morning at 4:30 or 5:00. Then we had mandatory breakfast, lunch, and dinner together. Eating together. Living together. Training together. Those things bond you and you also develop an enormous amount of respect for another. You see these people all the time and in various circumstances, and a lot of that comes down to everybody having to embrace the suck. We all, underclass and upper class, went through the same things at one point. Whether it's having to salute every single upperclassman when you're walking on campus or keeping your head pointed directly forward at all times, or having an upperclassman insist that you do this or that, they may be kind of inconsequential in the big picture, but they do what they're intended to do. They give you a sense of belonging and tradition. You know that the person who is making your life tougher than you would like in that moment also went through the same thing you did. Shared experiences are what bring you closer. And really, when it comes down to it, everybody wants to see you succeed.

There's a saying at West Point, "The history we teach was made by the people we taught." The instructors at West Point are former West Point graduates, ROTC members, and active-duty officers. And just like my dad encouraged us to get as much education as we could, so did the Army. Many Army officers and others go on to get master's degrees and PhDs while serving. My sister was among those. And so the saying that history at West Point is made by alumni means more to me than some because of my family history at the Academy. She graduated from there, as I said, then for two of my years there she served as an instructor. For obvious reasons, I couldn't enroll in a class she taught, but while she was there teaching, she had already been in the military for ten years and checked up on us. Now, I say "us" because my younger brother had also gotten into West Point. He's only ten months younger than me, so he was just a year behind me in school. Because of that minimal age gap and for a lot of other reasons, Wrendon and I are super close. He's among my closest friends, and we still talk several times a day.

So, when I was at West Point, I had that figurative team and family all looking out for me. Not only was my sister an instructor, but quite a few of my sister's classmates from 1993 were there teaching as well. It's a kind of small world there, and I knew that my sister was keeping tabs on us through them as well as checking with us all the time. She'd been through the experience at West Point herself, so she was always a great resource we could rely on for anything. For us, being the little brothers, that meant leveraging all the advantages we could. I don't mean anything underhanded or anything like that. But my sister had a car. At that time, cadets weren't allowed to have one on campus. So, with D'Hania in possession of a car, Wrendon and I both became very popular cadets. I have many fond memories of going with her on weekends to the Palisades Center mall in Nyack, New York. We'd just hang out together, and the rest of the time in those two years, she was doing everything she could to check in with us and make sure that her little brothers were okay.

After Wrendon graduated the year after me and cross-commissioned into the Navy, and I had completed my aviation training and was flying Apache helicopters, we had another kind of family reunion in 2006. We were all stationed in the Middle East, in Iraq. My brother was aboard a ship in the Arabian Gulf. My sister was in Baghdad's Green Zone, and I was flying missions over Baghdad proper. She actually surprised me one time by taking a helicopter flight up to Camp Taji to visit. She was still the big sister looking after her little brother. That was unforgettable. She's still that role model to me. She still watches out for us.

She wasn't the only one who did that. As a helicopter pilot, I have to rely on my ground crew to keep my aircraft operational. One of my crew chiefs was Corporal Brandon Bender, an enlisted man from Alabama. Essentially, he was solely responsible for maintaining and repairing my helicopter. I knew that I'd better treat him well because my life is in his hands, right? Seriously, though, I did develop a bond with this guy. We couldn't have been more different. He was a white guy from the Deep South. His family didn't have a lot of money for college, and Brandon saw the military as a way to better his station in life. Still, we just clicked for some reason. We had a good time and often engaged in deep conversations. He would explain certain things to me in a way that I didn't necessarily understand or came to from a different perspective. Over time, we got so comfortable with each other that we would make really off-color jokes about one another and such. There was no politically correct agenda that we had to adhere to. We were friends who came from two different worlds.

There was another gentleman by the name of John Fuller who was a warrant officer in my unit. He was one of the youngest pilots in it. He was also the most tactically sound among us. I flew the bulk of my combat missions with him. I'd eventually do fifty-five altogether. Needless to say, multiple times we were in sticky situations. In an Apache helicopter, you're either in the backseat or the front seat. So you and your copilot rely heavily on one another. John now lives in Texas. One of my political supporters walked up to me a few years ago and asked, "You know the name John Fuller?" I said, "Well, I know *a* John Fuller. He's the best pilot I've ever seen in my life." He told me, "That's the guy that works for me flying on my ranch."

I said, "You mean Vanilla Face flies for you?"

This ranch owner looked a bit confused, but I went on: "Well, please tell Vanilla Face that Chocolate Face says hello."

I don't know if in the Army today we'd get away with using those nicknames, but that was how we addressed one another. John and I are still good friends, and I'm going to visit Vanilla Face on his ranch soon. I'm sure that we'll talk about 2006 and how up-tempo that mission was.

STEPPING UP

At that time, our unit had two helicopters in the air 24/7. We were overflying Baghdad proper with that frequency because of how often

we were receiving notification from the ground about troops in contact. We had to react quickly to come to the aid of any ground units.
We didn't have the time to spool up, take off, and arrive on target in a
reasonable time frame. We had to be there *now*.

One day, we got a troops-in-contact call. Normally, Baghdad is so
small that it only takes about twelve minutes to get on station from
where we were. This time it was a coalition outpost that was under
attack. I entered the coordinates into the GPS, and I saw that we were
thirty minutes from the location. That was ridiculous. I wasn't sure
if we should fly all the way down there. Wasn't the other aircraft we
had aloft closer? Our commander insisted that we go, so we followed
orders and flew all the way down there. We ended up staying on station for seven hours. An Abrams tank had hit an IED. The ground
troops were getting lit up pretty good. We were taking and returning
fire. Seven hours is a long time to keep a helicopter engaged and we
refueled a number of times to continue to do so.

I was really proud of the four pilots on that mission. I was pretty
sure that we saved some American lives that day. That's always the best
feeling. That's the reason we were there.

After we returned home, the sergeant major of that ground unit,
and their commander, sent us a flag that they had flown on behalf of
our helicopter crew. They also included a certificate that stated their
gratitude for the lives we saved that day. I appreciated that gesture
and the confirmation that we had done our ultimate job. I'll never
forget receiving that flag and the perspective it gave me. I don't know
the names or the faces of the troops we helped save that day. I don't
know what might have happened if we hadn't showed up. But we did
show up. Just like those guys on the ground showed up. That's what
you do. That's what my dad taught me. That's what my teachers and
coaches at St. John's taught us. That's what my instructors at West
Point, my commanding officers downrange, and my sister and my

brother taught me. You show up. You do your job and you go above and beyond what's expected and what's needed.

That sergeant major and commander went out of their way to find out who was overflying their position that day. They got our names. They tracked down my home address in Texas. They sent a personalized note. They thanked us for saving the lives of people who were otherwise anonymous to us. They weren't really anonymous, though. They were brothers and sisters at arms. So, in reality, it wasn't really a job, and there's a reason why we call those efforts we all undertake a "mission." A job is a thing you do. A "mission" is a life you choose and the actions you undertake to ensure that lives and ways of life are preserved.

I'll never forget receiving that flag. Even more so because a long time later I was at an event in Houston. A man approached me and introduced himself. He went on to say that he was the father of one of those infantrymen on the ground that day we overflew for seven hours. He thanked me for preserving the life of his son. He couldn't imagine what his life would have been if he'd lost him.

Like so many military people, I was willing to die for my country, for every single American. I'm not quite sure that same American would die for me in the same situation. But that's okay. That's the reason we put on that uniform. That's what makes this situation of the 1 percent serving on behalf of the other 99 percent work. That's what makes it so special.

★★★★★★★★★★★★★★★★★★★★★★★★★★★★★★★★★★★★★★★

A lot of veterans in Wesley's position who spend time overseas in places like Iraq and Afghanistan come home and feel a sense of devalued purpose. They wonder if their own mission of protecting this country is even appreciated at all. No, I don't mean the discount at Applebee's or the occasional awkward, but genuine, "Thank you for your service" at the local Tractor Supply. They see that a lot of Americans are seemingly ungrateful for the small things. The twenty-seven different fast-food joints within five miles in any direction, the comforts of air-conditioning, sleeping in on Saturdays, seeing their loved ones' faces almost anytime they want, the touch of their spouse's hands, the silly laughs tickling their babies, watching the sun set over a place called home. To many of us, Americans who haven't experienced what combat or even a relatively safe deployment is, well, they haven't seen behind the curtain. They're taking security for granted, they aren't grateful for the spoils of such a prosperous society, and they don't understand what it takes to make this land free for the next generation.

That right there is where we veterans can go disastrously wrong. First, we have to acknowledge our true mission and what may result from successfully accomplishing it. Our mission isn't to be lauded as heroes, or to awaken Americans to what they are taking for granted. We were those same people with the same limited perspective before boot camp. Our mission is to fight our enemies abroad, away from home. Our mission is to stand in the gap, to hold the line to secure victory before the fight ever makes it to our shores. If we accomplish our mission, which we have done in historic fashion, then how can we be surprised by, or even hold against our brethren the very ignorance of war we fought to preserve?

Pearl Harbor and 9/11, while two very obvious outliers, were catalysts for national patriotism and a unified country, but I'll take peace and the preservation of innocent lives if all I have to pay is the frustration of being one of the few who do understand what's behind the proverbial curtain of American culture on any given day.

Second, and perhaps most importantly, we have to understand the hard work and sacrifice that's happening here at home every day while we're away, and especially when we get back. Americans work hard. They fight rains and winds to keep the power on, they stay up nights saving lives in ambulances, they run headstrong into burning buildings, they hold the hands of the dying, mourning and desperate to comfort them. They work tirelessly to cure illnesses; they work thanklessly to deliver packages, teach children, cook food, and provide for their own families. We can't lose sight of the often benevolent yet fiercely fighting spirit that lives within each American. We have to remember that we aren't fighting for freedom alone; we're fighting so that these people, the American citizens we share a life with, experience freedoms fully. What good, after all, is a freedom without a people to live it? Wesley understands that. He accepts, and loves, our true mission: to serve and protect Americans.

★★★★★★★★★★★★★★★★★★★★★★★★★★★★★★★★★★★★★★★

WHAT WE FIGHT FOR

I remember coming back home between deployments. When you do, you always want to take in as many tastes of home as you can. There's a restaurant in town called Barnaby's, one of my favorites. I really wanted to go, and the woman I was dating at the time agreed to go with me. It was morning and we drove over. When I pulled into the parking lot, I saw a few guys outside. I recognized one of them as a buddy from high school. They were sitting on the hood and the bumpers of the car, and I could see immediately that they were a little worse for wear from the night before. He spotted me and said, "What's up, man? What are you up to?"

"I'm doing good, man. Doing good."

"Dude, I went out last night. I had a rager. I had an awesome time. I'm just still feeling it. What about you?"

"I just got back from Baghdad two nights ago."

He looked at me and said, "I'm such an asshole." I remember laughing so hard because seeing him enjoy himself, hearing about his partying, and knowing that he was there for a morning-after breakfast when he'd sit with his buddies and try to reconstruct what happened the night before was one of the reasons why I chose to do what I did. Seeing him again after all that time made my day. I told him not to feel so bad. And I meant it. I was glad to see him. We'd been through some things together at St. John's and we'd made our choices and moved on. But still we had that time in our past, and I was really, genuinely glad that he was living his best life. Because that was what I was over there fighting for.

That's why I later ran for Congress. In 2018, we had the fewest number of veterans serving in the halls of Congress in our history. That has rapidly changed since then. When you see this many veterans getting involved politically, that's kind of the canary in the coal mine. The reason we've stepped up is that as a country, actually, we aren't doing very well. Our country is sick. We're losing the very values that the American soldier fought to protect; we're clearly heading in the wrong direction. That's when you see combat veterans, who, by the way, as members of the military are taught to be apolitical, and serve regardless of who the president is, start to run for office again. So when you see this, this influx of veterans running again—and to be honest with you, the overwhelming majority of them are Republican—you start to see that, hey, we're the guy that just fought for something. I'm willing to die for something, and we want to keep it going. So we can no longer stand by and be apolitical at a time like this, when we're realizing that we're watching what we fought for slipping through our fingers. I think that's why we're seeing so many combat veterans running for office. We still want to look out for the people to the left of us and to the right of us. We still care deeply.

I remember 9/11, when the towers fell. A week later you couldn't go online and buy an American flag. George W. Bush had the highest approval rating of any president in modern history. After 9/11, that level of patriotism, the level of loving the country, the level of like, yeah, America is not perfect, but we're the best in the world, was so prevalent. It's the reason why my classmates didn't leave: we knew that we were going to go to war, because we didn't want anybody ever attacking us again, because we wanted to keep our country safe. But we're losing that now. For some it's not cool to be an American, and we're systemically racist. The system is inherently bad. Capitalism isn't good, they say.

But I say wait a minute, wait a minute, wait a minute. This is what sets us apart from the entire world. It's up to the combat veterans to get it back. Because we realize a lot of bonds in this country have been broken, but a lot of people in this country are sick of that. We need to go back to how we felt post-9/11, when we were united and fought for and not against one another. We all know what it's like to feel kinship, like a family, like a team, like a unified, focused group that is striving in the same direction, with the same goal in mind. Bonds can be broken, but they can be put together again. That's why I served then and continue to serve today. That's what my family has always been about.

To Free the Oppressed

STAFF SERGEANT NATE BOYER

★ United States Army ★

"I really felt the urge to go
somewhere to fight for those who
couldn't fight for themselves."

★★★★★★★★★★★★★★★★★★★★★★★★★★★★★★★★★★

In 2016 the quarterback of the San Francisco 49ers, Colin Kaepernick, made headlines and started a very controversial movement by choosing to sit on the bench during the playing of our national anthem before their final preseason game. Like most veterans and patriotic Americans, I was pissed.

I thought, Who's this entitled millionaire trying to claim oppression and disrespect our country like this? I preach a lot about grace. It's something I believe in applying, and quite honestly wouldn't have made it without. But some things hit you hard, and this was one of those things that really just sparked a visceral reaction in so many of us. Shortly after, I saw a link to a *Military Times* article written by a guy I'd heard of and admired, Nate Boyer. Nate was a former Green Beret and NFL player. I read his words and in an instant my anger was transformed to curiosity. I won't recite Nate's words, but they're worth a Google. Instead, I'll say what I took from them. Nate didn't agree with Colin. He didn't excuse an obvious sign of disrespect and he laid out well why that flag and anthem mean so much to those of us who've buried our brothers in Arlington National Cemetery, under that flag and to that tune. But Nate also offered something new.

His article was an open letter to Colin himself. Nate asked questions, offered to understand, and asked to meet with Colin to discuss the issue. I was taken aback at the maturity and emotional intelligence Nate conveyed in his letter. I needed to meet this guy. I reached out to him immediately through mutual friends. I didn't hear back for a week or two. Colin had reached out to Nate as well, and at Colin's invitation, Nate had gone down to San Diego to meet Colin before the next game. Nate didn't convince Colin to stand with him out of respect for our fallen, but he did get Colin to acknowledge why it matters to us. He got Colin to kneel with good posture rather than lazily sitting. The idea was to have a purposed pose, some middle ground between non-observance and respect. Nate stood at attention with his hand over his heart beside a straight-backed, kneeling Colin Kaepernick.

The result was headlines and reactions from every angle. Some called Nate a sellout, while others said Colin was appeasing and weakening his protest. For me, I simply wanted to meet Nate and talk. I'd been inspired and wanted to know more. I was living just north of Austin, Texas, and Nate, a former University of Texas football player, was in Austin shortly after meeting Colin. So when we finally connected, he invited me to join him and some friends on a dove hunt conveniently taking place at the midway point between us. Like many relationships in my life, college football and hunting were once again at the forefront of what would become another important bond forged by adversity and grace. Nate's story, including becoming famous as the veteran who convinced Colin Kaepernick to kneel rather than sit, is unique and impactful.

★★★★★★★★★★★★★★★★★★★★★★★★★★★★★★★★★★★★★★

NATE

Like a lot of us, in my younger years I didn't feel really purposeful. I didn't do much of anything for others. After high school, I eventually worked on a fishing boat and all sorts of odd jobs. I enjoyed a lot of life experiences. I wasn't a dirtbag or anything, but I certainly didn't feel like I was doing anything for anyone else on a daily basis. In 2004—so obviously this was post-9/11—I heard what was happening in Darfur, where the Sudanese government was engaging in ethnic cleansing. Their forces were carrying out the most horrific activities: massacres, executing civilians without due process, setting fire to towns and villages, forcibly removing populations from the tribal lands they inhabited. I had read quite a bit about the conflict and also how relief organizations were really shorthanded. They needed people, and I thought, I'm people, and I'm willing to help.

That was the first time that I really felt the urge to go somewhere to fight for those who couldn't fight for themselves. I applied to go with some of the nongovernmental organizations (NGOs) like Doctors Without Borders, Catholic Relief Services, and a couple of others. I was rejected by them all. I couldn't volunteer with them because I didn't have a college degree. I didn't have any special skills that were deemed necessary to really be of help over there. So I ended up flying myself over there, and eventually talked my way into volunteer opportunities. What I did was really quite simple: I helped build out the refugee camps and tent shelters. I distributed food rations and played soccer with the kids.

I didn't meet any Americans at the camp I was at. I met some Belgian workers, and French Canadians, especially since I was in Chad, just across the border from Sudan, and that was a French-speaking part of the world. I didn't speak French, so that made getting to know my fellow volunteers well pretty hard. But that wasn't a problem with the Chad locals and some of the Sudanese refugees. Even with the language barrier, I felt connected with them in some way. A lot of them were so grateful that an American would recognize the problems there and want to help, even if I was an American who didn't exactly know what I was doing and had little to offer aside from my time and a little bit of elbow grease.

As I said, they were very grateful, and they wanted to hear all about America. They were awestruck by the fact that somebody would choose to leave America and come help them. That hit me because I felt very fortunate to be able to be there. I didn't do anything to earn the privilege of being an American. I just happened to be born there; I was lucky to be American. That wasn't something I deserved. I just got it.

★★★★★★★★★★★★★★★★★★★★★★★★★★★★★★★

Most Americans who know anything about football know much of Nate Boyer's story, particularly those who support and love our military. But, like most inspiring people, there's a lot more to his life and career than his exploits on the gridiron. Following his stint in Darfur, Nate joined the US Army in 2005 and by December 2006 he had earned his green beret as a member of the Army's Special Forces. By 2008, his unit, 10th Special Forces Group, was in Iraq. He also did two tours in Afghanistan. Once he left the Army, Nate checked out of Fort Carson, Colorado, and drove south, all the way to Austin, where he enrolled at the University of Texas at the ripe old age of twenty-nine. The consummate optimist, Nate had decided to play college football at one of the top programs in the country. There was just one problem: he'd never played a down in his life. But, not unlike his decision to simply buy a plane ticket to Chad when NGOs wouldn't accept him, he didn't let that technicality stop him. He taught himself a valuable specialty skill of long-snapping and convinced legendary coach Mack Brown that he was an asset to the team. Nate went on to play all five years of his time in Austin. He earned numerous awards for his contributions to the community and for his excellence in the classroom. After graduation and the end of his collegiate football career, he played briefly in the National Football League, earning his way onto the Seattle Seahawks, despite not having been drafted.

Knowing Nate's accomplishments, you see how his motto—

"Anything Is Possible"—is not just words, it's an ethos, a creed to live by. He's taken on big adventures in the outdoors, volunteered his time for various charities, and plays a role with veterans service organizations and other not-for-profit enterprises. Now a filmmaker and Hollywood actor, he uses his talents and unique position to write and tell stories that highlight the struggles of both veterans and athletes, as well as most Americans. Nate is an "actor" in every sense of the word: it's truly his actions that make him special.

★★★★★★★★★★★★★★★★★★★★★★★★★★★★★★★★★★★★

GAINING PERSPECTIVE

Being around the refugees and the people from Chad opened my eyes to so many things. I gained a lot of perspective on that journey. I bonded with some of the locals and some of the kids. Some of those kids had lost their fathers, who were murdered. Some of them had witnessed their mothers being raped and had their village burned to the ground. But they were in that refugee camp, playing soccer with other kids they didn't know and they were smiling and having a good time because they had an actual soccer ball and they got to eat that day.

One experience that has stuck with me was my last week in-country. I was getting ready to head back to the States, but I didn't have much of an idea about what I was going to do next. Then I got malaria. I'd been taking my antimalarial, my doxy (doxycycline), and all the other preventative meds, but I still got it. I had to go into semi-quarantine. The people at the camp didn't want me around the other workers. I was feeling pretty lousy physically, and then this local family offered to take me in. The father's name was Étienne. They lived in a little mud hut and put me up in a small little room within it. I had a cot to sleep on, and about all I could do for three or four days was lie there. I couldn't keep any food down. I couldn't sleep. I was simultaneously freezing cold and simmering hot, sweating bullets and having my teeth chatter. I had COVID this last year and malaria was much, much worse. I trusted Étienne and he gave me medicine and I took it. They did everything they could to take care of me.

The family gave me a little transistor radio and put it next to my bed. They brought me tea as well. The son and his cousin would come by and together they all tried to help me get through the worst of it, get me back on my feet. Eventually I was able to stand, and then, with their help, I was able to go on short walks to get my strength back. I remember Étienne sitting with me and the two of us were listening to Bob Marley. I also met one of Étienne's nephews, who, like the rest of the locals, wanted to know more about America. He told me that he was interested in joining the American Legion. I knew what he meant. He was familiar with the French Foreign Legion and assumed that we called our American military the legion.

Eventually I got better and returned home. I wrote to Étienne and his family. I sent him some blue jeans, and for, I think it was his nephew, I sent him a guitar. His had been stolen, and I wanted to replace it. So I did that for Christmas that year. I still wonder how they're doing and if I could track them down again. His nephew wasn't the only one I met who wanted to join the American military. The process wouldn't be easy, but if they could get citizenship, it seemed like a good thing to aspire to.

DE OPPRESSO LIBER

Often while I was in bed listening to the transistor radio, the news was on. I lay there hearing about the Second Battle of Fallujah and the Marines going in there while I was just trying to regain my strength. The reports inspired me. I was getting a brief play-by-play about these

Americans risking their lives for the Iraqi people. I started to think seriously about joining them in that effort. Then, shortly after I got back home to the States, I learned about the motto of the Army Special Forces—*De Oppresso Liber*. To Free the Oppressed. That really spoke to me. That's the mission that I wanted to be on. It just sounded perfect for me.

Then I started to learn more about what the Special Forces community does. Unconventional warfare is hard to strictly define because it encompasses so many elements. But part of the mission set was to assist foreign internal defense. That meant fighting alongside and living alongside, training alongside, and becoming brothers in arms with Afghan and Iraqi warriors. They want to live free. They have a similar mindset to us. So the idea of living with Indigenous people while serving in the military was similar to what I'd been doing in Darfur. That really appealed to me. That was what I wanted to do. I wanted to go somewhere and understand the culture and help build alongside these people and help them get themselves from under the oppression they were experiencing.

So that's what I did in joining the Army and then as a Green Beret. On my first deployment in Iraq in 2008, the Iraqis were holding elections. Prior to that, we'd been working day in and day out with the Iraqis. It was a difficult mission because it was hard to know whom to trust. We were trying to help them rebuild their country. Part of that was them holding those elections. They were a part of turning over power to the people. All of it is complicated because, really, we weren't at war against Iraq or Afghanistan—we were working against the terrorist organizations within those countries.

WHAT IT MEANS TO BE A MAN

Army Special Forces includes a small team of fighters called Operational Detachment Alphas (ODAs). One of the guys in my ODA, whom I'll call Brad, became a good friend. He was a great leader and an inspirational individual. We got to know about one another's lives. He had married really young but that hadn't worked out. Later he met another woman, a single mother whose child had some pretty tough challenges. I remember sitting on a rooftop in Iraq one night, around a fire pit, talking with my buddy about this woman and her son.

He told me that he had been very hesitant to really fall in love again. He had told himself that he'd never get married again. But then he met this woman and he fell for her. Then he met her son, and he felt immediately that he was going to be a part of that family. He knew he was going to marry this woman and adopt the boy. That was what he wanted to do, needed to do, and being around the two of them had just made him a better man.

I remember thinking, Wow! I am such a child. I was twenty-six or twenty-seven years old at the time, and I looked at Brad and saw what it really meant to be a grown man. He was somebody that I wanted to follow. He wasn't much older than me, but this guy was already a team leader in so many ways. He was the most selfless individual, someone who was always willing to help everybody else. He did that on the battlefield, too. He wasn't the only demolition guy, but he'd be there cutting strip charges for us so that, when we went out on a mission, we'd have them. He wasn't the comms guy, I was, and yet he'd be there helping me. Whatever it was, wherever it was, it didn't matter. He was there lending a hand. He was the model of the truly honest American hero warrior. He was somebody whom I wanted to model myself after and struggle to be like every day.

When we were going after a high-value target, we'd have to cordon off an area and split our twelve-man team into groups of two. I always seemed to end up with Brad as my wingman. As dangerous as it was at times, and as crazy as it was, he was always fun to be around and I felt safe with him. I felt empowered. I felt braver than I would normally be. He never hesitated. We would have to kick a door down and search a place, and the family would be scared crazy. We'd conduct our search and then as we left to move on to the next house he'd take a bit of time to reassure that family. That's just who he was. I don't know why it is that we always seem to lose the good ones. The best of us. He was certainly one of them.

I still wear a bracelet that his wife made after his passing. I wasn't there, but the night before, he called me. By this time, I was playing college football for the University of Texas. I was with the Texas National Guard but wasn't deployed. I was back home and had just finished the football season and I was given the Disney Spirit Award on ESPN.

Brad called me because he'd seen the awards presentation. He said he was calling to find out if I was going to run for president the next year. He was joking with me, of course. Then he told me how proud he was of me. He was the guy who had convinced me that if I was going to play college football, I shouldn't just go to a small school or a junior college. "You're a Green Beret," he told me. "You've got to go big." That stuck with me, and I did what he advised. The next day after that phone call I was contacted by another former Special Forces teammate and he told me, We've lost him. I stood there and my knees went dead with the shock of learning that sad news. A bad day. But I, and a lot of other people, try to live on in his honor.

I had the honor to be asked to help carry his casket with five other pallbearers. After the funeral, because he had specified this in his will, we all went to the pub and had kegs of beer just as he had spelled out. I have to admit I'm not always the best at maintaining relationships. I have a lot of passions and pursuits and things that motivate me, and I have challenges I seek out. That often doesn't leave time for relationships. But we made that postfuneral gathering happen, and I saw a lot of guys that I hadn't seen for two or three years. We picked up right where we left off. The cool thing about the communities I'm involved in—athletes and veterans—is that you went through some pretty challenging experiences together. You developed a lot of respect for one another. So when you see them now, it's like riding a bicycle, man. You don't feel awkward and do the small-talk thing. You have a raw brotherhood that not very many people get to experience.

A VISION OF THE GOOD LIFE

Brad has been gone for ten years now. I think of him every day. I have conversations with him every day. What we experienced, not just he and I, but a lot of veterans, is rare.

That moment we shared on that rooftop is rare. It was surreal to have, essentially, the world on fire all around us, and for us to have this positive conversation about life and the future. With all that going on? Everything is bleak and we're talking about him getting married and adopting a kid and building a life? That's a very unique experience. Not that I want there to be situations where people are struggling and dying, but to be in a place where you feel like everything you do matters, and it does, is special. We were fighting for those who can't fight for themselves. So to share that experience with others is a very rare thing. Maybe it happens in immediate families. Brad became my family in a matter of months.

★★★★★★★★★★★★★★★★★★★★★★★★★★★★★★★★★

Nate isn't just using a turn of phrase when he says "we always seem to lose the good ones." I think the good ones put themselves in more danger to save others, or they do their job so well, we always want them on our team. They're selfless in their pursuits and perhaps that puts them in the middle of the chaos of combat more often than the rest of us. For me, that "good one" was Gunnery Sergeant Floyd Holley. Floyd had just married his longtime partner, Chrissy, a few weeks before our deployment to Afghanistan in March 2010. He had two stepkids he loved with Chrissy and all four of them were beautiful, talented, and kind. We called their family "The Incredibles." Floyd and I got along very well. We shared hobbies, mostly working out and racing dirt bikes, and I looked up to him.

When we got to Afghanistan, he and I were the only ones eager to find a way to continue our physical fitness training in any way we could. That turned into several hours lifting sandbags and running while the rest of our platoon was smartly resting. After a few weeks we were dispatched into two-man teams across our area of Afghanistan. I didn't see Floyd for a few months, until late July. We were reunited when both of our two-man EOD teams were selected to assist in Operation Roadhouse 2, the push to take Safar Bazaar. The night before we began the operation, Floyd and I got in one last workout in what was the closest thing to a real gym either of us had seen since those early weeks of our deployment. As the two of us enjoyed the sound of real iron plates sliding onto a real bar over a real bench, we didn't have much to say.

Then Floyd broke the silence with a joke: "Damn, dude, you've stayed strong . . . must be the push-ups." I laughed and explained I'd always had a strong chest. Then the conversation picked up between sets of bench pressing. He and Chrissy were having a baby shortly after we all returned and he was excited. I asked him what he wanted it to be, boy or girl. He said, "I don't care, man, I just want it to be healthy."

We started talking about the op ahead and I could tell he was a little worried about our safety. I'd been there working IEDs for almost six months. Floyd had been there the whole time as well, but he had several years and a few deployments on me and saw the sparkle in my eyes when I talked about taking apart IEDs. That's when he gave me the most important piece of advice I'd get in my Marine Corps career. He smiled and said, "Listen, Triple J, if you've walked down on one IED or a hundred, you're an EOD tech who's done what few in the history of EOD have done. You've touched a bomb, an IED. Don't go looking for opportunities to die. Don't be scared, do your job, but don't get addicted to doing things that kill you and not dying. Eventually, you'll lose that game."

I got what he was saying. We have a lot of autonomy in our job as to what things we should deal with up close and personal, especially with robots. Floyd was looking at the rest of his life, a baby on the way, a wife, two kids already half-grown, he had unfinished business. The next morning, August 1, 2010, with several dozen vehicles carrying a few hundred Marines south through the desert east of the Helmand River, we were Oscar Mike.

Floyd's team broke off and took the high ground just outside the city while my team and one other EOD team supported the main effort. We cleared streets and buildings for five days, then, on August 6, my luck ran out as I stepped on an IED, resulting in the loss of my legs and a medical evacuation. Floyd and his teammate were moved down to fill in for my team after my injury. A few weeks later, I was lying in a hospital bed in Walter Reed, fresh with open wounds and tubes running from everywhere. I was woken up from a midday nap. I can't remember who said them, but the words are as vivid today as they were over a decade ago. "Joey, Floyd was hit today. He didn't make it. He's gone." And that's how that goes.

That's how it went for Nate. You can't change it, it comes

as a phone call, it really just doesn't seem real. We last saw our brothers smiling, cracking jokes, or telling us some sage advice for the road ahead. They were solid like oak, a stalwart source of wisdom and reassurance, and then bam, a phone call wipes them out of our lives forever. It's not fair; it doesn't make sense and shouldn't happen. But that is war, and we are warriors. So, we go on living our lives, we take care to remember them, we share stories and yearly texts with their families, and we live our lives knowing they gave up their lives so we might have more smiles, jokes, and stories in our own. So then we bear the solemn responsibility to make our remaining time on this spinning ball of irony mean something. We find a new purpose in their sacrifice.

When it comes to finding purpose, Nate didn't need to look further than his buddies attempting to leave elite military units and transitioning to a civilian life. A lot of emphasis is placed on the physically wounded, such as amputees like myself. But there are several invisible wounds that are just as difficult to overcome. The difficulty in transition is a psychological hurdle that even affects other professions, like professional athletes whose careers are ended seemingly too soon. Nate, along with TV personality, sports reporter, mixed martial arts devotee, and fitness guru Jay Glazer, wanted to do something to help these two unique groups of individuals manage that transition more successfully. So together in 2015 they founded a nonprofit charity aptly named Merging Vets and Players (MVP). As the name indicates, they pair athletes and military veterans. In a workout at a local gym, they sit down and guide discussion about the difficulties they face.

★★

HELPING OTHERS WITH THE JOURNEY HOME

Jay has been around the fight game and football for a very long time. He also has a great respect for men and women in uniform, those who are willing to go out and fight. He related to me that he lost a best friend on 9/11. Jay was in New York on that day and the loss of that friend affected him greatly. He was in lower Manhattan and searched through the rubble for his buddy. He went to different hospitals checking to see if he'd been admitted. Amid all the chaos of the day, he remembered these two fighter jets passing overhead. Of course, that's a very loud and intimidating sound. But he remembered an overwhelming feeling of safety and security coming over him. Like, oh, man, they're keeping us safe. And that stuck with him.

In his role in training athletes and others, in being in the pro sports area, Jay had encountered a lot of athletes who were struggling with transitioning and finding their greatness again, remembering who they are and understanding that they got where they had because they'd outworked the world to get the opportunity to play on the big stage or to fight in the arena. I met him when I was trying to get a chance to play in the NFL and he trained me up for that.

We shared an understanding that what goes on in sports and the military and the struggle with no longer wearing the uniform is very similar. We don't compare the two: sports are games and war is war. But losing the identity that you had, that sense of purpose, that team, is something that individuals in both worlds share and face difficulties with. You have to keep in mind that for a lot of them in both realms, it happens to them when they're very young. It's not on their own terms and it frequently happens in a flash. You get cut. You get wounded. You no longer figure in the game plan. You're no longer a part of the mission. Some of us, like me, we're lucky that we make the choice ourselves. But we still don't know exactly what's coming next.

Athletes and military personnel have a mutual respect for one another. So, with MVP, we bring the two different teams together. We help them walk that walk together. That lets them know that they're not alone. It also exposes them to people with a different background, a different career, and different stories, but who can still relate to you. We try to get them to understand that you're not the uniform you wore. You put that uniform on. Yes, it was a part of who you are, but the essential elements of you are still there. You did a job. You were the person underneath that uniform. Those qualities you had are not gone.

★★

At first glance you might think Nate is some sort of a jack-of-all-trades. He seems to have done it all. But digging deeper, you see he's simply a man with a servant's heart, a disciplined mind, and hands that won't sit idle. The latest challenge he's taken on is writing, directing, and acting. All of this came full circle when he wrote, directed, and appeared in the movie *MVP*. Produced with the help of Hollywood action star Sylvester Stallone, it tells the story of a retired NFL player and a homeless veteran.

Whether it's creating a film, writing a book, or sitting on a rooftop around a fire, the primal urge to connect with one another remains an important part of what it means to be human. For an individual like Nate, who has experienced the best and worst of humanity, his perspective is necessary and enlightening. But perhaps the most important thing about Nate's innate ability to adapt to any medium to serve others is the question it poses to anyone who reads his story: When it comes to making the world around us a better place, if Nate can do all this, what will you do?

★★

"Treat a Man as He Should Be"

—★ ★ ★—

LACY GUNNOE

★ United States Air Force ★

"Instead of proving people
wrong, the real power is proving
those who believed in you right."

★★★

In 2017, I was working at an amazing place called Camp Southern Ground. This state-of-the-art summer camp for children is special. At Camp Southern Ground, kids on the autism spectrum can go to summer camp with kids of common abilities and feel like they fit in. The passion project of my good friend the country music star Zac Brown, the camp was also designed to serve veterans in the off-season. Zac hired me, along with a civilian named Jake Dukes, to sort out what that veterans program would look like. I didn't know it at the time, but this would be one of the most valuable learning experiences I would ever embark on.

I took the mission—find or develop a way for CSG to serve veterans in a meaningful way—very seriously. At first I was only cautiously optimistic about the team I had to work with . . . seeing as they were all "nasty civilians." But Jake and the team quickly won me over. We spent hours talking out how we might serve veterans and finally landed on a weeklong experience that challenged veterans in self-discovery, physical obstacles, mental toughness, and teamwork. We built, on paper, a great week of activities and guided discussions that would hopefully allow veterans leaving the military to see themselves as "fitting in" to civilian life, much as CSG showed kids with challenges how they can fit in as well.

There was just one problem: it was on paper. Actually, there was another problem: Who was going to help us do it? We decided to reach out to our own network of friends and acquaintances to fill the spots of our first "pilot" week. To me, this meant reaching out to all my wounded and ground combat veterans. That's my experience and where I felt such a program should be focused. But Jake understood, or perhaps slightly stumbled on a greater truth. Ground combat experience is only one of many ways service members find themselves a bit lost, and certainly not the only way they can establish bonds. So as I struggled to fill every spot with someone from my personal network, Jake politely suggested a local vet he knew, Lacy Gunnoe, of the Alabama Air National Guard, based in Birmingham, whom he'd met while volunteering with a nonprofit. I had my reservations at first: this guy wasn't blown up, he didn't run through the streets of Baghdad or Kabul, what does he have to offer guys like me? But maturity won the day and I agreed to take a phone call with Jake and his friend Lacy. And boy, was I wrong.

I can't recall the phone call verbatim. I don't need to. I know how I felt as it ended. As Lacy talked about his experiences, and why he wanted to help administer this program with us, I could hear the passion and honesty in his voice. He cared. I didn't yet know the details, but I knew this guy had a story and I was eager to hear it.

★★★

LACY

For a majority of my Air Force career, I served as an instructor pilot, including instructing at the Air Force's largest pilot training base, where I trained future pilots in the T-37 and T-6 aircraft. This assignment remains my favorite because I also had the privilege of serving as the squadron's "mayor." As part of my additional duties as the mayor, I was responsible for our "roll calls." You may have heard of this tradition held in flying squadrons, primarily held within the fighter community. This sacred gathering is held in the "heritage room," the proper term for squadron bars, where new pilots earned their call signs and many shots of Jeremiah Weed bourbon whiskey may or may not be downed. This tradition has been passed down from World War I, as many pilots did not return, and the mayor would read off the names to toast those who did not and celebrate quickly, only to fly out again the next day. As the mayor, I wielded a gavel as we started exactly, to the second, on time. If someone was not present, accounted for with a call promptly at start time, or if a note attached to frosty beverages was not left it would be noted to be paid upon the next roll call.

I attempted to maintain order even with my two enforcers, but after the time hack (a military term for synchronizing our watches) and start of the events, the fun was hard to control. Essentially, I was the leader of the debauchery, and it *was* debauchery. I served as mayor for three years, and every quarter we would name new people who had to get up in front of the group and tell a joke, who were quickly booed regardless of their humor. Eventually we would assign those pilots a call sign that might entail a cryptic acronym to ensure the name patch could be worn in public, but I can tell you that some of that is a little inappropriate.

But those roll calls brought us together and it was the closest unit I was ever a part of. We all had to go through it at some point, even the nonfighter types, but that shared experience is like another application of adhesive. Lars "Yeti" Hubert was one of my commanders when I was the mayor. The previous commander had counseled me for a few things and I felt defeated at the time. Yeti was there, pulled me into his office and re-vectored all my thrust in the right direction. Later, when I had to move on to my next assignment, Yeti was my commander. He knew that Birmingham, Alabama, was my number one choice, but I also knew no spots were available there. I'll never forget being in my flight commander office that day when Yeti walked in. He said, "You know, Lace, I wish I had a whole squad of guys like you." He handed me a letter. In that letter were my orders to report to

Birmingham. Yeti had pulled some strings, called in favors, or perhaps sold one of his children (joke!) so I could get my first choice. I will never forget it. His wife ensured that the spouses were just as close. They gave relentless support for the wife of one of our fellow pilots who eventually died of cancer. This family loved the Tiger Squadron like we were their cubs. He still checks in on me every now and again and I am still trying to earn the kind words he shared in the office.

Here in Birmingham, I've gotten to meet some other people who've experienced real bonds of brotherhood. Newton Duke was a POW from the Korean War and his experience changed my life. Newton buried his fellow POW brothers with the same spoon that he ate his food with. While at his home he showed me that spoon he'd kept all those years. He also shared what he went through as a POW, the evil pain of hunger, sorrows of men lost, but also the hope he felt when, walking back into freedom, he saw a comrade wrap himself in an American flag like a blanket and step into a truck to go home. Newton Duke has been a big blessing in my life and reminds me of the sacrifices we make and how we can be of service to others. He wasn't my instructor, but he was my teacher. I mourn his recent passing while remaining grateful for the lessons he taught me.

★★★★★★★★★★★★★★★★★★★★★★★★★★★★★★★★★

I can't say with certainty, but I have to imagine the first man who used a sword taught the second man what he learned, and in doing so, became the first in a long history of military instructors, those among us who have learned a skill, put it to action, survived mistakes, and ultimately completed a mission. Without these individuals, and their desire to selflessly and patiently teach the next generation, none of us would ever achieve feats of heroism in battle, save a life, or do a job. I've had the pleasure of being taught skills by some great men. First, my dad, who taught me how to lay brick and block, and perhaps more importantly that I didn't want to do that forever. Then there were football coaches, history teachers, drill instructors, and finally my EOD school instructors. One of those left a mark that changed my life forever.

One of the toughest sections of EOD school is called "AIR." This is where we learn all the ordnance deployed by aircraft as well as all the explosive hazards associated with operating a military aircraft, like the rocket pack under an ejection seat that only deploys if the ejection doesn't go well. This part of school is exceptionally hard and many of the students who fail out of EOD school do it in AIR. Having made it through the first few sections of AIR, I was testing on a specific piece of ordnance on the final day of the course and my instructor was Staff Sergeant John Hayes. He was a stone-faced, quiet Marine who was known to be strict, but fair. Unlike some of the other few Marine instructors in the multiservice school, he didn't care to converse or make friends with any of the students. He was there to do a job and that was to see if we had what it takes to do *the* job downrange and with live explosives.

As I went step by step, following the information provided to me, reading the proposed scenario, and deducing how to properly render safe the ordnance in front of me, I began to apply hand tools and procedures according to the protocols I believed were applicable. One of these procedures called for taping a fuse in a way in which it couldn't function. Essentially holding down a spring with tape. I took a six-inch strip of tape and applied it exactly where I should have.

Finally, after a few hours I was done with my practical

application test. I looked at Staff Sergeant Hayes for any kind of expression or nod to say, "You passed." None existed. Instead, he had me sit on a bench outside the instructor's office. I sat there for hours, watching my classmates come through, seeing the smiles of relief on their faces as instructors quickly reviewed their performance and told them they'd passed. Finally, with about thirty minutes left in the school day, Staff Sergeant Hayes appeared from the office, visibly bothered. He looked at me and said, "If a bomb blows your leg off, are you going to apply a Band-Aid or a tourniquet?" I looked at him with what had to be an expression only seen when a deer stares directly into the headlights of an oncoming semi . . . and then it hit me . . .

"Oh," I said.

"Yeah, dumbass, 'oh.' I hope you've learned something before we're on the battlefield together because I'm gonna want a tourniquet."

He threw my test packet at me, and it said "Passed."

I was confused, but I took the win and left.

The next day another instructor pulled me aside and said, "Hayes saved your ass yesterday, you better do him right. He argued that you did exactly what the procedure said, but you were supposed to wrap that tape around a few times. I guess he sees something in you because if you fail a test now, he's on the hook."

Staff Sergeant Hayes taught me that when you have an opportunity to do what's in black and white, to fail a student or overlook a teammate, sometimes you have to look at the bigger picture, recognize something worth investing in, and ultimately put your neck on the line for them. That's what EOD is all about. A few years later that interaction would come full circle for us both. While recovering at Walter Reed from losing my own legs, I got another call about a Marine EOD tech who'd just come into the intensive care unit missing his legs. It was Staff Sergeant Hayes. He was in bad shape. I did as I'd done for several of my brothers who'd come in after me. I rolled down to the ICU in my wheelchair and spent the next several hours with him so he wouldn't be without a friendly face while his family made the trip to DC. In those hours I couldn't help but remember what he'd told me about applying Band-Aids to tourniquet problems. I wasn't there to literally apply his, but because of his patience and belief in me I did my job in Afghanistan with an added level of attention to detail.

Lacy Gunnoe's roll call story and the assigning of names gets repeated under different circumstances all the time among those in the military and civilian life. We may use terms of endearment, seemingly inappropriate nicknames, or anything in between, but the granting of a name serves as a sign of inclusion—you belong and the identity you share with us is different and special. You were one thing before you came to be with us and now you are something different and better. I struggle to imagine what men like Newton Duke and his fellow prisoners of war had to deal with, but I'm sure that they had their own version of a mayor or roll call all for the purpose of holding on to themselves, and forming a bond.

★★★

COUNTRY ROADS

The best gift my family gave me was a work ethic. I joke that like Chris Farley's character in the *Saturday Night Live* sketch, I was raised in a "trailer" down by the river. It's true that I was born in the middle of nowhere in southern West Virginia. Although my parents' divorce hit hard, each of them had a real influence on me. My mom was one of seven kids and was the only one among them who graduated from high school. She ran her own hair salon. She also rode a motorcycle to high school and was prom queen. My friends called my dad "Jimmy Hart, the Mouth of the South," like the professional wrestling manager of that name, and his contagious personality always had everyone laughing. He was also an outstanding coach, who pushed us all to be our best. I've never seen him dip, drink, or smoke in my lifetime but have seen him serve his community and work harder than anyone I know. After they divorced, I remember how hard it was being alone a lot and Dad showing me he only earned about nine thousand dollars a year. While we were limited on the financial side, we were not limited with access to riding motorcycles, ATVs, hunting, sports, and well . . . cutting firewood or working way too early and way too late.

While I appeared confident, I didn't have a true belief in myself. If it weren't for other people believing in me more than I believed in myself, I would have never gotten to college. My high school guidance counselor had to help with financial aid or else I wouldn't be where I am today, and my mom had to force me to complete the college application. I had a tough time in high school after the divorce; before it I was the student body president of my middle school. My parents' divorce messed me up. I started wearing hoodies, switched to rap music, and dyed my hair different colors—anything that was unusual in my area because I wanted to be different. Of course, I wanted to fit in, too, like you do at that age.

I drove my dad crazy by getting my ears pierced and I remember being at graduation surrounded by so many that loved me, but feeling utterly alone. I spent a lot of time with my grandparents and became determined to not be like all the other kids in that area. One thing that set me apart from a lot of them is that I did get to go to college. Looking back, that may have saved my life.

If it weren't for my uncle Melvin, I'm not sure I would have survived at West Virginia University (WVU), but I am certain I would not be in the military. Uncle Melvin was a major in the United States Air Force. Before that, he was a US Marine. He became a Marine because he failed out of Concord College; at least that's how I interpreted it. He went into the Marines, came out, went back to college, and got straight A's. The Marine Corps had taught him about discipline. After going to Officer Training School in the USAF, he took an assignment teaching AFROTC at WVU. He became the commandant of cadets, running the ROTC program there.

I'll never forget this. One morning, he pulled up outside my dormitory in this beat-up brown 1970s Toyota. It had "Highwayman" written down the side of it. He picked me up when it was way too early in the morning after I'd been out way too late the night before. He took me out to the track on campus. A few other guys were there wearing AFROTC T-shirts above their gym shorts. We did push-ups. We did sit-ups. We ran. We did the Air Force physical fitness test. I talked with some of those guys, and I thought, I don't belong here. When I spoke to the ROTC leadership other than my uncle, I got the feeling that they didn't think I belonged there, either. Even though they didn't say those words out loud, I knew. And that's all it took. I may not have believed in myself that much, but the power of proving people wrong is pretty potent. One of the greatest motivators in life is to have someone tell you, You can't do something, you don't belong, you can't do this. It gives you something to prove. I wish I knew then that instead of proving people wrong, the real power is proving those who believed in you right.

MOST IMPROVED

In the second semester of my first year at WVU, I was getting up early, taking out my earrings, and joining those guys out on that athletic field and track.

Uncle Melvin, I knew, believed in me, but I was still struggling in that environment. Still, at least I was making an effort. I wasn't loving what I was doing, but I kept showing up at the right time, right place, right uniform, and with a decently right attitude. I also recognized something. My dad had pushed me pretty hard, but he had at least showed up for me. A lot of the people I knew growing up didn't have parents who did that kind of thing for them. I started pushing some of the ROTC members who needed help. I realized I loved doing that. I loved encouraging them, so I created Motivational Enthusiastic Attitude Training (MEAT) sessions to do workouts and run while singing "jodies" to get fired up before official training. I wasn't a stellar performer myself, but I remember earning the Most Improved Cadet award at field training and a few physical fitness awards. I think I got that Most Improved Cadet award more because of how bad I was when I first started. But this award, and the support of my leadership, were the reason I was assigned in charge of physical training (PT). It gave me the fire to introduce those MEAT sessions and start to push others toward their best.

So, I went from being the guy who was dragging his ass one early morning because his uncle drove him out there to being the one chanting out the cadence while running and doing calisthenics. I was the one leading the group. I went from feeling like I didn't belong to feeling motivated to ensure that everyone else had the opportunity to belong.

Fast-forward to just before I graduated from the ROTC program. We were all formed up in the gym where NBA legend Jerry West had played for WVU. I was in my ROTC uniform, no more dyed hair, no more earrings. The commander came out to close down the leadership laboratory session and said that someone was not in proper uniform.

I thought for a minute and looked around, thinking, Wait a minute? Someone's out of uniform? Who?

The commander looked at me and said, "It's you."

I was still confused. I knew I had the right uniform on, my dress blues.

It turned out I wasn't in the right uniform for a pilot candidate. The commander tossed me a flight suit. I was now a member of another group, this one trying to earn their wings. For a boy from a holler in rural West Virginia, this was a huge deal. Things like this didn't happen to guys like me—unless your name was Chuck Yeager! Once again, I experienced the sense that I couldn't do it, that I wouldn't belong. On the outside I would don the mask of confidence while on the inside I was fighting doubt. I'd have people believe in me to get to that point, but at each stage, I lacked belief that I could actually accomplish the next step. I'm still friends with many of the cadets, and I had Uncle Melvin to thank for getting me in the Highwayman and supporting me throughout my time in AFROTC. Off to active duty I went, and I was learning to fly a single-engine Cessna being taught by a World War II veteran, Hal. Earlier than anticipated, he sent me up to solo. Inwardly I doubted myself. I watched him walk away, and he didn't even look back as I taxied out toward the runway—what a savage. I did it, and I like to joke that old pilot lived long enough for me to figure out how to land the thing safely.

All seemed good in my world. I was a brand-new lieutenant. I was learning to fly. I reported to work on September 11, 2001, and my life and profession would be changed forever. We had Air Force pilots flying intercepts on airliners and escorting them down to land. That's when the gravity of what I was training to do came home to me. I was there with guys I'd enjoyed having a beer with and joking around with and now they were scrambling and launching—to shoot down civilian aircraft if necessary.

★★★★★★★★★★★★★★★★★★★★★★★★★★★★★★★★★

I can understand and identify with Lacy when it comes to a humble background. I too grew up poor, in a rural, seemingly forgotten part of the country. Ironically enough, I also grew up in a holler. We didn't have the river, though. That makes me laugh. My parents knew I could be something "more," but with no one in my lineage ever graduating from high school, college wasn't even a part of the conversation.

But, like Lacy, I had other people in my life who knew what I was capable of even before I did. My best friends, Keith and Chris, each with dads who were career military, pushed me. On the morning of September 11, 2001, I was in gym class lifting weights. One of our coaches came in and turned the TV on and didn't say a word. We watched, confused for a few minutes, then at 9:03 a.m. we watched as the second plane hit its tower. I went through my school day somewhat ignorant to what it all truly meant. I was fifteen years old and had no idea what would come next or how historic, and tragic, the morning's events were. But that afternoon, lying on my back on a grass field, in my football pads, stretching next to Chris, my coach said, "Men, look at this sky . . . there isn't a plane in it. Today you all train for a football game that may or may not happen this Friday, but not long from now many of you will be training for a war that will come from all this. Take care of each other, fight hard for each other. This country needs all of you."

That's when it hit me. I had no idea Chris and I would

both end up in Iraq six years later, or all that would transpire
for each of us, but I knew what kind of men we were training
to be. And that bond between us, between our football
team, between all of us as Americans that day, that's what
even the fiercest of enemies can't break. That's what kept
Lacy going even when he was unsure of himself, what kept
those POWs sane through years of isolation and torture,
and perhaps even what kept that World War II veteran
calm and confident during Lacy's training. They believed
in each other and, in turn, believed in themselves.

★★★★★★★★★★★★★★★★★★★★★★★★★★★★★★★★★★★★

PEOPLE WHO BELIEVED IN ME

Shortly after 9/11, I wound up doing my next phase of pilot training
at Columbus Air Force Base, in Mississippi, at the start of 2002. I
had good hands, but struggled with the fire hose of information and
of course, the inner talk of not believing in myself. My instructors,
Captain White and Major Smith, pulled me aside and told me about
all the reasons to stay in the program when I knew the protocol was
to send me home and on to another assignment. They expressed their
belief in me and encouraged me to stick with it, and I did. I earned
my wings as a pilot in the USAF and went on the become an aircraft
commander flying a KC-135 and doing five deployments all over the
world.

As I did that, I realized that I was a part of a bigger team, flying
in support of ground troops, and Marines on the ground, while the
ground crews and support personnel that helped us succeed in our
flights were amazing, dedicated individuals. One of the great things
about the Air Force is that we didn't always have the same people

My dad, the oldest of three sons, was stoic in some ways and a complete cutup in others. He stood at five feet eight, but he had no trouble commanding respect from his six-foot-tall son. I respected him because he had the intellect and patience to learn any skill necessary.

Joey's dad when his son was a toddler, a newborn, and a newly pinned Explosive Ordnance Disposal technician.

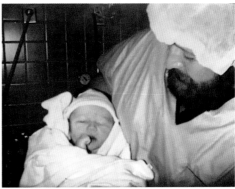

★ ★ ★

Dad knew bonds weren't
something you forged lightly
or threw away cheaply. For a
Marine, those bonds become
more than merely shared
circumstance or convenience.
He taught me that a bond is
a responsibility to come home,
to recover, to be there for the
people you love.

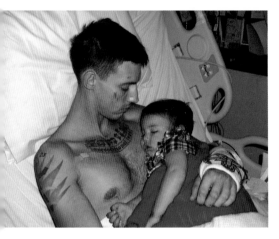

Above: Joey with his wife,
Meg; son, Joseph; and
daughter, Margo. *Left:* Joey,
after his injuries, holding
Joseph. *Below:* Joey and Meg.

GREG WRUBLUSKI

Greg Wrubluski is that rare Marine who rose through the ranks from enlisted to officer—what we call a "mustang." What makes Greg special is that while his rank changed, the type of man and Marine he is didn't. The price you pay for leading can be high. But because of the high bar Greg set, other people stepped up to follow his example. His brothers have gathered around him for myriad group texts and hunting trips, conversations about football and life. He was there for us and now we're here for him.

Left: Greg in Herat Province, Afghanistan, and (*below*) hunting.

Greg and Danny Ridgeway.

AMOS AND ADAM BENJAMIN

Amos Benjamin stands a head taller than most folks, and if I didn't know he was a Marine, I'd probably think he was a pro football player. Amos's older brother, Adam, served with me and many of my friends in the EOD community. Adam was killed in action in Afghanistan, but his legacy lives on within our group of professionals and also in his very big little brother, Amos.

Left: Eighteen-year-old Adam and five-year-old Amos. *Below:* Amos and Adam as adults.

Amos with his wife, Courteney, and baby Liam.

DANIEL RIDGEWAY

Daniel Ridgeway has been at my side through many a hunting trip and adventure. We are brothers for life. We even fight like it in passive-aggressive texts from time to time. But we love each other just the same. When anything in life gets too much to handle, we are there for each other.

Left and below:
Danny and Joey.

Danny hunting.

Choosing to serve offers people a path to a chosen family, an interwoven network of brothers and sisters who will have your back in adversity—not the family one is born into but blood brothers nonetheless. It's a family that's one phone call away for the rest of your life. The military offers an escape from an alienated society to one built on lifelong bonds.

Joey and Daniel Greer.

Above: Danny Ridgeway in Afghanistan and (*left*) on the "long walk" searching for IEDs.

Above: Ralph "EJ" Pate. *Right:* Danny and EJ.

When Amos Benjamin's older brother was killed in action, Amos found his brother's friends coming to him for support, rallied by their commanding officer, Greg Wrubluski. Greg had found a family in the Marines when his own relatives didn't bother showing up. That same give-and-take is true in so many stories in this book.

Amos with Danny and Greg.

Joey with Amos and Danny.

★ ★ ★

WESLEY HUNT

Wesley Hunt spent eight years in the Army as an Aviation Branch officer and H-64D Apache Longbow helicopter pilot. Honorably discharged as a captain, he now serves as a dad, husband, and U.S. congressman. For Wesley, military service is a family tradition. He attended West Point with his sister, D'Hania, and brother, Wrendon. Wesley's father, after twenty-three years in the Army, finally retired as an adjutant general.

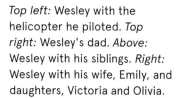

Top left: Wesley with the helicopter he piloted. *Top right:* Wesley's dad. *Above:* Wesley with his siblings. *Right:* Wesley with his wife, Emily, and daughters, Victoria and Olivia.

NATE BOYER

From volunteering to help refugees in Darfur to serving as a Green Beret in the Army Special Forces, Nate Boyer has always sought a life of service and challenge. Nate is still taking on challenges, from his football career to new ventures in film.

(Courtesy of Connor Mendez)

(Courtesy of University of Texas Athletics)

Top left: Nate receiving a Special Forces team patch in Afghanistan in 2014. *Above:* Nate returning from patrol in Iraq in 2008. *Left:* Nate leading the Texas Longhorns out of the tunnel at the Cotton Bowl in 2014. *Below:* Nate training an Iraqi Special Forces soldier in 2009.

★ ★ ★

LACY GUNNOE

Lacy Gunnoe grew up in the mountains of West Virginia and struggled to imagine he could ever do anything important. Mentors like his grandfather helped him believe in himself. He found the Air Force and became a pilot, flying big planes and teaching young trainees. His military career has pushed him to do things he didn't think were possible—now he works to make sure others have the same realization.

Above: Lacy, Joey, and Jeff McDonald. *Right:* Lacy with a requalification class.

Left: Lacy and his wife, Kaleigh. *Below:* Lacy teaching a class at Church of the Highlands.

Aaron Hale's patriotism and love of creativity have been dominant themes across his life. When he first joined the Navy, he worked as a chef. After 9/11, however, he knew he wanted to do more and enlisted in the Army, ending up in Explosive Ordnance Disposal.

Left: Aaron with Joey.
Below: Aaron cooking before the bomb blast.

Aaron cooking at Walter Reed days after the blast.

★ ★ ★

Despite injuries that cost him his sight and an infection that took away most of his hearing, Aaron has shown his indomitable spirit through new creative endeavors, from starting a fudge business and traveling as a motivational speaker to living as an athlete and adventurer and, finally, serving as a loving husband and devoted father.

Aaron with his wife, McKayla, and sons, Cameron, Wyatt, and Owen.

Aaron making fudge as Cameron observes.

Jacob Schick is one of those guys you just want to be around. He has a certain humble confidence that makes him as approachable as he is respected. After getting out of the Marine Corps, he has devoted his time to helping others heal and learn to open up about the challenges of life "back home." Through that work, he's ended up in some pretty surprising places, including playing a role in Clint Eastwood's film <u>American Sniper.</u>

Left: Jacob. *Below:* Jacob and his wife, Ashley.

Jacob with Bradley Cooper and Clint Eastwood.
(Courtesy of Warner Bros.)

★ ★ ★

STACY GREER

Daniel Greer was killed in action by the bomb that took my legs. Daniel has been by my side, and his widow, Stacy's, for the past twelve years. In this book, Stacy tells Daniel's story, describing the bond she shares with him and their son, Ethan, today, as well as the many people who have stepped up to support their family in the years since Daniel's death.

Above: Daniel in Afghanistan.
Left: Daniel and Stacy's wedding.
(Courtesy of Cade and Marcia Truitt)

Joey with Ethan and Stacy.

★ ★ ★
KEITH STANCILL

Keith Stancill is one of my two high school best friends, along with Chris McDonald. We all went to Iraq in 2007 and came home in 2008. After my injury in 2010, they were with me the whole first year. The bond you share with brothers who have known you that long is a bond that remains unbroken for life.

The three friends in high school and after.

Joey with Chris and Keith.

★ ★ ★

Chris's dad, Jeff McDonald, was a Marine, football coach, teacher, father, and friend. At times he was all those things to Keith and me. He was a warrior to the day he died, not because of the fight left in him but for the love and care he had for us as his adopted sons in war.

Jeff and Joey.

Joey and Keith.

Left: Keith with his wife, Allana, and his kids, Brian and Aspen. *Above:* Keith with a puppy.

working with us, but we had to trust each new individual to know and do their job. That meant that we had to develop an enormous amount of belief in a lot of people. Something that produces bonds in combat and elsewhere in the military is the amount of trust you place in others and they place in you.

Pilots often make great roommates. Our house had four pilots and at least one was always gone. One of my best friends since 2003 was my roommate and we spent time on the road together. Being a kid from small-town West Virginia, I wasn't exposed to too much of that. Joe taught me a lot about travel, experiencing the world, and he encouraged me to save money. Over time, I came to think of him as a brother. We hosted our families together, celebrated weddings, supported each other with deployments, loss of family members, and went on to have two assignments flying together. He was a great pilot and great leader and remains an even better friend. After twenty years of friendship, that old roommate, a true wingman, was one of the first to hold my newborn son as he and his family hosted us at the beach just a few weeks before I wrote this.

I am blessed to have formed bonds with others whom only the military could fiber together. Brothers with better stories than my one and who live such inspiring lives. One whose wife still tells the story of my deploying for her husband with their newborn in the NICU. She proudly tells of me going against the commander's expectations, and I humbly smile as I see their son today, healthy and a heck of a soccer player—also our neighbors a few houses down. Bonds of military brotherhood mean that when you have the opportunity to really help, you do it. So, flying as a tanker pilot on that deployment was a privilege. It wasn't a sacrifice. I know there's no question that he and Joe and others in the flying community would have done that for me.

LEGACY OF SERVICE

I learned the value of service from my grandfather, who was a water well driller. Pawpaw, whose name was Lacy, was the biggest servant I've known. He loved our little mountain community. He would take a branch off a cherry tree and use that forked stick as a divining rod to find water underneath the surface. He'd mark the spot and then he'd set up the drilling equipment there. There was a lot of poverty where we lived, and he was a man of faith. So he was known for his generosity, not charging families with kids, people whose lot in life put them in a position where they couldn't afford it.

It was the example that he set, and my family has set, and others throughout my life set that influenced my career decisions. That's why I became an instructor pilot just like Captain White and Major Smith. I wanted to pay back the people for all the grace they showed me and all the belief they had in me. The instructors who had invested in me and while I thought of quitting, they pushed me forward. They saw something in me that I couldn't see, that I chose to see in others.

When I was an instructor, I had my Kitty Hawk moment. I call it that because a lot of people know about the Wright brothers and how they went to Kitty Hawk, North Carolina, to test out their aircraft. They'd done a lot of their developmental work back in Ohio, but the environment for them to really succeed in flying was in the sand dunes in North Carolina. That was the case with me, too. I had found the right environment for me to serve others. Over the years when I served as an instructor, I did what those other instructors had done for me. I did my best to serve, lead, and inspire others to be their best. I shared with them my story, my lack of belief, and encouraged them to believe in themselves. As an instructor, I felt like I was where I belonged, doing the work I should be doing. That's when I realized, on the other side of the table, sitting in the instructor seat, that I didn't just look confident on the outside, but I truly believed in myself. I earned a few awards for the work I was doing, but it was me being of service to others that got me there.

I was able to change my mindset because others believed in me. That's what I wanted to do for other people so that the chain of belief could keep gaining links.

I've met others who followed a legacy of service, too. I once had a trainee whose name was David. He always came in for the day early and left late. He always poked his head into my office before going to the flight room to ask me if I needed help with anything—take out the trash or whatever. I always told him no. I tried to make it clear by my tone that my office was holy ground and he shouldn't enter it. I tried to be assertive, sarcastic, whatever, to discourage him from stopping by my office. He would just smile and nod and walk away. I hid my smile and kept thinking, What a good kid. He was servant-mindset kind of guy. He was the one who always cleaned up in the flight room.

Yes, David was a good guy, but he and the rest of his class weren't performing well. They weren't earning good grades. They weren't studying as a team. Consequently, because they were struggling, so was David. I had to figure out what to do with this group.

One afternoon, I got everybody to stand at attention. I walked out of the flight room and went down the hall to where a display case sat. Inside that glass case, pairs of wings sat on shelves. These were the wings that would be presented to them if they passed. They'd be pinned to their dress blues at graduation. At that ceremony, you also get wings that are separated into two halves. You keep one and you present the other half to someone of your choosing, someone who played a significant role in your life. The only time those two halves are paired again is when they're placed on the pilot's coffin.

I walked back into the flight room and told the students to close their eyes. I took the wings I'd taken from the case and scattered them across the table at the front of the room. I then told them to open their eyes.

"What was that?" I asked.

They collectively told me that they thought it was their wings. I told them they were right and then asked them who they planned to give the other half of their wings to. One trainee said he'd present them to his girlfriend. I hid my eye roll but understood she had supported him during training. I continued going around the room. Eventually I got to David, who said that he was going to take the other half of the wings and put them on his father's gravestone. I had known that his father had passed and had flown in his guard unit. I also knew David wanted to graduate and return to fly in his dad's home unit. What I learned while he was speaking was that his dad had gone to pilot training in Columbus. His dad had attended training in the same unit we were in and potentially the same flight. Now David was there where his father had once been.

I got it then. I understood why David wanted to be there helping out, taking out the trash, feeling more connected than others to this space. I thought, perhaps David was there early and there late because the longer he stayed, the more time he was spending with his father. I felt David had something much larger than just pilot training on his mind. He was there to preserve and strengthen the bond he had with his father. He believed in something bigger, a larger connection.

You could feel something in that flight room shift once David made clear why he was there. A lot of the others in that trainee class were there hoping that they'd be able to move on to fighter pilot training. They could be a part of the elite. Be the tip of the spear. They were there wanting to get something for themselves, competing with others in the class. But that wasn't David's reason. He had no intention or ambition to serve in a way that served himself; he was going back to his guard unit. He wanted to connect and serve while honoring a legacy of service.

After that, those trainees turned around and started to help one another. They helped David. They bonded and now it wasn't just about themselves; it was about the person to the left and to the right of them. They needed to be able to trust that the best person got put in the best plane to make sure that the mission got done.

I eventually moved on from being a flight instructor there and on to instructing in the KC-135 in Birmingham. One day, I received a text. It was from David, a picture of a trophy. He'd graduated from pilot training. The trophy was presented to him for earning the Distinguished Graduate award. I couldn't help but think of all those people in that trainee class who had decided to really bond together. They had poured themselves into one another. They had believed in each other and in something bigger than themselves. And, man, when you're in a room where people have faith in themselves and a larger cause, that's winning. That brings you together in such a powerful way. That is what wins hearts and minds.

I believe that my faith in God teaches me that. I try to lead with my heart in whatever way I can because I believe that each of us is created to do something bigger. If I can play just a small part in helping someone believe that they can do something greater than they first thought, then that's the greatest currency I can ever possess. The level of impact you have on the lives of others is how you measure success.

"TREAT A MAN AS HE COULD BE"

One last story of a unique bond. As a new instructor pilot, I walked into my flight room and spotted a man who looked out of place—I'll call him Diego. He was older than the rest of the class, who were all in their early twenties. I asked him a couple of questions and it was clear that he didn't speak English well. He had attended a crash course in the English language in San Antonio, Texas, before being assigned to basic pilot instruction with us. He was a part of the American Liaison Program (ALP). The US helps train pilots from other countries to build relationships and rapport for future endeavors.

Diego was struggling a bit in our class, with his training and with English in general. That's crucial because we have to maintain radio contact quickly with all the aircraft. It's hard enough for native speakers of English to focus on their flying and their communications, so it was nearly impossible for Diego. Several instructors came to me and said that the situation with Diego could put me in a dangerous position as a new instructor.

I sat down to speak with Diego to better assess where we were at. He walked in and his body language said it all. Slump-shouldered and unsure of himself, he sat down across from me. I looked at his grades for his recent flights and they did not look good—plenty of "bloody" grade sheets covered in red pen marks. He was not trending toward graduation. I could tell he was doubting himself. I told him that we were going to fly together. Let's just go, have a good time, and focus on a few basic maneuvers. I just want to get to know you better and see how you're progressing. I didn't tell him not to kill me, but I was thinking that.

I doubt if either of us had too much fun on that ride. He couldn't do any of the aerobatic maneuvers.

We landed safely and debriefed again. Having seen how he performed, there really wasn't much to say or for me to know. I felt bad for the guy. He was not going to pass. He'd come to this country and would have to return a failure. Then I thought of a quote from leadership expert John C. Maxwell: "It's not how much you know, it's how much you care."

So, based on that, I asked Diego to tell me about his family, just to have a normal conversation. I could see him ease up a bit. He and his wife or girlfriend had a brand-new son back home in his country. He was sending his paychecks home to them, but otherwise, communications with them was difficult in 2008, using the military internet and Skype. I knew that some of the other instructors had been rough on him. I told him something I'd read, a paraphrase of Goethe. I looked him dead in the eye and said, "If you treat a man as he is, he'll remain as he is. If you treat a man as he could be, he'll become what he could be." I thought of the people who'd done the latter for me. I wouldn't have been in that room and in that position if it weren't for them.

I couldn't be sure if Diego fully understood what those words meant. So I sat him down at my desk and showed him the quote written there. I also showed him the computer screen where all his grade sheets were recorded. I showed him the place where I was to enter my grade for the assessment I'd just done with him. It was a "Red Block" due to his last sortie being a poor one, but his new grade was blank. I entered "Excellent." I went through the rest of his scores and changed them all to Excellent. He sat up taller with each one. His chin rose. It was like I was putting air in this man's soul. I asked him how he felt about these grades and he told me he felt good. I then said that now he had to earn them. The next day, he had mastered those three things. No matter what all went wrong, he had to have X, Y, and Z down pat. He was starting to get the maneuvers down. That progress continued for the next few weeks and the change in Diego was obvious. When we had briefings together, he was much more confident and professional.

Ultimately, Diego made it. He made a few mistakes, but he qualified to graduate. We were all happy for him and he earned it. We had a little party for him, and someone brought in a cake to celebrate. We also asked Diego if he wanted to say a few words. He did. He raised his right hand slowly and saluted me awkwardly as I sat at the same computer where our bond had started. He repeated the Goethe quote to me. "Treat a man as he is and he will remain as he is. Treat a man as he could be and he will become what he should be."

A few years later, he sent me a message with a few pictures attached. Inside were photos of a smiling Diego, his family with their son growing up, and him with some other men standing inside an aircraft. I recognized one of them as the president of his country. Diego had gone up to fly their version of Air Force One.

Some bonds of brotherhood last a lifetime; some are moments in time. In some cases, you may not see or hear from someone for long periods. They aren't in your life all the time. But I tried to tell people that the impact you have on others is your greatest asset; so believe in others. You may not know immediately how that bond of belief and trust has transformed over time. But in some way, somehow, it will come back to you in unexpected ways. One of the things I've noticed is that with people you served with, even though many years have passed, when you connect again, it's like you're right back with them in that time in an instant. Bonds may be visible or invisible, but when you have faith and you put faith in others, it doesn't matter. They're real.

And by the way, I just went on Facebook and looked up Diego He's still flying. He's still confidently doing great things. But most importantly, knowing him like I do, he's most happy being back home with his family.

★★★★★★★★★★★★★★★★★★★★★★★★★★★★★★★★★★★★★★★

My dad used to say, "Son, anything worth doing is worth doing right." Those words are surely simple enough, but over the years I've learned just how hard they are to put to practice. Working in the trades, he always had manual laborers who

were . . . less than upstanding citizens. Tiger and Eugene—
those were their real names—were two of a kind. They were
all but disenfranchised from regular society, with no driver's
license, no permanent address, no real reason to show up or
be men of their word. But they showed up for my dad. They
worked hard and they were a part of his team. In high school
I worked with them on weekends and eventually led the
team when my dad wanted a day off or needed to work on a
different job.

I asked my dad, "How do I get Tiger and Eugene to work
hard for me like they do you?"

He laughed, thought for a minute, and said, "Son, I make
you wash my trucks every week."

"Yeah," I said.

"What do I always tell you?"

I thought . . . and said, "Well, you say don't bust the rust
unless you're going to polish the chrome."

"Exactly," he said. "Everyone has something worth
investing in, worth polishing a little. Sure, you have to be stern
and set expectations, but if you get in there and work with
them, show them how it's done, and show them you believe in
them to do it . . . they'll do it. Don't just bust them down for
being simple; build them up for working hard, too."

That's what Lacy was doing. He knew some of his students
weren't going to simply thrive in the same ways most of his
other students were. But he also knew he couldn't just tear
them down. He couldn't teach them how to do it correctly by
simply pointing out what they were doing wrong. He couldn't
build them up to polished chrome if all he did was bust the
rust. Lacy understood what my dad taught me, that everyone
has something worth investing in, worth believing in. And for it

to be successful, they have to first believe in themselves, and when in a class or platoon or on a team, they have to believe in each other. That's the kind of bonds created by good teachers, and I think it's safe to say that Lacy Gunnoe is a damn good teacher.*

★★★★★★★★★★★★★★★★★★★★★★★★★★★★★★★★★★★★★

---

* The views expressed in this chapter are those of the author and do not reflect the official policy or position of the US Air Force, Department of Defense, or the US Government.

SHOULDERS TO LEAN ON

— ★ ★ ★ —

Those people are my family. I would do anything
in this world for any one of those men and
their families. I don't care what it is.

—Greg Wrubluski

I was able to change my self-doubting mindset
because others believed in me. And that's what
I wanted to do for other people so that chain of
belief could keep having links added to it.

—Lacy Gunnoe

★

When I joined the Navy, I learned what it meant to be a
part of something that was so much bigger than me. I
underwent a major transition as a result of serving. I truly
loved it and really enjoyed having brothers to the right
of me and to the left who were unified in a great cause.
It wasn't as simple as just putting on a uniform. It was
seeing people from all walks of life coming together.

—Aaron Hale

Perseverance Is a Choice

STAFF SERGEANT (RET.) AARON HALE

★ United States Army ★

"I'd been living for me. It
wasn't until I really learned
to serve others that I found
my joy, my purpose in life."

★★

There are several specialized jobs in the military. Some are highly technical, some deal with logistics, and others are more combat focused. Only a select few encompass nearly all aspects of warfighting. Explosive Ordnance Disposal, or EOD, commonly referred to as the "BombTechs," is one of them. Every branch of service gets to decide for itself who can become an EOD tech, and how they are approved to enter the job field, but we all go to the same school. EOD school is located (ironically) on an old bombing range owned by the Air Force near Eglin Air Force Base in the panhandle of Florida. The school is operated by the Navy. The Army sends half of all students there, and the Marines primarily teach the most relevant section to today's wars: IEDs. It's truly a collaborative effort. If you know anything about the different branches of service, you know that rivalry and even trash-talking each other is a big part of our culture. However, just as the highly technical knowledge and ground combat application of the job requires united training that crosses traditional lines of division among service jobs, so do traditional rivalries get put aside in light of the job's dangerous nature. Marines are always proud Marines, and soldiers proud soldiers, and so on. But being an EOD tech means something all on its own. It's truly a title that's earned, and so going to this school with all four services in your class creates bonds and relationships that far surpass service rivalries. We call it the "EOD community" for a reason. It's somewhat of a fraternity, if you will.

One of the non-Marine students I grew to know and love was unique in so many ways. My first memory of Aaron Hale was on an otherwise unmemorable day in the middle of EOD school. My grandfather had unexpectedly passed away and the few days I spent at home for his funeral meant I was behind on our very fast-paced curriculum and had to pick up with a different class that was a week behind mine. After starting the day with a new subject and a new instructor, we broke for an hour-long lunch break. Being that we were in the Sunshine State, most of us ate our cold sandwiches or fast-food leftovers on a patio behind the schoolhouse. But Aaron Hale was not "most of us." He brought a small cooler, a bag of charcoal, and a lighter, and within the first five minutes of our break he was grilling a pork tenderloin complete with asparagus and squash for sides. At first I laughed and thought, as I bit into my homemade ham sandwich, How high-maintenance can you get? But then he surprised me. He turned to me, smiled, and said, "Well, this is too much food for me. Want some?" With a perfectly cooked slab of meat, I'd met a friend who would become a brother for life. I'm proud to share his story.

★★★★★★★★★★★★★★★★★★★★★★★★★★★★★★★★

AARON

We speak our own language in EOD. It's a brotherhood within the brotherhood of military service, like a fraternity inside the military. That sense of brotherhood is why I found myself at Walter Reed in November 2011.

I was in town because I was enjoying two weeks of R&R before resuming my eight-month deployment in Afghanistan. My whole family had gotten together in the DC area to see me. But while I was there, I learned that a fellow EOD team leader in my company on deployment in Afghanistan had gotten injured. He was at Walter Reed. Kiel Vickers and I were good friends, but even if we weren't, I would have gone to visit him.

When I got to Walter Reed, I found out that Kiel was still in the intensive care unit. In fact, that day he was being operated on, which meant he had only recently gotten to the States. I wanted to know as much as possible about what had happened to him, the nature of the injuries, what kind of surgery he was undergoing. I asked a floor nurse if she could tell me, but of course, for privacy reasons she couldn't let me know anything except that he was expected out of surgery soon. If I liked, she said, I could wait in Kiel's room and see him after he was out of recovery. Of course, I was going to stay as long as it took to see him.

I went into the room. The bed was neatly made and on a chair in the corner sat a pile of clothes from the Wounded Warrior Project or some other organization. There was a pair of shorts and a hoodie. There was one shoe.

It didn't take a rocket scientist to figure out why where was only one.

Awhile later, Kiel was wheeled into the room. He was on a rolling gurney with the sheets tucked in tight, and I could see that he had an intact leg and half of the other. When he saw me, he lit up. "Hale! What are you doing here?"

He had thought I was still in-country in Afghanistan, and now there I was in his hospital room. He had a huge grin on his face. I don't know if it was the effects of the medication he was on, but more likely it was just Kiel's personality. We talked for a bit and then he said, nodding toward his lower body, "I think I kicked myself in the face with own boot!" He busted out laughing and I joined him. That was amazing. I mean, there are some things you just have to laugh about, and that's part of the bond we share, that sardonic humor.

Then he said, "You want to know the worst thing about it? Ruined a perfectly good calf tattoo!"

Two weeks later, I would be in that same unit at Walter Reed being treated by Navy doctors, going through my own ordeal with my lights out forever. I remember lying there feeling sorry for myself knowing that there wasn't anything they could do to help me see again. I was literally and figuratively in a dark place. I was fighting all those what-if demons. My head was still all wrapped up in gauze and it felt like a swarm of bees.

I heard somebody come into the room, and then Kiel's voice. "Hey, dude, give me your hand."

I thought, Why the hell does he want my hand? What's he going to do?

"Check this out."

I felt him grab my hand and the next thing I knew I was cupping his chin, feeling something rough and scratchy against my skin. I recognized it as his beard.

"Dude," he said, and keep in my mind my entire head was swathed in bandages and I'm now permanently blind, "you have got to start growing your beard. You and me, we're going to do it. Beard brothers!"

I chuckled. It took me a second to get what he meant. You see, even in the hospital, the Marines have a liaison officer there and if you tell him that you're doing okay, he will instruct you to be clean-shaven just like you were on base. He'll even hand you a razor. However, we, as Army soldiers, did not have a liaison, so Kiel was enjoying the liberty of not having to meet every regulation and was driving the wounded Marine EOD techs in the unit nuts. His energy was infectious and him wanting me to join him as a beard brother was exactly what I needed to get me out of that dark place. That's what brothers do for one another. They don't always ask; they tell you what's best for you.

★★★★★★★★★★★★★★★★★★★★★★★★★★★★★★★★★★★★★★

The concept of brotherhood goes far beyond male bravado or acts of masculine performance. A brotherhood is a shared experience, and a reliance on others to be there for you, to understand what you're going through, and to offer help when you need it. In fact, the brotherhood of EOD, regardless of service, includes many women who do the job heroically alongside their brothers in arms. Aaron and Kiel found a relief, even humor in their shared sacrifice, but Aaron learned the concept of mutual reliance and dedication much earlier in life. Long before joining the military, the major figure in his life who got him started on a path of exploration and adventure was actually his mother. She endured a pair of difficult marriages, but she managed to create an atmosphere so positive that Aaron says that he loved his Ohio childhood, despite his parents splitting up and later Aaron not getting along with his stepfather. Aaron's father moved to California, where Aaron spent his summers, loving the beach life, very different from suburban Ohio. She taught him a sense of perseverance and optimism, and while her freewheeling creative spirit wasn't as much for discipline, he started to pick up the idea of a mission and life of service from sources that ranged from war movies to coaches.

That mix of creativity and discipline meant Aaron had an unusual trajectory in the military. There's little about Aaron's life and outlook that fits into a neat package of standard expectations. I recognized that shortly after we met. Learning his background also made his penchant for tasty meals at lunchtime make a lot more sense. Aaron had enlisted in the Navy and spent six years there serving as a cook. Deciding that he wanted to play a more direct (combat) role in the defense of the country he loves, he moved from the Navy to the Army with the explicit goal of becoming an EOD technician. Aaron lives by a simple, yet effective, credo: No More Excuses— Accept the Challenge. Despite sustaining injuries that cost him his sight, and later developing a serious infectious disease that also took away most of his hearing, Aaron continues to love life and engage with it fully as a veteran, a successful businessman, motivational speaker, athlete and adventurer, and as a loving husband and devoted father.

I'm proud to call him a friend, and a brother.

★★★★★★★★★★★★★★★★★★★★★★★★★★★★★★★★★★★★★★★

MAKING THE BEST OF IT

My mom was an eternal optimist. I have no memories of her ever complaining. I was the oldest and I wasn't always the most grateful for what I had. For a time, after my parents divorced, my mother was a single mom raising three kids, and she never complained about her situation. Along with that, she never had a bad thing to say about anyone, even though she didn't have the best marriages.

On the other hand—and I'm not blaming my mom at all—she wasn't the best disciplinarian. I took some advantage of the fact that she wanted me to be able to express myself. She allowed me to go to school wearing the most ridiculous clothing and haircuts! I think I was in the fifth grade when she asked me if I wanted to get my ear pierced. I hadn't even considered it before. I went ahead and did it and I think I was one of maybe one or two other guys in the school with any piercings. We were way ahead of the trend. I thought my mom was the coolest. I wasn't alone. A bunch of my buddies had a crush on her. I had, and still have, a terrific relationship with her.

My mother also led a lot by example. Still to this day, I'm an avid reader, and I got that from her. Every time we sat around the kitchen table, our conversation gravitated to the latest books we were reading. Today, even if I'm on the phone with her, that's still the case. I get great recommendations from her and vice versa.

She also taught me the value of work and saving money to get the things you want. If there was something I desired, she would tell me—and my dad did this, too—that I would have to come up with half the amount and they'd cover the rest. One example of this also shows how she encouraged my creative side. I wanted to go to Australia and New Zealand as part of the student ambassador program. Tickets for the flights were expensive and we couldn't really afford them. But my mother and I came up with the idea that I could raise some money for it by selling some homemade arts and crafts items. She and I went to the craft store and bought grapevine wreaths, the conical mini-Christmas tree shapes, and some wood and other supplies. I made these really gorgeous-looking holiday scenes and strung lights on them. This was when I was in high school. I took some of them to school and I walked right into the teachers' lounge and sold them. I made enough money to go to Australia and New Zealand on the student ambassador program.

Later, when I joined the Navy, one of the things that attracted me to that branch of service was the opportunity to travel and to experience different cultures. My first duty station in the Navy was in Naples, Italy. When I was on shore duty, I would hang up my uniform at the end of the day and go into the city. I wanted to learn the language, eat the food, learn how to drive like the crazy Neapolitans who think that traffic lights, signs, and lane markers aren't regulations, just helpful suggestions. There are some service members who have the attitude that the rest of the world should be more like America; they aren't comfortable with anything that different. A lot of them ended up stuck inside. We called them "barracks rats." That wasn't me at all.

A lot of that goes back to how, when I was kid, my mom encouraged my creative side.

While I was serving in Italy, my younger brother was in an accident that left him with severe head and spinal injuries. He was in a coma for a month after that, and after he awoke, he had to go through all kinds of physical and occupational therapy so that he could walk and talk and feed himself again. My mother dropped everything and moved in with him during a rehabilitation that sent him from Ohio to Colorado. That's what you do when someone you love needs your help. I don't think it's a coincidence that we refer to the place we come from as our "mother country." That's the kind of feeling we have about it, the deep emotional attachment that bonds us to it. Again, I saw what my mom was willing to sacrifice, without complaint, to bring her baby back toward the life he once had. She has this incredible capacity to respond to the worst circumstances with calm and perseverance.

DOING THE RIGHT THING

I went to Revere High School in Richfield, Ohio, in the late 1980s and early '90s, it was an amazing era for music. After school, I worked at the Blossom Music Center, a huge outdoor concert venue in Cuyahoga Falls. I loved hanging out after the shows and listening to all the different bands. My artistic affinities—music, TV, movies—are very eclectic. I could sit and watch *Magnum P.I.* and then flip the channel to Turner Classic Movies. I liked all kinds of movies, but especially ones about World War II and Vietnam, since I always had an interest in military history.

Some of that came from the fact that both my grandfathers served in the military. I never met my maternal grandfather because he died when I was very young. My mother couldn't tell me much about what he did in the war because he never told her much. He served in an administrative capacity in the Army Air Corps. I'd seen pictures of him in his uniform but that was the extent of it. I knew a bit more about my paternal grandfather. He was one of those men of that generation who didn't talk much about their service. I know that he was in the Philippines.

The thing that I really admired about the men in all the war movies I like—*Tora! Tora! Tora!*, *The Guns of Navarone*, *The Dirty Dozen*, *The Great Escape*—was that they always did the right thing. They were always confident. John Wayne typified that, and I especially liked him in *The Green Berets*.

I also saw men like that in my community. In particular, I had a legendary football coach. Joseph F. Pappano was like a father figure to me and a lot of the other guys I played with. He was there for twenty-six years and after his retirement the football stadium was named for him. A lot of people respected him because he was successful—he led the Minutemen to victory in our rivalry game against Copley High School twenty out of twenty-six times—but I respected him because as fierce a competitor as he was, he was also an incredible mentor. He emphasized doing the right thing on the football field, knowing what our assignments were, accepting responsibility for our mistakes, and then doing everything we could to make sure that we didn't make them again.

Before Coach Pappano, I was coached in middle school by Coach Keys. He was a military veteran himself and a huge, muscular specimen. Despite what you might assume, he wasn't the stereotypical drill sergeant type. He was totally laid-back. He wanted us to do well, but if we made a mistake, he'd just laugh a bit and tap us on the back of the helmet and encourage us to do better next time. He exuded something that I'd see in a lot of other service members. He kept things in perspective. He understood that after what he'd seen and experienced, the rest of life's problems weren't that huge.

I wasn't with my dad all the time, but even so, I learned a lot from him. He was a successful entrepreneur and his work ethic and the disciplined approach he took to building business and employing people were a real positive influence on me. I saw what it meant to be a professional and how to conduct yourself and later I took those lessons with me into the military.

I grew up on twenty acres of land, and there was always plenty to do to maintain the property and take care of other chores. My stepfather would get me up early in the morning on weekends to split logs. I didn't like him. I didn't like having to roll out of bed that early. I did like splitting logs, though. Something about swinging and the physical labor involved appealed to me. It took me out of my literal comfort zone, my bed, and showed me that there were times when you just have to do the right thing.

The problem was, when I set that axe down, I also set aside those lessons. They didn't carry over into the rest of my life. Simply put, I was a bit lazy. I played football and lacrosse and did okay because I had a bit of natural ability and physical gifts. I did okay in school, B's and C's, but I didn't, as teachers and counselors are so fond of saying, "apply myself." We were doing okay financially, more than okay in comparison to some of the kids I grew up with, so I didn't work that hard. I loved life. I appreciated everything that I had, but I don't think that I really understood what it was going to take for me to be on my own.

That certainly didn't help when I enrolled at Bowling Green State University in 1996. Everybody else I knew there knew how to work and how to discipline themselves. I, on the other hand, was living in the moment and having a great time, not focused on the future at all. Two years later, I was done there.

Fortunately, I recognized my weakness and decided to do something about it.

A NEW LIFE OF SERVICE

I was eager to pay back the wasted tuition money I'd been given. I was also eager to be of service in the way that my mother was, so thinking back on those movies I loved and the men I admired, I figured that military service was the right thing for me to do. The military checked a lot of boxes for me: I could develop my core skills and values. I could learn to become a hard worker and become more disciplined. I could also eventually transition out of the military and go back to school and get my life on track. For me, it wasn't so much about serving the country. I loved America and was proud to be an American, but in a way, I joined the military for selfish reasons. What could it do for me?

While joining the Navy in 1999 did get me some of the things I wanted, I ended up getting so much more out of it. I found out what it really meant, in a non-Hollywood way, to serve a greater cause. I truly loved having brothers to the right and left of me who were unified in a great cause. It wasn't as simple as just putting on a uniform. It was seeing people from all walks of life coming together. Like me, some of them may have come into the military looking for something for themselves, but ultimately, particularly after 9/11, it was about what they could contribute to the defense of our country. In my case, I built bonds with a lot of different people over the years, but I also came to appreciate and bond with my country. As I said, I was always proud of America and being an American, but that relationship deepened the longer I served. I realized I wanted to do more for a country that had done so much for me.

At first, though, I had no clue. Until two months before I enlisted,

I never thought I'd ever be in the military. I liked it in the abstract but had no idea about the reality. I was always a bit of a loose kind of hippie kid growing up with my long hair. On that trip to Australia and New Zealand, I came back with a long duster jacket that I thought was supercool. I'd only discharged a weapon maybe once in my life before basic training. It wasn't that I was opposed to them. I just wasn't interested except for the one time I went into the woods with one of my buddies.

I didn't know about all the different jobs service members have. I thought it was like *Full Metal Jacket*. Everyone was a soldier; everyone was a rifleman. I thought that maybe you got to choose a collateral job, like being a reporter or playing in the band. I had narrowed it down to the Air Force or the Navy. I picked the Navy because I figured they had ships and they had to go to shore and shore meant beaches and beaches meant living like I had during those summers in Southern California. That would be pretty good, I figured.

I ended up with a job that let me express my creative side. I spent my first four years working as a cook. I eventually rose to a position where I was the personal chef of a three-star admiral.

When I started out, we were at peace. A lot happened from the time I enlisted in 1999 to 2004, obviously. It felt like one minute, I was cooking aboard ship for that admiral and the next, we were at war. I was watching events unfold in Iraq and Afghanistan from the ship in a similar way as the vast majority of Americans: on television through news coverage. I could only do that for so long. I knew that I had more to give than cooking. I know that every job in the military is important, but I also understood that I had skills and abilities that could be better utilized. I wanted to be closer to the action. I wanted to be more kinetic. I got a sort of compromise solution from the Navy. In 2006, I was sent to Afghanistan to run an Army chow hall that was operating as part of a Provincial Reconstruction Team.

★★★★★★★★★★★★★★★★★★★★★★★★★★★★★★★★★★★★★

Aaron joined in 1999, before the events of September 11, 2001, and before we were fully engulfed in a twenty-year war that would in many ways define our entire generation. He says he joined for selfish reasons, but having a very similar high school experience in the early 2000s and joining the Marine Corps in 2005, I'd say he joined for all the right reasons and just didn't know it yet. No matter how we get to military service, or what personal goals we think are driving us, we do it because there is something primally fulfilling in risking our lives to serve a greater cause. And there's something distinctly American to leave the comforts of middle-class life and college to do it. What impresses me most about Aaron is what we don't have in common. I went to the Marine Corps to improve myself, much like Aaron. But I did it in 2005, knowing war was very much on the table. Aaron joined two years before 9/11 and could have easily gotten out at the end of his first four-year contract and avoided the war altogether. Instead, he not only reenlisted, but sought opportunities that took him from the comparably charmed life of an admiral's chef stationed in southern Europe to feeding combat troops in Afghanistan. That is running toward the fire. That is patriotism in its most impressive form.

Aaron found fulfillment in the job he was doing to support combat operations. But he wanted to do "more" to be "closer" to the dangers that those around him were braving every day. He also got a message from home and another reminder of all the ways that bonds are formed and people can be of service to one another and make sacrifices.

★★★★★★★★★★★★★★★★★★★★★★★★★★★★★★★★★★★★★

JOINING EOD

While I was running that mess hall for the Army in Afghanistan, I also met some EOD techs assigned to the area. Regardless of the mission, regardless of the role of civilians in the operation, the Taliban and other insurgent groups were bent on limiting their effectiveness. If this was a battle for the hearts and minds of the Afghan people, then the message they were sending was clear: No good can come from foreign intervention. If you collaborate with them, you might find yourself suffering the same fate. In war, where the line between combatants and noncombatants was often invisible, trust was at a premium.

In talking with those EOD techs, I thought I saw a way I could serve in a more substantive way than I had been. After my return to the States following that tour in Afghanistan, I investigated the EOD training program further and applied for a change of job assignment to it. Unfortunately, my request was denied. Simultaneous to that, I faced another decision. My contract was about to expire. I loved being in the Navy, but being of greater service was more important to me. I let my contract expire and immediately sought out an Army recruiter and was accepted. It was considered a lateral move, so I didn't lose my rank (sergeant) and immediately went to basic training.

It wasn't until I really learned to serve others that I really found my joy and my purpose in life. It was about doing more with my skills, and serving in a greater capacity.

Following basic training, I entered into the EOD training program in 2009. There I found another family to belong to. Among my classmates was Johnny Joey Jones. He was in the Marines, but the various service branches send their EOD techs to the same school. That's why I say that there's more of a close-knit fraternity among us, since, first, there's relatively few of us; second, the job is very dangerous, so it takes a special kind of person to want to do it; and third, we often know one another from our earliest specialized training, and so despite serving for a different branch, we end up very close.

After graduation, I was assigned to Fort Drum, in upstate New York, near the Canadian border. It isn't just while serving overseas that you bond with others. Living together on the same base will do that, and in upstate New York in the winter, that bond is a kind of cold fusion. It's so cold that troops from Alaska are assigned there to do their cold weather training.

I wouldn't have to worry about that for long. My first EOD deployment was to the very hot zone of Iraq in 2010.

★★★★★★★★★★★★★★★★★★★★★★★★★★★★★★★★★★★★★★

That year brought the heat of midterm congressional elections in Washington, DC, the throes of balancing domestic politics and national security. President Barack Obama and his advisors decided to broadcast their intent to end the war in Iraq and withdraw many of the troops they had surged to Afghanistan in 2009, and reduce the size and scope of our involvement in both countries. Unfortunately, in Afghanistan the result was a reenergized fight from the Taliban, who believed they could seize on a perceived retreat of US forces from much of the country. With these factors at play, and the arrival of the Afghani "fighting season," the summer of 2010 proved to be the deadliest period to date for EOD technicians in the war on terror, my legs being just one example of the toll it took on our community. Thankfully, Aaron returned safely from that tour in Iraq. But the wheels set in motion that year would mean a resurgent Taliban and another deployment to Afghanistan for Aaron in 2011.

★★★★★★★★★★★★★★★★★★★★★★★★★★★★★★★★★★★★★★

THE INJURY

It was during that long, lonely walk about eight months into deployment that I was injured. The blast took away my eyes and cracked my skull in a couple of places and both my eardrums were blown up. The bones in my skull were so fractured that cerebral fluid ran out of my nose. Miraculously, the rest of my body, from the neck down, was virtually untouched. The explosion just hit me in the head, and, of course, you know us EOD boys have very thick skulls, so that's the best place to hit me!

But at the time, I was in a bad place, replaying events and wondering, Why me? Why did I have to mess up and get myself injured? I was down, because I was injured on December 9, 2011, and that was just shortly after being home and visiting Kiel at Walter Reed. When I met Kiel, I had been home for Thanksgiving and spending time with my son. My son was born on November 21, 2010, and so he was just a little over a year old when I was injured. As I was lying in the hospital, I was coming to terms with the fact that I'd been away from home for most of his life, and now I would never see him grow up.

Though there was nothing that could be done for my blindness, I got my skull patched up by the Army doctors at Walter Reed. I had what's called an encephalocele, which is when the brain is trying to escape through an unnatural opening in the cranium. They performed an operation that took some cartilage and part of my septum and patched the cracks and filled the holes. After my initial recovery period from that, I was sent to Augusta, Georgia, and a Veterans Affairs hospital there.

I underwent a few more procedures during the six months I was in Augusta. The hospital was the site of one of the sixteen blind rehabilitation units the VA has around the country. I was taught some skills to help me exist as a blind person. I learned how to use a cane to navigate on my own. I learned to use various accessibility devices that allowed me to communicate with people and to stay engaged with the world of the sighted. And so much more.

My mother was there to help me out, just like she did for my brother when he was so severely injured. Only four years after that tragedy, she had to deal with my injuries, and I remember telling her how fortunate I was to have such a strong, resilient mom looking over me.

I was married at the time, and as is the case for some military personnel, the life we chose came with a price. My wife and I weren't on the best of terms before my injuries, so we soon separated and then divorced. After that, though, along with so many EOD techs and other friends like Joey, I had other people to step into that void to help me out.

Sometimes the help came from unexpected sources. The organization Building Homes for Heroes stepped in to assist me with housing. I was, and remain, enormously grateful to the organization and all the people involved in making this happen for me. To not have to worry about housing, particularly for someone who is blind and needs some adaptations to a home to make it as functional as possible, was a huge relief. Without all those worries about finances and housing and such, I was able to better concentrate my energies on the reality I was dealing with.

I relocated to Florida, and it was there that Building Homes for Heroes found a place for my family and me. I chose Florida because even though the Army thought that I would medically retire, I had another idea.

LOOKING FOR A WAY TO KEEP SERVING

While I was recuperating and adapting, I learned about a handful of blind active-duty members of the military who were still serving their country. That was what I wanted to do. So, when I was asked where I wanted to retire, I said that I didn't. Instead, I had it in mind to become an EOD instructor. I knew that I couldn't return to being a tech—you couldn't be one if you were just color-blind, never mind sight-blind. But I was inspired to make that request because of the example set by others. One of them, Captain Scott Smiley, is blind but he commanded an entire company. Due to the number of wounded service people coming back from Iraq and Afghanistan, Wounded Warrior transition units had been established to help them make the transition to civilian life. Captain Smiley was chosen to head one of those units in the Pacific Northwest. I was impressed and pleased that someone without sight could remain active-duty and assume a company-sized command.

I also heard about Iván Castro, who was an active-duty Army Ranger despite having lost his vision. He served out of Fort Bragg in North Carolina as a recruiter for Special Operations. I can't deny that I was going through various phases of grief and loss—I was pissed that the Taliban had gotten the better of me, primarily—and that contributed to me wanting to not retire. I wanted to continue to contribute. I had been a team leader, and when you're accountable to the guys on your team and develop a bond with them, that doesn't just go away. I still wanted to help others, and the best way that I could do that was by becoming an instructor.

I requested that I be transferred to Eglin Air Force Base, located on Florida's panhandle. Being back among my fellow servicemen did a lot to improve my mental and emotional state. I was back in the giving-and-receiving mode with the military. I was determined to prove that even without my eyes, I was still a valuable member of the team. Proving to myself that I still had a lot of value helped me heal from some of the emotional and psychological wounds I'd experienced.

One of the things that I missed during my recuperation was being with other EOD techs and participating in some of the things we did that cemented the bonds of our brotherhood. It was great to have that again.

A lot of it was about traditions of the EOD community. If you violated one of the tradition's rules, you had to pay a "fine" in beers. One of those requirements we had involved having on your possession at all times a special coin that had the EOD insignia on it. At any time, under any circumstances, someone on the team could ask you to produce the coin. If you couldn't, your name and your infraction would be entered into the log. Most of the time, it was easy to have the coin on your person, and once you'd messed up once, you were vigilant about carrying it with you at all times. So, as time went on, the stakes got higher and the game more challenging. Catching someone without it became a goal and a badge of honor.

I heard a story once from my first sergeant about the extent to which a tech will go to win a coin challenge. When you were training with live explosives, you had to gear up. That meant putting on a bio-chemical suit that would fully seal around you. But underneath that, you wore a pair of special underwear made of a fabric that was saturated with beeswax. We often worked in hot, humid environments, even in training. But even without those environmental factors, that protective gear we wore made us hot and sticky, since our skin couldn't breathe. Once, this particular group had been out in the training area on a particularly warm day. At the end of the training session, they retreated to the shop and they all rushed into the locker room so that they could strip off those suits and that underwear and get in the shower to cool down. Nobody was really talking because they were so intent on getting into the shower ASAP.

The silence was broken when one of the guys stepped into the middle of the locker room. He was buck naked. He reached around behind his back, squatted a bit, and a coin clattered onto the concrete floor.

"Top that!" he said.

Now, you've got to respect a guy who would keep that coin up his butt. They all laughed and then gave him a golf-gallery kind of polite clap for being so willing to go the extra mile to be prepared. It's all about creativity points.

It's moments like that you remember and you miss when you're no longer a part of a team. It's not just the big things, like knowing that you're responsible for saving lives, that bring you close. Sometimes it's just something that someone pulls out of their ass.

Another way we bonded was really testing one another in coming up with explosive devices that presented the greatest challenge to disarm. After all, IEDs are limited in their effectiveness only by the creativity of the bad guy. So, to defeat their ingenuity, we had to be more creative than them in constructing them.

As part of our training, we were constantly building in our shop devices that could kill someone. They weren't connected to explosives, of course, but a buzzer or some other signal was sent when you failed to successfully disarm them. After going through homemade-explosives training, we went through electronics training, learning about sophisticated circuitry, microchips, and cell phones, and other remote detonation switches, like key fobs.

This could also be very funny. Inside every EOD tech there's a stash of caveman DNA. So, one of our favorite aspects of training was trying to trip one another up. At one stage, we learned about how disposable cameras could be used as a triggering mechanism. There's the button that you press to open and close the shutter. You can also press it down partway and a light will come on to let you know that the flash is charged. We would open those cameras up and find the capacitor inside that managed those functions. By attaching two tiny alligator clips to the ends of the capacitor, we could get the cameras to function as an explosive initiator or a little Taser.

Imagine the possibilities of a little Taser. During training, we'd take those disposable cameras and arm them so that they could shock whoever came into contact with them and closed the circuit between the two leads we'd attached. We were tricky about it, and hid these little shockers all around the shop, in the training classroom, and wherever else we could surprise the unwary. So, imagine a first sergeant sitting down on his office type chair in the classroom. We'd put a lead on one armrest and then on the other, with the device taped to the underside of the chair, out of sight. The first sergeant sits down, then puts both arms on the rests, and jumps half a foot as he gets a jolt and the guys burst into laughter.

Doorknobs were another favorite with great shock value. We also had a prank that involved the use of baby powder. We'd set up a trip wire and empty paintball rounds. You walk into a dark room, reach for the light switch, but just inside the door is the trip wire. Boom! The paintball explodes and fills the room with a cloud of baby powder.

All of those things kept us on our toes. They kept us communicating with one another—maybe conspiring with one another is a better way to put it. Regardless of whether you were the victim or the perpetrator, your actions brought you closer together.

We weren't always trying to "kill" one another, either. Sometimes we were trying to save our collective asses when we were downrange and staying at a forward operating base. We'd use our tech skills to make our lives more comfortable. The EOD teams would be living together in a large tent, big enough for forty troops to sleep in. We were much smaller units, three-man teams, so we had plenty of space. We'd also store all our gear in our tent—including robots and other classified equipment to aid us in all aspects of our mission.

Everyone needs some downtime, especially with the stresses associated with our line of work. Sometimes you just wanted to kick back and play video games or something. To do that and avoid detection by higher-ups in the command, we'd establish a perimeter using passive infrared sensors—a variation on the kind used in grocery stores or other places that swing a door open for you automatically. We'd use those to send an alert signal when someone was approaching our tent. We'd also sometimes use the video camera from one of the robots that were down for repairs to keep an eye on who was coming and going near our area.

That sort of close coordination was made easier because we already worked in such small teams. There were three of us assigned to work in support of a company-sized unit, sometimes even a battalion or a brigade. We got to know some of the other troops, but we interacted most with the members of our little fraternity. That also makes it easier for us to be tight-knit even now. We're not all alike; I think of EOD guys as either being the alpha-male jock type or the technology-loving nerd type. It doesn't matter which side of that line you fall on, you still have that bond built of shared experiences. A lot of that has to do with knowing that other people trust you to do your job well and to help save others from getting hurt.

THE LONG WALK OF RETIREMENT

After almost eighteen months as an instructor, I retired from the Army. The whole time I was back in with the EOD team, I was investigating how to become formally separated from the military. It took a lot of time and effort to figure out all the mechanics of that. I'm glad that it did, because continuing to contribute by serving as an instructor created a kind of buffer zone for me. I didn't stop cold turkey—that would be another way to put it. And once I did retire, I continued to keep active in the EOD community through social media. I'm active on five or six platforms or groups where EOD folks can get together to share their experiences and, sometimes, to ask for help. It can be as simple as saying, "I'm having a rough time right now," or "My memories are getting to me."

One of the groups is called "After the Long Walk." That's a reference to what we called it when a solitary EOD tech, oftentimes the team leader like I was, took the long walk toward an explosive device in order to disarm it. The area was cleared of other personnel once there was confirmation of a suspected explosive device. Unless you've been there, it's difficult to understand what that feels like. So, reaching out to a brother who'd been there and done that is often the best way to come to terms with whatever issue you're facing.

Last year a member of one of the Facebook groups I was on announced his plans to walk out into his front yard and take his life. He gave instructions on where the letter he left behind could be found. He thought everything through and then he did it before it was possible for anyone to respond or intervene. That death sent shock waves through the entire EOD community. But the rest of us were there for each other, and we limited the damage. We didn't let that experience linger; we didn't let it fester. So often suicides come in clusters, triggered by one incident. I guess our training taught us to defuse situations, to detect problems before they become something worse. That's why when someone needs help, we come together and swarm to help a brother or a sister get through.

People helped me get through the early stages of my grief, my initial anger and shock at losing my sight. If it weren't for them, my mother, members of the EOD community, I wouldn't have been able to get to the place where I realized that my future was mine to make. I was left with the reality that I was going to be blind for the rest of my life. Nothing was going to change that. So I decided that even though I couldn't see, I could still be me—the me that had wanted to be the best that I could to serve others and use the tools and gifts that I had. If I was going to be a blind man, then I was going to be the best blind man I could be.

I was fortunate. I had gone through the programs at the blind rehabilitation center. I had accessibility devices like my phone and my computer, which utilized screen-reader software. As soon as I learned how to get on the internet, I typed in the search bar the keyword "blind" followed by . . . you name it. I wanted to figure out how blind people got outside, ran, cooked, and on and on. A few names kept popping up in the search results. I learned about Erik Weihen-mayer, the first blind person to climb Mount Everest. Lonnie Bed-well, a former Navy petty officer, lost his sight but was eventually named *National Geographic* magazine's Adventurer of the Year, taking on some of the most dangerous white-water runs in the world in his solo kayak. He downhill skis, he climbs mountains, and he was the first blind person to kayak the entire stretch of the Colorado River, including through the Grand Canyon.

I reached out to Army Ranger Iván Castro and we talked and talked. He encouraged me to take up running and gave the goal of completing races like the Air Force Marathon, the Army Ten-Miler, and the Marine Corps Marathon. I'd never been a serious runner at all. I had no idea how to get started training and how to find a guide runner to assist me in navigating. I thought that Iván had done all these things himself, so I could do them, too.

I also contacted Erik Weihenmayer, who supported me in tak-ing on mountaineering adventures. The same with Lonnie, who got me into white-water kayaking and accompanied me on some trips. I wasn't blazing a trail; I was following the one that others had laid down before me. And I was fine with that. More than fine. I'm so glad that other people have supported me and instructed me and inspired me.

Part of my desire to expand my reach was fueled by complete terror. I was so scared of being trapped by my situation. I dreaded the thought of being stuck on the couch in my house feeling sorry for myself, crawling into a bottle or popping pills for the rest of my life. All of those possibilities scared the shit out of me. So I had to get outside, to breathe the fresh air and learn to move my body, even though I couldn't see where the hell I was going. We figured it out. There are ways to run on the road as a blind person, ways to kayak in white water, or to climb mountains. The world is still available to me. I kind of figured out a new way to make that true. And each time I look for higher mountains, or to run faster or run farther. I found that I can tackle more and better challenges.

The next step was to try to inspire others, which made me feel great. Having somebody say to you, "You helped me through a really hard day, just telling me about your hard day." I find fulfillment in accomplishing hard things. There's even more in helping others accomplish their hard things. That's really what fuels me now, because there's always that underlying terror of the alternative.

★★★★★★★★★★★★★★★★★★★★★★★★★★★★★★★★★★★★★

In some ways, I can understand Aaron's fears. To one degree or another, all veterans and in particular those who face the challenges of catastrophic physical as well as emotional and spiritual wounds face a long walk. The initial steps are the hardest, and even among the most courageous, we continue to rely on people in whom we can place our trust. The main product that we build when we form bonds with people is trust. Like Aaron, who places his trust in guides who help him climb mountains, navigate rivers, or complete marathons and ultramarathons, we rely on others to help see us through. We need them on days that feel like adventures and lift our spirits, or ordeals that try our patience and push the limits of our ability to persevere. For me, those people are the ones who rely on me in their own lives. People I have a responsibility to, like my family and my brothers. Knowing I still serve a purpose in their lives, like the mission at hand when walking down to an IED, helps me stay motivated and feel like I have a purpose in life. Especially when the daily pain and frustrations of my injuries get me down.

I admire Aaron's ability to place his trust in people with whom he's very close and those he meets on internet forums who volunteer to help him get in one of his daily training runs. Aaron was literally tethered to some of those people in the running community as they helped direct him and set the pace that he wanted to run. Those literal bonds don't constrict him or limit him; they set him free to enjoy the fullness that life offers. Trust, sharing the love of an activity you have in common with someone else, and literally showing up in person or online or on the phone are a kind of force multiplier. They extend our capabilities as humans and increase our enjoyment. I can never know exactly what it's like to be blind, but in the time I've spent with Aaron over the years, I've learned what it's like to have a vision for the future that encompasses an unrelenting desire to do more, to be more, to give more, and to experience more. He, like so many other veterans I know, wants just that—an opportunity. We don't ask that it be free of challenges, just that we get to face them on our own terms and with others there to offer support if we should somehow stumble.

> Unfortunately for Aaron, the harder he pressed to regain independence and tackle challenges, the more challenges life threw at him.

★★★

MEETING MCKAYLA—AGAIN

In 2015, things were looking up for me. I was divorced from my first wife at that point, and that was a tough experience to go through. Still, I had social media and my hopes. I joked at one point that as a blind person I was really having a hard time with the Tinder app. What was I swiping?

Speaking of awkward photos, I have one of my wife from when she was five and I was twenty and she was sitting on my lap. Mc-Kayla's mother and my mother were best friends growing up outside of Baltimore. McKayla's mom moved to Colorado and raised her family there. My mom, of course, was in Ohio raising her kids. Each summer McKayla's mom would drive back east to visit family in Baltimore, and that included a stop to see us in Ohio. It was on one of those trips that that photo was taken. Fast-forward to after my retirement from the Army. McKayla and I became Facebook friends. At first, we just messaged there, but then we started texting, and that led to phone calls. It evolved to the point where we were like middle schoolers swapping stories and laughing together for three hours on the phone. It was fun. But was it going to be more than that?

In 2015, I convinced her to come to Florida. It's a great place for a vacation, right? She spent the week here, and her vacation turned out to be an extended first date for the two of us. We had a really good time, but she was living and working in Sacramento, California, while I was in Florida. So, when she flew back home, neither of us really knew where things stood between us. We each had lives and work to get back to. The day she left for home, I flew to Nantucket to do a speaking engagement. When I returned to Florida, I got home and was feeling a little dizzy, a little fatigued, and lay down for a nap. Still, I was feeling pretty good. I was on the phone with McKayla when I had walked in the door. I wanted to keep talking with her, but given how I was feeling, I let her know that I had better rest and call her later. I woke up the next morning feeling much worse, so bad that I had to be taken to the hospital. The doctors determined that I had developed bacterial meningitis. I was really out of it for the next four days. I understood that this infection could cost me my already limited hearing. I was so sick that I was barely lucid and didn't have enough time or focus to consider what this bad break would mean for my future.

I woke up on the fifth day in the hospital, and thought I was still semiconscious and everything seemed like a fever dream. My mom was there. My sister was with her. So was McKayla. My mom had been in touch with her and let her know about my diagnosis. Mc-Kayla had dropped everything and flew back to Florida to be with me. For the next few days after I was released from the hospital, the three of them nursed me back to health. I had a long road to recovery, and now being deaf in addition to being blind was another obstacle to overcome. My mom and sister had to return home and attend to their own lives. McKayla stayed. She moved into my house and even had friends in Sacramento pack up all her things and drive them to her so that she didn't have to leave my side. I never asked her to do that, but she understood that I had deep roots in Florida, with my son here.

I understand now that there are probably better ways to get a second date, but it was worth it!

Sometime later, we got married, and today, in addition to my eldest son, McKayla and I have twins. I also have my hearing back to a high degree due to a cochlear implant. I'm grateful for that, but the implant helps with my hearing, not with my balance. As I get fatigued, my vestibular balance gets bad. That has limited me to some extent with my running—I mostly do it on smoother surfaces and terrain. It's sometimes hard for me to hear people in windy conditions, too, so communication with running partners can be difficult. But we all manage.

The same is true at home. I love being a dad. It is so much fun. My oldest is a little guy for his age; he's almost twelve now and he's super athletic. I've never known another kid his age who has a six-pack. He's also superfast and highly coordinated. He plays lacrosse and runs cross-country. I'd love to be able to coach him in either sport, but I recognize that that isn't in the cards right now. He's great with the twins and caring for them. He's also adjusted to having a dad who can't see. I may not be able to coach him in sports, but I'm trying the best I can to set an example for him in other ways. I may not be able to jump in the car and drive to his game or to a practice, but I can show him how to be responsible and hardworking and persistent. I'm not just a stay-at-home dad. Like my father, I'm an entrepreneur. I took my love of cooking and baking and turned that into a business making and selling fudge.

I am also a partner in a real estate investment company with Daniel Devine. He and I met while I was running that chow hall in Afghanistan on my first deployment. Danny was a member of the Navy's military police force. It's a good thing we were friends because there was a lot of black-market trading of Army Meals, Ready to Eat (MREs) for other foodstuffs. Nine Afghan nationals from the area were working as cooks under my supervision. They could get things at the local markets I didn't have access to through the US military. There were a couple platoons of Italian Special Forces there serving in the NATO reconstruction effort. I got to practice the language and trade MREs for things like espresso packs and vacuum bags. Sometimes they would go to their headquarters and come back with whole wheels of cheese and legs of prosciutto. Man, that was cool.

Danny and I stayed in touch after that first tour. Later, after I'd left the Navy, he got deployed to Afghanistan again. It was on that deployment that he was on patrol and just coming back inside the gate of the forward operating base (FOB) and a car bomb exploded. The blast threw him against a concrete wall. He was knocked out, came to, and then engaged the enemy. He downplayed his injuries and completed that tour. It turned out that some serious damage to his brain and spinal cord had been done. It only showed up when he exhibited problems with his memory. Today he's still active duty and in the process of being medically retired. He's stationed in Pensacola, about an hour from my home, and I got back in touch with him. We started hanging out again. He's a single dad with two kids, and with all that's happened to each of us, all the things we have in common, we picked up right where we left off all those years ago with our friendship.

I know that a lot of service people struggle with retiring from the military, and the what-do-I-do-next question is a very scary one. I saw an opportunity where Danny could be of help to me and I could be of help to him. Along with the confectionery business I run, I decided to get into real estate, acquiring properties, renting some, fixing and flipping others. There are some limitations to being blind in the real estate business, so having Danny as someone whose judgment I trust is invaluable. We are partners in that. I'm still doing public speaking, though I have so much to keep me busy that I'm being more selective about what I do. I still love to cook, and during lockdown, McKayla encouraged me to post some cooking videos on TikTok. She directed and served as the camera operator with her iPhone. We called them Aaron Hale's Cooking Without Looking. I had created three sourdough starters at the beginning—I'm very good at killing yeast—and it grew (pardon the pun!) from there. We posted every single day through a lot of lockdown and had 150,000 followers. It generated attention for our fudge business, but now that quarantine is over and life has gotten back to normal it's hard to find the time to do them. Besides, with Dan on board and the real estate business needing a lot of attention, I've shifted my emphasis a bit to trying to figure out how Dan and I can produce content to help people better understand real estate and financial freedom. I'm also developing a podcast idea because, let's face it, I run the risk of being the only person without one!

That doesn't mean that I've abandoned cooking entirely or ever will. One of the ways that we form bonds with one another is through sharing meals together. That's true with family and friends, and it's true with people with whom we serve in the military. It's also a way that we show appreciation for the people we care about and who care for us. Back during my first deployment in Afghanistan, my team and I were responsible for providing three meals a day for four hundred to five hundred people involved in that PRT work. I would also prepare midnight rations for the troops staying up through the night doing late patrols, so that when they came in, they would have something there waiting. During the holidays, after everyone else had cleared out of the kitchen, I would go in there and make all kinds of desserts. I'd also bake decorative breads. At Thanksgiving and Christmas, especially, I wanted to make it special for those who were away from friends and family back home. For one Thanksgiving while overseas, I formed a cornucopia out of dough and baked that. Danny remembers that, and he always brings it up because sharing food and what we've created boosts morale. It didn't just do that for the people I was feeding; it did it for me.

After developing meningitis, while I was still being treated and had yet to have my implants put in, I was living the life of a deaf and blind person who was seemingly drunk because I kept staggering around with my balance so impaired, I leaned on what I knew best. I trusted that I could pull it off again and boost morale among my family and friends and me. I decided to prepare the best Thanksgiving meal anyone had ever done. I invited the whole family and got started cooking. Weeks in advance, I baked cookies and pies and stockpiled them in the freezer. I made batch after batch of fudge.

McKayla noticed a couple of things. First, I was making a lot of fudge. Second, she was seeing me smile for the first time in quite a while. I'd had a second helping of being in a really bad place after developing meningitis. Why was this happening to me again? Hadn't I paid my dues by losing my sight? Hadn't I had my fair share of bad breaks?

But cooking and baking and sharing food with others was very therapeutic for me. Especially at Thanksgiving. It reminded me that I did have a lot to be grateful for. The funny thing is, the more fudge I produced, and the more it started to pile up around the house, Mc-Kayla had to start sneaking it out and giving it to friends and neighbors. Not that sneaking it out so that a blind guy wouldn't notice was some great feat! But in the end, so many people enjoyed it that we got the idea that we could sell and profit from it.

That's the thing about bonds we develop. They benefit all parties who share them. They remind us to be grateful, that despite whatever pain and struggle we've been through, we've been given a lot of gifts, too. That's what you need to think about; I'm very fortunate to have the people in my life that I do. That's why whenever I learn of someone else in need, I do everything I can to be there in some way for them. Compassion and empathy are ingredients we always have on hand, and if a neighbor or friend is in need of them, we can always lend them.

★★

From his dad moving out when he was a child, to a war sparking up just as he found a calling in the military, some might think Aaron is cursed with bad luck, or that maybe he should've given up. Those people fail to see Aaron for who he is, or perhaps life for what it is. The story of Aaron Hale is nothing less than the story of triumph in the face of adversity. We all suffer in life. Some folks get sick, some folks have car accidents, house fires, bankruptcy, or lose a loved one too soon. But people like Aaron Hale see these struggles as part of life, and they use them as opportunities to grow, to love life even more and show those around them how much we're all capable of. Aaron doesn't quit because things are tough, and because he still shines as a beacon of hope to so many of us who are lucky enough to share a bond with him, he has inspired countless others to do the same.

★★

Helping
Others Heal

— ★ ★ ★ —

CORPORAL (RET.) JACOB SCHICK

★ United States Marine Corps. ★

"If talking about my experiences
and exposing my vulnerabilities
will help others, then that's
what I do. That's what warriors
do to help their brethren."

★★★

Jacob Schick is one of those guys you just want to be around. He has a certain humble confidence about him that makes him as approachable as he is respected. Those qualities may appear more and more fleeting among folks, especially men, these days with society seemingly always on the edge of being offended or people simply receding to the background on their own terms with work-from-home jobs and online shopping. Meaning people like Jake truly leave an impact, a wake in the water if you will. And I think we need them now more than ever. Jake isn't simply outgoing, he's authentic, and that attracts people. Jake is also a Marine Corps combat veteran, an amputee, and perhaps mostly importantly to our friendship, a country boy with a similar upbringing. Jake grew up between Bossier City and Shreveport, Louisiana, then moved to Texas shortly before he became a teenager. I guess I could call him a Cajun cowboy of sorts.

In Texas, football is a big deal. Not just the glory of scoring a touchdown or some storybook version of kissing the homecoming queen, but more so a part of coming of age for young men, a cultural duty to your town and community. In small towns in Texas, in Georgia, Ohio, and indeed across the South and Midwest, football gives you a purpose. It offered Jake exactly that at a time when he needed it most. As he's told me several times, if not for football, and his responsibility to his team, he likely wouldn't have had the motivation to go on to graduate from high school. But Jake had his sights set beyond high school—joining the United States Marine Corps. Jacob was very tight with his grandmother, his MeMe. Besides teaching him how to carry that humility and pride simultaneously as good men do, she shared with him stories of Jacob's grandfather, a Marine himself, who fought at Iwo Jima in World War II. Near the beginning of his senior year in high school, Jacob achieved that greater goal and enlisted, and by June 2001 he was ready to put his glory days of high school football in his rearview mirror and join a new team, one with an even greater sense of purpose.

He enlisted using the buddy system, with his high school friend and teammate Danny. Enlisting together at the same time, they would be in the same platoon in boot camp. It's sort of a ploy used by the military to ease fears or concerns in teenage boys hesitant to leave home. Although they weren't scheduled to go to boot camp until December of that year, the terrorist attacks on September 11 accelerated that process and Jake and Danny reported to boot camp at the Marine Corps Recruiting Depot in San Diego just weeks after that horrific day. Having enlisted to be an infantryman, Jake went to the School of Infantry (SOI-West) at Camp Pendleton, California. Immediately after boot camp, he trained to be a rifleman in an infantry unit.

Jacob served with the 1st Battalion, 23rd Marines, and deployed to Iraq in 2004. It was then and there that the true nature of service and sacrifice came into focus. He knew that he had good role models at home and within the Marines teaching him to be a good friend, leader, Marine. "One team, one fight" was prominent among those lessons. Sometimes it felt more like an abstraction, something whose meaning you *just about* but don't quite know, but in Iraq it transformed into reality. He saw that slogan lived out every day in ways large and small, just as he had so often at home.

★★

JACOB

My grandmother went by the name MeMe and was, hands down, the epitome of a matriarch. She could be stern. She wouldn't always say a whole lot, but when she did, everybody listened. She wasn't a big woman, but she was very sure-footed, very secure in her own skin. From her, I learned a lot about self-confidence and carrying yourself with pride and being proud of your name and where you come from. And you knew that if MeMe loved you, she loved you in the biggest and best way possible. I was fortunate that I was the youngest grandchild and she conferred her love on me that way. In her eyes, I could do no wrong. If MeMe loved you, she loved you all the way and that's how she was with me and me with her.

She told me a lot about my grandfather, who didn't say much of anything, ever, about his service in World War II. I also had an uncle, who joined the Marine Corps, following in his father's footsteps. Both of them had left the Corps as corporals. I had plans on becoming a mustang, an enlisted man who rose through the ranks to become an officer. I wanted to raise the bar, and that was partly due to MeMe's influence and my don't-settle-for-less personality.

I learned a lot from MeMe about sacrifice and giving back for the betterment of others from her. When I was young, I spent a lot of time with her going to nursing homes in the local area. There I'd help her hand out cupcakes and other things to the patients. We'd also go to the Veterans of Foreign Wars hall and do similar things. MeMe had such a servant's heart that she was eventually named president of the VFW Auxiliary for the entire state of Louisiana. I got to see all sides of that woman. She could be stern, but she was a nurturer, too. She wanted the people in those nursing homes and those veterans to know that they hadn't been forgotten and that they were loved. I'm very, very grateful for her because she was one hell of a mentor and a leader.

MeMe stepped up for me since my parents got divorced when I was young, and though we moved away to Texas, she kept in touch. I don't think she ever owned a computer or sent an email, but she wrote me hundreds of letters. I still have most of them. She was great about sitting down and putting thoughts and feelings and emotions on paper. Up until I went to boot camp, I must have gotten at least one letter a week from her. She continued to write to me, and though I wasn't as good about it as she was, I'd write her back—the only person I ever really did that with. She remained a strong presence in my life, if from a distance. When I got wounded and was flown out of Iraq to Maryland, my dad told me not to expect to see MeMe there. She had always told me that if God had intended us to fly, he would have given us wings. She meant that, and she wasn't going to climb in an airplane even for me. I understood and accepted the limits she had. She died at the age of ninety-six.

GETTING INTO TROUBLE—AND OUT OF IT!

With my buddy, Danny, ours was a bond that was up close. When we enlisted together, the recruiter told us not to let the drill instructor know that we'd joined under the buddy system. We got tight as soon as we met. He loved the outdoors, loved hunting and fishing, and so did I. He loved football and hated school and I loved football and hated school. We both believed in working for what we wanted. I'm not sure Danny would have joined the Marine Corps if it weren't for me. I may or may not have applied peer pressure, but if I did, I'm glad. He was a good Marine, a damn good human, and an even better friend. Unfortunately, he died in a car wreck, a single-car crash. I've been to a lot of funerals and that was definitely one of the harder ones I've had to go through. Danny was one of those guys I got to experience pure joy and love with. It's so hard to find that these days.

Danny and I did everything together. I even tried to talk him into going into infantry like I did. Except he chose artillery. I got to mess with him a lot about that because he would say the two were nearly the same. I'd tell him that they weren't and not to say that. Anyway, we were thick as thieves. I remember one time in high school just after Danny had gotten a new truck (well, one that was new to him). He took his girlfriend out for a ride in it to this place that we called the hills late one night. I was at home with the girl I was seeing at the time. My phone rang and Danny was on the line, freaking out. He had gotten that truck stuck. He knew his parents were going to kill him. He said, "Jake, I need you to come out here and get me out of this situation. I don't know what to do. It's stuck. Won't move." Danny didn't have a tow strap with him because those things were expensive. I thought about it for a minute and remembered a teammate of ours that didn't live too far from the hills. He was better off than us, and I figured he likely could afford one, so I headed out to his place. Turns out he didn't have one, but he searched his garage and came up with an orange outdoor extension cord.

I didn't know if it would work, but I had to give it a shot. Next, I had to find Danny. This was before GPS locators could help track someone accurately. I knew he was in the hills, but which hill, I had no real idea. I drove all around and eventually found him. When he saw me, he ran up, all emotional, thanking me, saying I couldn't imagine what this meant to him. I told him to calm down a bit and save the emotions for once we had fixed the problem. I'd never extracted somebody before. I looked down at that thick slimy mud and thought, There's no way I'm crawling into that to secure one end of the cord. In the end, we tied it up about the differential and the other to my front tow hook. Lo and behold, that extension cord held and we got him out of there. You would have thought Danny won the lottery, he was so excited. He knew he was in trouble because his parents had been trying to call him.

I'll never forget that nightmare because it was one of those situations when two dumb kids are trying to figure something out. We were hoping that we could prevent his parents from killing him, and I wanted to help my buddy out. We had our driver's licenses and that's the ultimate mode of freedom at that age. What would have happened if they took that away from him, even for a little while?

FRIENDSHIP AND LEADERSHIP

I would have done anything for Danny, and he would have done anything for me, no questions asked. That closeness actually made things difficult at first in the Marines. In boot camp, because of the buddy system, we were guaranteed to be in the same platoon. I quickly became a squad leader, but Danny didn't. That caused some tension because as squad leader, I had to sometimes tell him what to do. He didn't like that, especially when I had to do it in front of the other recruits.

One night after lights-out Danny came over to my rack—as a squad leader, mine was up in front of the squad bay. It was about midnight and Danny asked me to pull some strings so that he wouldn't have to stand fire watch. I told him no. He had to do his turn just like everybody else. He said that he was really tired. I told him that everybody was tired. He got pissed and told me that was bullshit and that I was letting this squad leader thing go to my head. I called the scribe over and told him to put Danny on fire watch until I said otherwise. Danny blew a gasket and started yelling that I couldn't do that. He knew that if he went and complained, things wouldn't go well for him. So, for the next few days and nights, Danny stood fire watch off and on and he was a walking zombie until I took him off it.

Our friendship looked to be on the rocks. He didn't have much to say to me for the rest of boot camp. Come graduation day, we were on the parade deck. When I heard the final word of the ceremony, "Dismissed!"

I turned and the first person I saw running toward me was Danny. He was crying like a baby, he was so happy he'd accomplished that goal. He didn't say a word and neither did I. We were back to being Danny and Jake. That's one of those times I'll never forget. He knew I was being hard on him for a reason, a good reason. Later on, I'd hear him tell that story to other people and admit that I was right. He'd laugh about it, and I was surprised he'd bring it up. He would even talk about it when he came to visit me in the hospital, and that was good emotional medicine for me. I was grateful that he did that before he passed.

A DEAL WITH GOD

In the summer of 2004, I was deployed into the Sunni Triangle in Iraq as our primary area of operation. I was in charge of a reaction team, a quick reaction force. We got a call, early morning, before daybreak on September 20. All the other guys had already bedded down. I was still awake, trying to come down off the adrenaline high of the standoff we'd just had a few hours before with about sixty-five Iraqi National Guard. There were only ten of us from the react teams, and with my Marine math, I knew we outnumbered them. We captured two high-profile targets that night and one of the weapons companies came in carrying all the big toys. The Iraqis pretty much surrendered right then.

Back at the command post, I was sitting in a Humvee with my teammate, Doc Daniels. It was his turn to be on watch, and I was there with him. We were looking down at the Euphrates River, counting flares, noting colors and patterns that insurgents were using to communicate. We'd turn that information over to the intel teams for them to decipher. After a while, I decided I'd better go get some shuteye. Murphy's law kicked in. No more that fifteen minutes after I had my boots off and lay down on my cot, another react call came in. I woke up, got the other Marines up, and had this bad feeling in my stomach. I walked out of the tent and that bad feeling rose up into my throat. I knew we were going to get hit.

I don't know how I knew. I have my beliefs. I think it's a cross between my grandfather talking to me from beyond the grave and God, but I knew we were going to get hit. I started to do things that I otherwise wouldn't have done because of this spiritual guide . . . or something, telling me what to do. So I listened to that gut instinct.

I went to my commanding officer's Humvee and got the bomb blanket out of it. I then went to the lead vehicle of the react team. It was a soft-top two-door, not the most up-armored of things, and I told the driver to get out. I took the blanket and spread it across the floorboards. I also took the radioman's comms and told everybody to button up— meaning if you were issued any protective gear at all, put it on. They had sensed that I knew something wasn't right after that. I jumped in the driver's seat and punched it. Three minutes later, we hit a triple-stack tank mine. As soon as the front left tire hit that top plate, it went down and struck the fuse, and the bomb went off. It blew me thirty feet above the top of the Humvee. I like to say I'm a Marine and believe in good form, so I came down on my head. I also like to say that because of God, I never lost consciousness and that allowed me to remember everything. I stayed awake and alert despite whatever shot I was given. It took the Black Hawk helicopter forty-two minutes to come and extract me. A long forty-two minutes, but at least I was the only one who sustained serious wounds. I wouldn't have it any other way.

I sustained multiple compound fractures in my left leg. I had to have my right leg amputated below my right knee. I lost part of my left hand, had burns, shrapnel wounds. I never tell people that I "lost" my leg. I know where it went and I still have the ability to go get it. The worst of it, especially immediately, was that I broke a bunch of ribs. It's painful, but there's literally nothing that can be done to treat it. You don't want to sneeze. You don't want to laugh. You don't want to take in a deep breath. I remember lying there on the deck waiting for the guys to get to me and doing a self-assessment. I could only see out of my left eye because my shatterproof goggles had in fact shattered and gone into my right eye. It would take a few months for me to regain vision in that one. My left leg was twisted around itself and my tibia was exposed. My right leg looked normal, but it hurt, and I knew it was broken. My left arm was mangled and my left hand was hanging down nearly from my elbow. I knew it was bad. I was bleeding badly. I made a deal with God. *All I ask is that you don't take me in front of my brothers. Don't allow my family to watch me die. As soon as the skids of that helo leave the deck, I'm all yours.*

That's how much of a bond I felt with those guys. They were my brothers, my family. Those Marines were who I was hoping to protect that night, and not just from the enemy but from my loss.

BAND OF BROTHERS

I can't say enough about the bond that forms with Marines. I was fortunate that after I was stabilized, I ended up at the National Naval Medical Center, later combined into Walter Reed National Military Medical Center, in Bethesda, Maryland. Obviously, it was a naval installation, and so I got to see other Marines there every day. I was only there for three months, and every forty-eight to seventy-two hours of that time I was in an operating room undergoing some kind of procedure or another. Having other Marines around made a huge difference for me. I was fortunate that I got to know the assistant commandant and the commandant of the Marine Corps. They showed up for me, and having the biggest bosses do that says a lot.

Through some connections, I was able to avoid being transferred to what was Walter Reed Army Medical Center, in Washington, DC. My dad had a bad feeling about the place, and I trusted his gut. We were able to make the case that I'd be better off at Brooke Army Medical Center in San Antonio. I'd be close to my home and my family. They couldn't afford the expense of all those flights out to the east coast. As it turned out, my body couldn't afford being moved out to Brooke so quickly. My body started to shut down, but I got back on the road to recovery again thanks to having family around. I tell people that 50 percent of the reason I suffered that immediate setback at Brooke was that I was the only Marine at an Army installation. The trauma of being called a "soldier" and not a "Marine" was way too much for me and inevitably some shit hit the fan courtesy of me throwing it.

Things were going on much as they had before. I was still in real bad shape, going through procedures in the OR, regular skin grafts and debriding/scraping off of skin, being isolated to avoid infection. I was not in a good way at all. But at least I was close enough to home that MeMe could come and visit me. She walked into the hospital room, looked at me, and touched me on my face. She said, "Well, baby, I guess God doesn't want you and the devil won't have you."

I said, "Well, you know what, MeMe? I'll take it."

We sat there and spoke for a little bit and then she looked at my dad and said that she was ready to go home. That's just how she was, a homebody, and I still feel her presence to this day, and she had such a major impact on my life and my faith. She taught me how to live a life well lived. She didn't have to show up every day to let me know that she was there with me and for me.

But while that support helped, recovery was a huge struggle. There was the physical pain of enduring forty-six operations and twenty-three blood transfusions. There was the emotional, mental, and psychological toll of a post-traumatic stress disorder diagnosis and a traumatic brain injury. I wasn't my prior self in lots of ways. Physical pain reminds you that you're alive, but the mental pain tests your will to stay that way. I felt guilty. I felt angry. I felt regret. I was bitter. I hated the idea that guys I cared so deeply about were still out there fighting and in harm's way while I was disabled and practically chained to machines that kept me alive. There was an end in sight, but it wasn't the outcome that most people hope for. I felt hopeless and helpless.

THE POWER OF SHARED LAUGHTER

Then, one day, a family member, my aunt Becky, was visiting. She said, "Jake, you know there's another Marine here."

I looked at her and said, "I want to go see him right now."

She tilted her head at me and said, "I don't know what the regulations are. I'm not sure you can do that."

"I don't give a shit what the rules are or what anyone says. I want to go see him right now."

By this time, I was pretty sure that the nurses there had been playing rock, paper, scissors to see who lost and had to deal with me. And God bless them, I was that bad of a patient and they endured a lot with me. So whatever nurse lost that round had to come into the room to confront me with the bad news. I wasn't in any shape to be moved to visit another patient. He wasn't in any shape to come and see me.

"I don't care what you think. I want to go see my brother right now!"

The nurse sighed and shrugged. At this point, the only part of my body that was close to fully functional was my right arm. So, to get me out of the bed and into an electric wheelchair there was this miniature crane that could lift me up, out, and then into a mobile machine to get me to the burn ward.

By the time I got to that floor, I had learned that my Marine brother's name was Ty. He was in really bad shape and I should be prepared for that. His entire body was covered in bandages, and I wouldn't be able to see what he looked like. I was told that he had lost his lips, his nose, his ears, the front portion of his cranium. He had other injuries as well, but I wasn't really listening to the litany. I just wanted to see this Marine, and I was sure that he wanted and needed to see and hear from me.

I went into the room, and the fear of infection, especially with a burn victim, was a big deal. From that short distance, I could tell that this was a huge dude.

I said, "My name is Jake." A nurse attending Ty leaned over and put his ear right next to Ty's mouth.

He introduced himself through the nurse.

"I just wanted to come check on the Devil Dog."

After that, we started to compare injuries. We both had external fixators on—him on his left arm, me on my left leg. All these rods and pins were like construction cranes keeping our bones in place. I showed him the stump of my right leg. He showed me his left leg and he wiggled his toes, just to be cute. I could tell this guy was a joker, and I was so grateful to have another Marine with me there. I told him to hang in there. I told him I loved him. I let him know that I was going to be there for him and come see him every day.

But as soon as I left that room and was alone, I started crying. That was the first time I'd done that the whole time I was wounded and recovering. I lost it because I knew that the doctors and staff had already told Ty's family to get there as soon as they could to say goodbye to him. They didn't think he'd last another forty-eight to seventy-two hours. Knowing that, a whole flood of emotion came pouring out of me. Mostly it was anger. I wanted to go back downrange and get revenge, not only for me, but for my brother Ty.

But by the grace of God, Ty made it and defied the odds. He and I got very, very close in the hospital. We also caused some chaos there. He would help me with my physical therapy and occupational therapy, and I'd help him. He was disfigured by his injuries, but he'd be behind a curtain so whenever someone came in to visit who didn't know about his condition, he'd never mention that he was severely wounded in combat. He just wanted to put people at ease.

When I was discharged and doing outpatient stuff, I'd still come by all the time. I'd pick him up and go off grounds to grab a meal with him. He'd get in my truck and turn the radio and crank up—I can't say music, but this noise, this thrash metal. He knew I'd let him get away with playing that stuff. He was the only person I let touch that radio dial. Despite how physically disfigured he was, he had such a pure heart that everyone was instantly drawn to him. He had to wear a helmet all the time to protect his skull, but he was so open, and not about protecting himself from people. He had gotten hold of a Texas license plate that said TY, and he superglued that to the back of his helmet. He'd wear T-shirts that said things like, "Keep staring; I'll steal your girlfriend." I've never met anyone who went through such a life-changing event and took it in stride so well.

About ten years ago, the day after Christmas, Ty passed away. I've gotten a lot of tough phone calls, but that was one that really rings up. The world lost a beautiful person that day. His parents were grateful that they'd gotten ten more years with their son than they thought they would. As soon as I got that call, I told his parents I was on my way. Over the years our families had grown close, and I dropped everything to be there. He also had a buddy named Vic, another Marine, and we all got tight, too. The night before the funeral the two of us showed up at the funeral home. We carried in a case of beer and sat next to the casket. We told the funeral director that we needed some music. He said okay, and told us what they had. We said no, we didn't need any of that. We had brought our own. So we sat there next to Ty, not talking, drinking beer and listening to thrash metal all night long, paying respects to our brother. Ty made my time in the hospital much less arduous because of the kind of human he was.

I remember one time on the birthday of the Marine Corps, the tenth of November, Ty and I were still in the hospital. But we wanted to celebrate that anniversary like any good Marine would. It was a huge deal for us. Vic came over to the hospital and took us to a bar in San Antonio. There weren't a lot of people in the place, but we had a few drinks in us. We were sitting at a high-top, and out of the corner of my eye, I saw Ty look up. He had lost the vision in one eye, and he was turned, cocking his head, with his full arm and half arm raised, looking shocked and pissed-off.

I thought, Oh no. Here we go. We're about to get in a fight.

I then saw he was looking at a guy sitting by himself about to light up a cigarette. It was hanging off his lip and he was bringing the flame up to it.

"Really, bro?" Ty said to him. "The last time someone smoked around me, this is what happened."

The poor guy looked at Ty, opened his mouth, and the cigarette fell out. Then he dropped the lighter and just *ran* out of the bar.

I laughed so hard, I lost control of my body and fell off the stool and plopped to the ground. It felt so good to just laugh like that. That's what Ty could do for people, bring that kind of relief and sense of joy. Vic played a big role in my healing, too. He showed up for both Ty and me, and having those two Marines with me helped me immensely.

SHARING SCARS

I also learned, over time, that by sharing my story, I've been able to heal and to help others do the same. MeMe had to share those stories of my grandfather with me because he wouldn't, or couldn't, do it himself. The same with my uncle Jack, who served in Vietnam. I've found a lot of victory in becoming vulnerable and not remaining hostage to my pride. I had a turbulent childhood, and I've had a lot of people in my life, including me, who've struggled with addiction and substance abuse and mental health issues. You're not supposed to talk about those kinds of things, was the lesson I was taught. I thought the same thing about my PTSD diagnosis and my TBI. I had these visible wounds that I could talk about, but not the invisible ones. And as hard as it was to heal physically from getting blown up, it was nearly as bad coming off the drugs I'd been prescribed to deal with the pain of those physical injuries. I went through the hardest time of my life getting off them. I'm a man of faith, but God and I had a lot of shouting matches. I lost every one of them. I'm glad that I had something to hold on to, something much bigger than myself.

It wasn't just God. I feel like I owe it to the people who can't hug their daughter, wife, brother or sister, mom or dad, to live a magnificent life. So if talking about my experiences and exposing my vulnerabilities will help others, then that's what I'll do. That's what warriors do to help their brethren. Sharing those scars can be very healing. MeMe kind of got that ball rolling. She took me to her Rotary club to speak about my experiences. It wasn't easy. I opened myself up to questions and answered them honestly, but it was really, really hard. After I did that the first time, though, I felt better. Every time after that, I felt better still. I knew that I was truly healing and starting to make strides in my mental well-being.

A PLOT TWIST

But that all came in stages. At one point, I was approached by someone who wanted me to be involved in an HBO documentary. They wanted to interview me for it. Right away, I was against it. A local Rotary club was one thing, but this was the big-time entertainment industry. I didn't want to be someone's show pony. I figured that whoever was involved in this was doing it for their own gain, their self-interest. I knew who James Gandolfini was. I hadn't seen his show *The Sopranos*, and I just assumed he was like the rest of the people in Hollywood. But I eventually agreed to meet him, and he was one of the most genuine human beings I'd ever encountered in my life. He loved all the way and loved deep and cared so much. I agreed to do it, and it was such an eye-opening experience to learn how many people in the entertainment industry get such a bad rap. They really do care and want to make a difference. One thing led to another and all of a sudden I'm in the movie *American Sniper* with Bradley Cooper. That allowed me to meet Clint Eastwood and work in one of his films. If when I was seven years old and hanging out at MeMe's house, you'd told me that I was going to be in several major movies, I would have laughed in your face. Stuff like that doesn't happen to people from Shreveport, Louisiana. But it did. And it wouldn't have if I had made the choice to end my life. You never know what's going to come down the line, and you never know what opportunities you're going to have and how many people are willing to lend you a hand and want to hear your story.

Bradley Cooper and I share a bond and he's absolutely become family. We just have this soul connection. Sometimes people shy away out of fear of rejection from responding to that. I'm grateful that I've been able to change my mindset when it comes to that. I just want to love and to be loved, and those are the two objectives that we have from birth until death. I'm fortunate that I have a partner, Ashley, who makes me a better man and a better father and a better leader. I'm grateful for that. It's a cliché but it's true—behind every strong man is a stronger woman. In my case that's spot-on.

TACKLING A BIG PROBLEM

I know that I'm one of the fortunate ones, and going all the way back to MeMe and my grandfather, I learned that you don't just give thanks, you give back. So, in 2013, a handful of us got together to take on a major problem in the veterans community—suicide. A 2012 study by the US Department of Veterans Affairs reported that twenty-two veterans a day took their own lives. We were all aware of the toll being taken in our community because we all had friends who had committed suicide. We had talked openly about it for years, but when that study came out, we decided that enough was enough. Things started small, with us instituting the 22 Pushup Challenge. That went viral all around the world, with everyone from celebrities and professional athletes to entire brigades here in the US and elsewhere in the world taking part. We're coming up on the tenth anniversary of the creation of what we now call the One Tribe Foundation. We've expanded beyond the veteran community to combat suicide among first responders, law enforcement officers, and frontline medical workers and their families. We don't just treat the individuals but rather the entire family.

Having been down the road I've been, I understand how important it is to earn their trust first. We let them know that our only goal is to help them live a life well lived. They're worthy of living well. I can understand some of the reluctance they have in coming forward to ask for help. It isn't easy. I remember feeling pissed-off at God and the world. I felt like I had been robbed of my right as a warrior to die on the battlefield. I'd gone through the very humbling experience of being a member of an elite unit and then, in a nanosecond, not being able to go to the bathroom on my own. During our workup and training, we never really talked about being wounded and surviving. We would either live or die; the thought of being wounded and how to go on after that wasn't really discussed.

Since I was wounded and I did survive, I spent a lot of time asking not so much "Why me?" as "What's the reason for this? What is my life meant to be like now that I have another shot at this life? What does this radical shift allow me to do?"

So that's the transition I made, with the help of so many others, to do the work that I believe God put me here to do. If there's one other thing that I would like people to understand it's this. Yes, the number of veterans and others who take their own lives is horrific and we have to continue to work toward solutions to this growing problem. But what the numbers don't often show is that for every one person who takes their life, there are many others who benefit from programs like ours and the many, many others out there who help veterans and others. Help is out there. Hope is out there. Success is out there. It comes in lots of ways, shapes, and forms, and you just have to be open to it. We're successful in nontraditional therapies. That's what we do best but that's not the only way to be a force multiplier for good.

I know that it's hard to be open. I remember the first time I met Joey. I was speaking at a fundraiser. He waddled up to me on his two prosthetics and said, "Hey, man, you know what guys like me call guys like you?"

I eyed him suspiciously, wondering where this was going. "What's that?"

"Paper cut."

I didn't laugh. I knew what he was suggesting: because I'd only lost one leg, my wounds weren't that bad. I said to him, "I sure don't remember it feeling like a paper cut."

He smiled at me and said, "Listen, man, you know it's funny. You just have to let yourself feel it."

The thing was, he was right. Joey's infectious personality and good ol' Georgia boy demeanor won me over right then. It was like he understood that we were part of the same club, that we'd been through many of the same things and that only we could fully relate to one another that way. More than that, though, he was treating me like I was just another Marine: giving a guy a hard time, letting him know that nothing was off-limits. We were both just one of the boys and no matter what had happened to us, that was never going to change. I wasn't only a wounded warrior, I was a brother, and that's how I was going to be treated. I wouldn't want it any other way.

★★★★★★★★★★★★★★★★★★★★★★★★★★★★★★★★★★

Jake's experiences before joining, during deployment, and even in recovery were eerily similar to mine. But I didn't know any of that about him when we first met. I just saw a guy who was as visibly motivated as he was injured. Balancing the scars and prosthetic leg was a smile, words of conviction, and most importantly, an infectious hope.

Our friendship has shared adventures over the years. I moved back to Georgia from Texas (where I met Jake) in 2016 to work for Zac Brown and his gamut of businesses aside from his music. I had just completed a custom motorcycle with a sidecar and hand controls and Jake had just gotten a similarly adapted trike to ride himself. I got a call one day from a mutual friend in Austin, Brandon Hatmaker of reality TV fame, asking if I and a few other veterans wanted to join a charity ride from Texas to Georgia, with fundraising stops in Houston with Marcus Luttrell; in West Monroe, Louisiana, with Willie Robertson from *Duck Dynasty*, and in Atlanta with Zac Brown, my boss. I quickly got a thumbs-up from Zac and called Jake to be one of the other veteran riders.

Always up for an adventure, Jake responded, "Well, I haven't ridden this trike more than a few miles at a time and you want me to ride across the country in three days with you? Sure, man, let me clear the calendar." After the first full day of riding, we ended up at the Houston event until late evening. Knowing that both Jake and I needed more rest than the experienced riders we were with, we opted to go back to the hotel a little early with two of the older riders. As we rode across town on a four-lane highway and reached the high point of an overpass, the clutch went out on my bike. The motor was revving but the rear wheel wasn't moving. I was at a dead stop in the middle lane, at night, with cars passing on either side at full speed. I couldn't get off or push it myself and knew I was in danger of getting hit. All of a sudden someone still wearing a helmet started pushing me from behind. He got me moving pretty quick.

Assuming it was our friend Steven, I said, "Thanks, man. Did Jake and Jeff stop, too?"

He responded, "Bro, I am Jake, and steer this thing straight to the right because I'm pushing us with one good foot and a prosthetic that's about to fall off."

I was speechless, I was so surprised. That's who Jake is. He's the guy who risks his own life to save yours. The guy who drops everything to ride across the country and raise money for your buddy's charity, the guy who goes hunting with you in the swamps of Maine and gives up his own opportunity to hunt so the guides can help you get yours. For as long as I've known Jake, I've known a brother who picks up the phone when you call and asks few questions beyond when and where you need him. We might have recovered at different times, but through our shared experiences covering the same obstacles on the same ground, we are forever bonded in both our hardships and successes.

★★★★★★★★★★★★★★★★★★★★★★★★★★★★★★★★★★★★★

A Family I Didn't Expect

— ★ ★ ★ —

GOLD STAR WIFE STACY GREER

★ United States Marine Corps ★

"In a way, it's like I've landed
in some kind of safety net.
So many people and so
many organizations are
all entangled together."

★★★★★★★★★★★★★★★★★★★★★★★★★★★★★★★★★★★★★★★

I first met Daniel Greer when he and his unit arrived in Afghanistan in the summer of 2010. I'd been there for a few months already and he was there on his first deployment as a combat engineer. I could tell by the way he talked that he must've been from around the same part of the country I was from. In the Marine Corps, your accent and favorite sports teams are a big part of your identity. Growing up in the foothills of the mountains of northwest Georgia I spoke with a certain Appalachian twang myself, and a University of Georgia Bulldogs G was always present on a hat or shirt in my foot locker, even on deployment.

As I introduced myself to Greer, I asked where he was from. As he explained that he was there with a reserve unit out of Tennessee, where he was from, my excitement turned to disappointment. "Oh," I said, "you're not a nasty Tennessee fan, are you?"

With a big smile on his face, understanding my reaction, he yelled, "Go Vols!"

In that moment, the thought crossed my mind that I might have more in common with the Taliban laying bombs in the village nearby than with this new guy with a similar timbre to his voice, but all that skepticism was washed away as each day he impressed me with his genuine personality, work ethic, humility, and love for life.

As I trained him on the IEDs he would be searching for as a combat engineer in our area of operation, he taught me valuable lessons on being a new father (something we had in common) and a good husband (something I hoped to be soon enough). In fact, some of my fondest memories from my entire eight years as a Marine are my conversations with Daniel as he told me about his life in Tennessee with his newborn son and the love of his life, his wife, Stacy.

★★★★★★★★★★★★★★★★★★★★★★★★★★★★★★★★★★★★★

STACY

As soon as we got to Germany, we went straight to the hospital and straight to his room. I was there with my cousin Amanda, Gunny Sergeant Estrada, Daniel's dad, Kris, and his cousin Jacy. As weird as it sounds, even though they told me on August 8 that Daniel was brain dead, that they'd done three different brain tests and they were all negative, I was still clinging to some hope that when I got there, they were going to be wrong. And he was going to be okay. It was August 11, and I was the first one to go in there to see him. He had a white bandage around his head and he was all wrapped up. He had a hospital gown on, but he looked just about the same otherwise. His feet and his hands were just a little bit swollen, and his left eye was super swollen and purple. But he was on a ventilator.

I just looked at him and thought, I just want to be with him, you know? But I knew he was not there. I knew he was gone. Like 100 percent I knew it. I didn't want to believe it. But I knew it was true. I was looking at him and I said, "He's not here. He's in heaven."

It was hard to know that we were going to have to take him off that ventilator. To look at him, his injuries didn't seem all that bad. At one point, a nurse pointed out that he'd also broken his leg. She lifted up the sheets and the gown, and I could see that they'd done surgery on it. His femur bone was broken and even though they knew he wasn't going to make it, they had fixed his leg. Just like they would have if he had survived. That's how much they cared about him.

★★★★★★★★★★★★★★★★★★★★★★★★★★★★★★★★★★★★★★

I can't say I know how Stacy felt seeing Daniel in that hospital bed in Landstuhl, Germany. But I know how it feels to see a man so honorable, so selfless, so courageous lying motionless on the battlefield. And I know the helpless feeling of wanting to help him, feeling responsible for him, and knowing there is nothing you can do. In that way, Stacy and I are forever bonded over the events of that fateful day and the precious life of my friend, and her love, Corporal Daniel Greer.

On August 6, 2010, my teammate and I were awoken by Daniel Greer. He asked us to come check out some IED components he and his team had found. We were executing a maneuver titled Operation Roadhouse 2 in the town of Safar Bazaar, in the Garmsir district of Helmand Province, Afghanistan.

We were an effort made up of about three hundred Marines and soldiers, mostly infantry, supported by an Army route-clearing unit as well as a similar Marine Corps combat engineer unit, a six-man group of Marine EOD (bomb) techs, and several medical personnel.

The town was just far enough into the desert that US and NATO forces had mostly ignored it in their ten years of operating in the areas along the Helmand River. Opium poppy was the cash crop of the Taliban, and most of it was grown here in this region. But there was another resource flowing into the market in this area. With little more than drone footage and human intelligence, higher Marine Corps decided the town of Safar had become a Taliban outpost primarily effective at funneling IEDs, or what were coined in the early years of the Iraq war "roadside bombs," into the region. Corps leaders hoped that by securing the town we could cut off the bomb-trafficking upstream and ultimately save thousands of lives.

To avoid civilian casualties, we made sure the town knew we were coming days in advance. All of the civilians and Taliban fled the village. However, seeing as how the major function of the town was to stockpile IEDs, the Taliban left a minefield in their wake in the hopes of inflicting as much harm on us as possible, long after they departed. My teammate and I were assigned to provide EOD support to the main effort, while two separate platoons of Marines, each with its own EOD team, broke off to 1) clear a route for casualty evacuations if fighting got tense and 2) clear an overwatch position on a nearby hillside.

This left my two-man team as the only EOD support for the two teams of engineers working exhaustively to clear the city buildings and streets of IEDs. From August 1 to August 5 my team found, rendered safe, disarmed, and blew in place more than thirty IEDs. Each one involved hands-on procedures, meaning we knelt over the IED and cut wires or placed explosives. I worked hand in hand with Daniel Greer's team and when he woke us up on August 6 to come check out what they had found, I knew it was important.

Ironically, Daniel and his team were clearing a storage unit directly across the street from the walled enclosure that we'd made home base the first day of the operation. Having first cleared several blocks of city streets and alleyways, they'd just begun opening doors and clearing buildings. We'd mistaken the storage units for a hostel due to constant traffic seen by drone surveillance, so when they went to clear them, Daniel's team was surprised to find big, open rooms mostly empty. But one was filled with pieces of US ordnance presumably recovered from the battlefield and now repurposed as IEDs and used against us. As we worked to identify and document what they'd found, my teammate picked up a very big flare called a LUU-2, which is deployed from an aircraft and used to light up the sky over a battlefield at night. I recognized it from EOD school and as he set it down behind a short retaining wall across the back alley of the storage unit, I remembered how simply moving one of these could be very dangerous. As my teammate walked a few dozen yards away to link up with other Marines and request their support in documenting forensic evidence from the components and materials we'd found, I leaned over the wall to check to condition of the flare. Daniel stayed near me to provide security for me as I worked. After inspecting the flare by leaning over the retaining wall and shining my flashlight onto its fusing apparatus, I stood up and took a right step toward Daniel. With that step, both of our lives were changed forever.

I immediately felt weightless as the world around me was enveloped in a cloud of tan dust. After a brief silent moment, I felt the *thud* of my back landing on hard-packed earth. I had stepped on an IED and it had blown me back about thirty feet. My lips felt as if they had busted open from the inside out; my face was beginning swell. I looked down and my legs were gone. Now what? I thought. I remembered the tourniquets strapped to each of my shoulders and reached up with my right hand to grab one, but as I reached, I realized my right forearm had been all but blown in half and I had no feeling or control over my hand. My left arm was twisted behind me. I was lying on it. I realized in that moment that I needed help. I looked down past my severed legs and saw Daniel lying thirty yards in front of me now, whereas just moments before he was right behind me. He was motionless, lying on his belly, and seemed to be unconscious. Marines eventually got to us and immediately began administering lifesaving steps. They took Greer off on a stretcher and then me. As my eyes swelled shut, I just kept telling the Marines, "I'm sorry I let you down."

I came to a few days later, on August 8, 2010, in a hospital bed in a US Army hospital in Germany. After a brief conversation with the nurse attending to me, I realized Daniel wasn't going to make it, and his family was on their way to say goodbye. I didn't know it then, but two things were as imminent as the dangers we faced in Afghanistan: 1) I would grow to love and bond with the beautiful family Daniel left behind, and 2) that feeling of seeing my friend lying on the battlefield just a feet away, with no way to help him, was one I wouldn't bear alone.

★★★

A FIREHOUSE FAMILY

The first time I met Daniel, he was wearing a Class of 2003 T-shirt. That was the year he graduated from high school. My roommate, Bonnie, and I were hanging out together with some friends, and Daniel came over with a friend of his who happened to be a friend of my roommate. I took one look at him and that T-shirt and said, "Oh, Lord, you are making me feel so old!" I had graduated in 1997. I was living in Ashland City, Tennessee, and working. I had my associate's degree in graphic design and was working for the US Army Corps of Engineers in that field. The funny thing is, I had that initial interaction with Daniel and then I completely forgot about him. He was just a kid fresh out of high school and nothing more to me at that point. It's funny to think of that now. I never considered this at the time because he was just too young and all, but boys do mature later than girls, and so our age gap was likely larger than just those five years. I'd be proven wrong later, but in any case, I went on with my life working and dating. That's a whole 'nother story! But the gist of it is that I met more than my fair share of immature young men at that point in my life, so many that I had just about given up hope of finding a guy I could rely on.

A couple of years passed, and I was still living with the same roommate. We went out to a little bar one night, just hanging out. We were standing at a high-top and somebody tried to squeeze past her, and the next thing I knew, she was yelping and hopping. A beer bottle had gotten dropped on her toe and she was in a lot of pain. We didn't want to go to the emergency room, but we knew a few of the guys down at the local fire department. We drove up and she hobbled out of the car and into the fire station. It was a volunteer department and a few of the guys were there. They agreed to take a look at her foot. One of them happened to be Daniel Greer. At first I didn't recognize him. I just thought that he was kind of cute. I had no idea I'd met him three years before. Our friend Kenny was the one we wanted to see to take care of my roommate's toe.

Daniel and I and all the rest of us talked for a while that night and exchanged "nice to meet you" farewells. I didn't think I'd see him again, but over the next three months, he became more or less a regular part of our group that hung out together. Since we were close to Nashville, music was a big part of the scene, and one of the places we went to a lot was called Silverados. I love all kinds of music, and Silverados was the place where we went to go line dancing. Daniel was a good dancer and we partnered up a bit. We were all just friends spending time together, and it was all just about having fun. Every time I was with Daniel, that's what it was—fun.

I started to get to know more about him. I wondered what he was doing volunteering at the fire department, and he told me that his aim was to get hired as a full-time paid firefighter someday. To increase his chances of getting accepted he was doing volunteer stuff and he was enrolled in and attending an emergency medical technician training class. I was taking classes in the evenings at Austin Peay State University, in Clarksville, and that's where he was going for his training, too. We started to drive out there together, and that's when I first started to get to know a little bit more about him.

He was living in Pegram, a town of about two thousand people, west and a little bit south of Nashville. It's only about twenty miles away, but it was very different from the big city. Daniel told me that he was living with his grandfather. He didn't go into details, but he said that he needed to help out his granddaddy every now and then. That was just like Daniel, always wanting to help out. Also, his parents had divorced and his dad was in Kentucky. His mom had a three-bedroom house, and Daniel has a brother and a sister who were still living at home, so I guess he wanted to give them a bit more space. He was the oldest, and Dylan and Mikaela followed him. Mikaela was much younger than Daniel, by thirteen years, and you could tell he was a proud big brother and Mikaela just adored him. I'd eventually see pictures of him, and of course, him being the oldest and his mom working, he had to take care of her a lot of the time. I could tell from those photos that as much as those kids aggravated one another, they really loved one another, too. They were really close.

DANIEL'S MISSION

What impressed me about Daniel even more was that he had a vision for what he wanted to do with his life. He'd done the volunteer firefighter thing, he worked as a 911 dispatcher, and he was going to EMT school, all with the intent of getting a job at the Ashland City Fire Department. He had a lot going on, but he kept his eye on that dream of firefighting. Whatever it took, going to EMT school and whatever else, he said that he was going to do it. Even back in high school, in addition to being a student and doing other kinds of volunteer stuff, he delivered pizzas to help out at home. I was impressed. He was a very responsible young man, and I knew more than a few irresponsible ones! Still, even when my friend Charlene told me that she thought that Daniel liked me—this was like back in middle school, when somebody "*liked*-liked" somebody else—I told her that he was young, that I was done with dating and guys and all that. You can't trust them.

But like I said, Daniel was different. Yeah, he was responsible and all, but he was also very funny. He had me cracking up all the time, and the more I thought about it, the more I thought that I really did like him, in that way. He was texting me all the time, asking me what I was doing and if we could hang out. By January 2007, he asked me out. I said yes, and it was a little while longer when I knew that I wanted to marry this guy. It wasn't anything really big or dramatic, but we had made plans for a Friday night a few nights before. It was just his friends and him coming over to my condo. We were talking and he said that he wanted to go buy a digital camera—remember those, before we had them on our phones? He said he was planning on doing that on Sunday and wondered if I would like to go to the store with him. I said that sounded good. I also started thinking that I needed a camera, too. Well, we had plans for Friday and Sunday. Then Daniel asked, "What are we going to do Saturday night?"

That just got me. I thought that if this guy wanted to spend that much time with me, I'm going to marry him. That's what I want. I want somebody to hang out with me every single day. It was just the sweetest thing anybody had ever done or said. After that we were inseparable. I'm sorry I'm getting choked up, but you know.

We kept dating and by September 11, 2007, he asked me to marry him. I have to admit I was taken by surprise. Not so much that he asked me, but that he chose that date. That was the worst date in history, but I can see now that at least there's one good thing I can think of that happened on the eleventh day of September.

By this time, Daniel had already gotten a job with the Ashland City Fire Department. He was feeling great about it. He was on top of the world. He *loved* his job, and he loved being a part of that brotherhood of firefighters. Also, shortly before I met him, he had joined the Marine Reserves. I'd eventually learn, after Daniel and I reconnected and got to be better friends, about a guy named Kevin Downs. They'd gone to high school together in Kingston Springs, and they were good friends.

★★★★★★★★★★★★★★★★★★★★★★★★★★★★★★★★★★★★★★★

Kevin Downs served as a sergeant in the Tennessee National Guard. He was only twenty-three when he was blown out of a tank in Baghdad in 2005. He eventually lost both his lower legs and had burns over 60 percent of his body. In time, he had to endure more than seventy-five surgical procedures. He lost an ear, and he lost the use of an arm. People described his injuries as gruesome, but Kevin's fortitude is awesome. He recovered well enough to serve as a volunteer football coach back at his hometown high school. He knows the game. He knows the price you have to pay sometimes for doing a job you love. He shared his story in an ESPN *SportsCenter* feature. He hoped that people could see him and be motivated by his story. Daniel was among those who were inspired.

★★★★★★★★★★★★★★★★★★★★★★★★★★★★★★★★★★★★★★★

THE CALL TO SERVICE

Kevin is such a good guy. He is so sweet. Because of what happened to Daniel, I've met a lot of catastrophically wounded servicemen and -women. It's amazing to me that they endure what they have. So, for Daniel, I think that Kevin's story was just another push in that direction toward joining the military. Obviously, he wanted to be of service and firefighting was one part of that. I didn't know him back in 2001 when the World Trade Center and the Pentagon were attacked, but his cousin Jacy, who was really more like a best friend, told me that that was when Daniel first started to talk about joining the military. He was too young to join then, and he still had that other dream to be a firefighter. But that was really what Daniel was like. He had to make good on the promise he made to himself and to others to get that firefighting job. He had to keep his word, and as much as he liked and admired those firefighters, he wanted to do even more for his country, to help an even larger number of people. Kevin's experience sealed the deal for Daniel. He was off to boot camp and then doing his regular rotations in the reserves.

By the time we were engaged, and in fact even before that, Daniel had completed his training as a combat engineer. I didn't know exactly what all that meant. I knew that the war was still going on, and that there was a chance that he would have to go fight in it. But I also knew that with his job back home, his day job as a firefighter, he could get hurt doing that, too. That did concern me, but seeing how much he loved his job, what could I say other than just pray, like, "God, please keep him safe"? Daniel was just so happy, and even when he would tell me about this house fire or whatever, I could tell that he was just glad that he was doing things to help people. Also, it wasn't like it was a job to him. He enjoyed it. He said that he loved to serve.

I loved that he loved to serve. I respected the fact that he really loved his job. That's such a rare thing. Once a month when he went to drill with the reserves, he loved that, too! I had so much respect for Daniel that I could never stand in the way of him being happy and fulfilled. More than that, he just loved life, everything that he did: he loved it. So many people can't say that, and whether it was when he was a kid and learned to shoot and hunt or later on, he just enjoyed things as much as possible. There are so many people who can't say that or didn't do that. I can't say that I've loved everything I've done.

I had a job, and as is the case for most people, it was just a job. I had good days and bad days. But I was also a mother. I had found out just two weeks after we were married that I was pregnant. Daniel loved being a father. He died at the age of twenty-five. It's sometimes hard to not think of all the things that Daniel has missed out on, especially being there for our son Ethan. It's hard to put it all into words. There were so many people who loved Daniel. At the fire station, he only worked every third day, so he had time on his hands. He loved to go fishing with another firefighter, Kenny Millett, and he would hunt with his shift partner, Dustin Shadowens, whose nickname was Little D. Those guys were always doing something.

THE CALL NO ONE WANTS TO GET

In January 2010, Daniel deployed overseas to Afghanistan. I knew that was going to be hard. I was still working and needed help with Ethan, so I moved in with my parents. Daniel and I kept in as much contact as we could, and he assured me that everything was going well. I knew he didn't want to worry me, and I tried not to worry. I tried very hard to not let him know that I *was* worried. He had enough on his mind without being distracted by how things were going back home, including if there were any problems. I had my parents, of course, that I could count on, and I absolutely adored Daniel's mother, Gina. His parents divorced when Daniel was in high school. Gina and I got along real well. She'd tell me that I was about the only woman Daniel ever brought home that she liked. I just loved her. The sad thing is that Gina died twenty-two months after Daniel was killed. On the death certificate, I imagine that it listed colon and liver cancer as the cause, but losing Daniel broke that strong woman's heart. It did mine, too, but somehow, I got through it all.

It wasn't easy, but I had a lot of help, starting from the day I learned that Daniel had been injured. I actually missed the call. I went in to work that morning and had a horrible day. It was just sucky. I don't know why, but I was just upset. By the time my lunch hour came, I wasn't thinking too clearly and I left my phone in the office when I went out. I work in the basement of a federal building and we don't get a signal down there, so it wasn't until I left work that I got a voice mail. Someone from Daniel's drill unit center wanted to verify my address. The first thing I thought was that maybe it had to do with our condo being up for sale, but then I started to wonder if maybe Daniel had gotten hurt. Then I was like, No. Don't think like that. They are just doing some kind of audit or something and weren't trying to trick me or anything. Back and forth my mind went. God would give me a few moments of peace and then I'd get upset again. I returned the call and again they said they just needed to verify my address. I gave them my parents' address and the woman on the other end of the line was very calm and said thanks and then goodbye.

On the drive home, though, my sister reached me. She knew that I was preparing to run a Yellow Ribbon five-kilometer race. She told me that I needed to get home and not go for a run. My son had a fever. She knew that was the only way to get me home without fully explaining: by telling me that my boy was sick. I didn't know the Marines had been trying to reach me all day.

It turns out the Marines had turned up at my parents' house, and that was why my sister was calling. They wouldn't tell her anything, but I figured it couldn't be anything good. By the grace of God, I finally got home. The three Marines from Knoxville came to the house to inform me of Daniel's condition. Only later did I realize that there was a whole set of procedures and things that go into a formal notification in person. A lot of it is kind of scripted. The words "severe brain injury" really stuck with me. Out of the three Marines, I only knew one of them. I don't remember the rest of what they said, just that Daniel was hurt.

★★★★★★★★★★★★★★★★★★★★★★★★★★★★★★★★★

When Stacy chose to unite her life and Daniel's, she was locked in and committed. I'm not sure she understood just how large her extended family would become. But I suspect she did, given that Daniel also had another group with whom he had formed strong bonds prior to entering the military. Not everyone who serves in the military comes out of the box ready to dedicate their lives to the military or to others. It may just be a coincidence, but I think that Daniel's home-state team being dubbed the "Volunteers" says a whole lot about the man he was and the life he lived.

For me, Daniel died that day on the battlefield. I saw the energetic, infectious light within him just a moment before the explosion, and then I saw his face void of that spark as he lay there facing me. But for Stacy and his family, the trip to Landstuhl, Germany, to be there as they removed the life-imitating machines and allowed his body to rest at peace meant a chance to hold his hand, kiss his forehead, and say goodbye. Something I wouldn't fully understand until I experienced it with my dad ten years later, after he fell lifeless in my house one early Sunday morning. As warriors, so much about our lives, and even our death, isn't about us, but about what we can do, or sacrifice for those who will enjoy it long after we're gone. Daniel left us all with our freedoms protected, but for those of us who knew him, he also left us with a legacy to uphold and live to honor. Daniel was already serving his community and saving lives as a firefighter and EMT. He had committed himself to helping those around him.

But he saw a need to serve more. He believed this country was worth sacrificing for, worth fighting for, and if fate saw it necessary, even worth dying for. As a father and a husband, he inspired me to live up to the example he set. As a Marine who sacrificed all those memories with his family to serve his country, he inspires me each day to live a good life and be a good man, father, and husband. As Americans, we owe it to Daniel and Stacy Greer to be a people worth dying for. As Daniel continues to inspire me after death, Stacy does so in life. Her strength to raise their son, continue living life, and share what she has learned with others going through similar tragedies should remind us all that we owe it to those who sacrificed for us to simply live this life and live it well. No marble inscription or folded flag, nor written account of Daniel's heroism, could serve as such a perfect monument to his life like the smile on her face when she talks about him. A true University of Tennessee fan, Daniel and his time on this earth were an embodiment of what it means to be a "Volunteer."

★★★★★★★★★★★★★★★★★★★★★★★★★★★★★★★★★★★★★★

THE EXTENDED FAMILY

Over the next day or so, I got updates from the personnel at the hospital. Eventually, on August 8, two days after his injury, I was told that Daniel was clinically dead, with no brain activity. I was sitting in the bathroom when I got that news. I was in a daze. I kept thinking that this couldn't be happening. This wasn't happening to me. Our son was only twenty-two months old. How could all this be happening?

Thanks to my mom, my dad, and my sister, I managed. My best friend (and former roommate) Bonnie was there, and she wouldn't leave my side for a second. She was answering my phone for me.

After we made the decision to let Daniel go, I had so many thoughts going through my head. I'd loved the fact that Daniel did almost all the decision making for us as a family. I loved being taken care of by him. I just kept thinking, Oh gosh, this is all on me now. I don't want to do this without you. How was I going to go on from there? Daniel was always so patient with me. I was the one who would always stress out over things, and he would help keep me calm. He was just perfect for me. We worked so well together. I didn't want to be alone. I didn't know if I could do it alone. I was about to turn twenty-nine years old and I'd waited a long time before I found someone like him and now I'd lost him.

I wasn't angry at him or anybody else at that point. I was just sad. For him. For me. For our son who was so young and would never really get to know his daddy. That really got to me. I didn't know what to do next.

When I was in Landstuhl, I met a really sweet lady named Vivian. We were all staying at the Fisher House there, where families of the wounded could stay. Vivian worked there and she was great. It's funny the things you bond over, but she was working there in Germany but also had a house in Coopertown, Tennessee, where my parents live.

We thought that was just so crazy. She helped us all a lot, and having someone there who'd been through this with all kinds of families and could answer all our questions or know where to go to help figure things out was amazing. I was only there a few days, but she kept in touch with me afterward and did some great things to help.

Back home, the chaplain of the fire department, Steven Sellars, was a huge help to me. In fact, I called him right after I found out about Daniel. The poor guy was on his way to dinner with his wife to celebrate their anniversary. He could tell I was really losing it, and he pulled over and talked to me and then came to the house. For the next two and a half years, he would show up at the house once a week for grief counseling sessions. He knew it was really hard for me to leave the house.

An amazing thing I found out later is that Daniel actually came to Jesus in Afghanistan seven weeks before he died. On June 18 he was in a firefight and was so shaken up afterward that it really made him turn to God. His cousin Matt received a letter from him on the twenty-seventh. In the letter, Daniel thanked Matt for a Bible he had sent and said, "I wear it when I go out on patrol. . . . I decided to try my hardest to stop being the old me, to stop cursing and being hard-headed, and to just be a better person. And after June 18, I know why. It's because God is helping me."

He had asked Matt not to tell me, because he knew I'd freak out, but of course, after what happened, Matt did tell me. And I'm so glad. I'm just so comforted to know Daniel is in heaven.

Also, immediately after learning about Daniel's death, I was put in touch with Joey Jones. He was in the hospital himself, badly wounded and all, on medication to help him endure the pain, but he talked to me. I needed to know exactly what happened. I knew it would change things, but having the truth instead of letting my mind run wild was really helpful. I'd never even met the guy and he was dealing with his own catastrophic injuries, but still he was willing to talk with me, to help me heal, to offer whatever comfort he could. That's how the EOD and Marines are. All of them were hurting in one way or another, but they set that aside to offer me help. I got so many calls and texts and emails. I can't remember how many or who all they were from. I was still in that daze, which lasted for quite a while. It was hard enough just to get through a minute, an hour, and then a day. Daniel died in August and his guys didn't come back to the US until November. They couldn't come to the funeral and I felt bad for them about that.

I wanted to be there when they returned to Knoxville. I went to meet the bus along with all the other family members and friends who were there to greet them. Daniel was the only guy who was killed during that deployment, and I wanted to be there because those were the guys that Daniel spent so much time with, knew so well. And let me tell you: every one of those Marines came up to me and hugged me first before they greeted their family members. They wrapped me in their arms and that all felt so good. I was bawling my eyes out. It was really emotional, and I knew that one of the guys who'd come back, Captain Nathan Opie, was seeing his baby son for the first time ever that day. That was so sweet. I was so happy for him. I know that for some of the guys it was hard for them to look me in the eye and say anything. I knew that they were probably feeling some kind of survivor's guilt or were worried they might say the wrong thing. I didn't want them to feel bad. I wanted them to be glad to be home, to have survived it, to have a chance to go on and live a great life. I saw a few of them looking at Ethan, and I knew what they were thinking.

A lot of the guys in the unit stepped up and kept in touch. Since they were reservists, most of them lived real close. They'd stop by. They'd have us over for dinner. Come Christmas, they'd bring presents for Ethan. Daniel was gone but the bond they had with one another was still there.

In 2020, on the tenth anniversary of Daniel's death, David Flowers, Daniel Wysong, B. J. Hyman, and nearly all the rest of the guys who had gone on the 2010 deployment gathered at David Flowers's place for a party. It was so much fun. Ethan looks just like his daddy. All the guys commented on that, and for them and for me, that was a really good thing. It was like they were looking at Daniel, like he wasn't gone at all. Of course, he was, and I knew that, but it didn't feel that way. I love hearing stories about Daniel and hearing people laugh. That was one of Daniel's favorite things in the world, making other people laugh. He wasn't alone in that. I remember one video the Marines made when they were back home. One of the guys was dressed like Tarzan, wearing that fur set of short pants. The cameraman was laughing so hard, the image just kept bouncing. They were like a bunch of young kids just cutting it up and being silly.

Nathan Opie, his commanding officer, was there. He is great about coming by. We spent Thanksgiving dinners with his family. He came to Daniel's mom's funeral. Any time I needed anything, or on special days like Memorial Day or the Fourth of July, they made sure that I had somewhere to be and someone to be with. I have Ethan and I have my memories, and it's great to always be with people who knew and loved Daniel like I did.

It has also helped that Vivian reached out to me some years after we first met and told me about another woman from my area who'd lost her husband. Her name is Chrissy Carpenter, and her husband, Andy, was killed six months after Daniel was. She lives in Dickson, Tennessee, and she's become one of what I call my "widsters," my widow sisters. We talk on the phone, we go on trips together—Legoland and other places—and we attend Gold Star family events. We share a bond with all those who've lost a loved one in war. It's great to be around people who've shared an experience that you have.

There's a bond between us, even if we've never met, that doesn't require any kind of introduction or explanation.

As much as I mourn the loss of my husband, I know that I'm really fortunate, too, and have gained a lot. So many people have touched my life in ways that I sometimes don't even know. I was really fortunate that an organization named Tunnel to Towers Foundation helped me pay off my mortgage. Since 9/11 they've been helping Gold Star families like my own and the families of first responders who've died by providing mortgage-free homes. They also build homes for catastrophically injured veterans and first responders. They are amazing. With Daniel having served in the military and as a first responder, we've all been well taken care of by people who understand and appreciate the sacrifice some of us make to keep the rest of us safe.

In a way, it's like I've landed in some kind of safety net. So many people and so many organizations are all entangled together. I love all the people I've bonded with. They've supplied me with so much support. Just a little while ago, I was back at the fire station, and one of the guys asked me if Ethan had talked at all about following in his father's footsteps. He hasn't, but I told the man that if Ethan ever expressed any interest at all, I wouldn't stand in his way. There was a training course coming up as a kind of introduction. I'm not going to push Ethan away or toward that life. I want him to choose for himself, but even with everything that happened, I'd be okay with Ethan working as a firefighter. They're called first responders, and that's what they do for other people as well as their own. The Marines do the same, and I'm grateful for all they've done to show me how much they care.

Bonds of
Friendship

—★ ★ ★—

SPECIALIST KEITH STANCILL

★ United States Army ★

"Nothing I experienced
before in my life, including
my military training, could
fully prepare me for what it
was like to be deployed for
fifteen months in Iraq."

★★★★★★★★★★★★★★★★★★★★★★★★★★★★★★★★★★★★★★

Few things form you as a man as much as your father does, and for veterans, as much as boot camp and the leaders you have while serving. But for me, right there with my dad and Marine Corps legend Lewis "Chesty" Puller were Keith Stancill and Chris McDonald. These were my two best friends in high school, then were my brothers through my first sip of alcohol, my first taste of love, my first time getting in real trouble, and my first heartache. We all joined the military to fight in the same war after high school, but long before we became brothers in arms, we were brothers in life, bonded through the shared experiences of having big dreams while growing up in a small southern town.

    By our junior year, the three of us were as inseparable as we were different. Chris was the son of a football coach, teacher, and Desert Storm Marine. He was studious, disciplined, and needed to be the best. I was the son of a brick mason and moonshiner. I had a wild streak and needed to be the center of attention. Keith was the son of an Air Force careerist who lived four states away. He was small, quiet, and mostly just needed to be left alone. With that in mind, it's only fitting that Keith is the one to tell you our story, and share the bond that will last each of us a lifetime.

★★★★★★★★★★★★★★★★★★★★★★★★★★★★★★★★★★★★★★

KEITH

I was back in Dalton, Georgia, where we all grew up. Chris had gotten me a job working gate security at the carpet mills for the same company he worked at. I got a call from Joey's mom. She was pretty shook up. She didn't have all the information yet. We didn't know that he was going to be okay. So, that was a pretty rough day. I can't remember the first time I spoke to Joey. His mom kept feeding us information. I just knew that he was in really rough shape.

The first time I saw Joey after he was injured, Chris and another buddy named Drew and I all went to see him in Walter Reed. This was after Joey was up and first getting to the point where he could move around. We spent a few days there and visited him as much as we could after he got home, trying to help him with everything as best we could. I felt a bit guilty about what had happened to him. I mean, this was my best friend and he had gotten hurt so bad. I had made the decision to join the Marines, Chris was in ROTC, and it seemed like Joey was influenced by the choices we had made. Obviously, he was an adult; he's got to make his own decisions, but still. It was hard not to feel guilty for what happened to him, but he made a great decision. He fit in with Marines and did great with them.

I'm sure that there was a period of time early on after Joey got injured that we treated him a bit different from before. That didn't last long. When Joey was first getting used to his prosthetics, he took me on a duck-hunting trip with some other guys from Dalton. It was dark outside. We didn't have flashlights on yet. The ground was uneven and Joey was counting on me to help him get from one car to the other so we could set out. He staggered and I didn't catch him. He fell to the ground and started laughing. He never blamed me for not catching him. He blamed himself. He never expected us to do anything for him. We just did what we could without trying to do too much. Sometimes that meant making fun of him. We poked at him a bunch.

★★★★★★★★★★★★★★★★★★★★★★★★★★★★★★★★★★★★★★★

The truth is, Keith and Chris did a great deal for me in the aftermath of my injuries. They did what you'd expect guys you've known since middle school would do for you. In his typical modest, understated way, Keith's refusal to take much credit for and downplay his positive influence and overplay his guilt says a lot about the bonds of friendship that developed among the three of us. We may not have said a whole lot to one another about what we were experiencing and feeling in those growing-up years together—well, I probably said a lot and Keith didn't say much at all—but it was the actions we took with and for one another that defined our bond, that made Keith, Chris, and me brothers in every sense of the word.

In ways more obvious to an observer, I was the wounded one. But we were all warriors, and sometimes the difficult thing about being one is that once you leave the battlefield, the fighting still rages on in your heart and soul. In our case, roles reversed. Keith and Chris felt a need to catch me, to help me. But I had the full resources of Walter Reed, and our whole community, there to help me. They had none of that. Yet they too were wounded and there were times I knew I needed to "catch" them. But more times than not, seeing as I was living in DC, still rehabbing, going to college and working, I wasn't able to catch Chris, and to a lesser extent Keith, when they stumbled.

I'm not alone in feeling that way. No matter how much effort we put into reaching out and helping our brothers and sisters who struggle with PTSD, with substance abuse, with financial hardships and busted relationships, when they fall, we feel it. We're shattered and we question why this had to happen again. We wonder what we could have done different. We wonder why words fail. We hope to do better next time, knowing that, unfortunately, and without a doubt, there will be a next time. In the future, we hope that our efforts will be enough.

Keith says that he's not a great storyteller. He says that he's not a big talker. But his actions speak loudest and tell the tale well. He was there for me, just as he's there for his family, for his wife, and for his kids. That he's reluctant to share all he experienced while serving his tour of duty in Iraq speaks volumes about him and his desire to protect those he cares about. He doesn't want them to treat him any different from before. He just wants to get on with his life and find enjoyment in the simple pleasures that too many of his brothers and sisters in arms were denied. Call it survivor's guilt, a coping mechanism, what have you: I think of it as quiet heroism, a way to honor those who fell and not stand in the spotlight yourself.

In the meantime, in the quiet moments, you can think about the time before when the falls weren't so drastic, when we landed on muddy football fields and forgiving mats recalling victories, and not the matches we engage in now, when we wrestle with bigger questions with greater consequences than bragging rights.

★★★★★★★★★★★★★★★★★★★★★★★★★★★★★★★★★★★★★★

CHILDHOOD

I was born in Little Rock, Arkansas, in 1986. My dad was an Air Force mechanic who mostly serviced C-130 cargo planes. I also had an uncle who served in the Marines. When my parents divorced in 1990, I moved to Dalton, Georgia. My uncle's family life didn't work out too well for him, either, and later he talked to me about how tough it was to have a good, solid life when in the service. He actually later discouraged me from joining the Marines for that reason. The funny thing is, when I moved to Georgia, I got to be good friends with Chris McDonald. His dad, Jeff, was also a Marine, and he tried to steer me away from going into the military, too. I guess I got to a place in life later on when I wasn't too good at taking people's advice. I respected both those men, so it's on me for being stubborn or whatever. Mostly, though, I think it was because I just didn't have a plan or see a real future for myself.

That wasn't because I didn't have any good influences growing up. A lot of the boys that I went to middle school with, and before that even in elementary school, played recreation league football. We weren't all on the same team. I was on the Eastside Mustangs and one of the other teams was Danville. I've forgotten their team name and mascot, but I do remember that one of the kids on that team was Johnny Joey Jones. We weren't friends back then; he was just another kid I went to school with and played against. I loved football, but I wasn't very good at it. It wasn't until I was a sophomore in high school that I finally weighed a hundred pounds.

I kind of just fell into wrestling. My mom wanted to keep my older sister, Tishia, and I busy, so she had us join the local Amateur Athletic Union wrestling program. It wasn't until you got into middle school that the district school had sports teams. Tishia wrestled and made a lot of little boys cry. Being a cheerleader, she didn't have time for wrestling after elementary school. Basketball was really big in Dalton, but I was too small to be any good at that. I took to wrestling, though, and really liked the idea that it was just me against someone else. I also liked the fact that while I could hold my own in other sports—baseball and football—I was really good at wrestling. Mostly it was one-on-one, though, and if you win nobody else gets the credit for it. It's always on you. If you lose, you aren't letting your teammates down as much as in other sports. You can push yourself as hard as you choose.

The biggest regret is that in my freshman year of high school, I quit wrestling. I got lazy. I wanted to go to parties, not practices. I didn't get along that well with the coaches. I had a really good coach when I was young, James Bethune. He coached me from the time I started until I entered high school. I think I had a hard time with the high school coaches because they weren't him. He was able to teach me and encourage me in a way they couldn't. Even though my dad was still in Little Rock, I don't think that I was lacking for a father figure. My dad and I got along very well, and spending time with him in Arkansas in the summer was good. I also had my grandfathers around. I did a lot of fishing with one of them. So it was bass fishing with my dad in Arkansas and trout fishing with my grandfather in Georgia. It wasn't just fishing; I liked doing anything outdoors.

BONDS OF FRIENDSHIP

My best friend Chris's father, Jeff, was my baseball coach and then in football, too. Again, he was a Marine and was the one who said I should think long and hard about joining the military. But seeing the kind of man he was, how good a coach he was, how he communicated with us and kept us in line and motivated, when I thought about all that later, whatever downside there was to the Marines seemed like no big deal. Also, Chris and I had met when I was maybe nine years old and we bonded pretty quickly. Before I knew it, with Jeff as our coach and Chris around my house or me around his all the time, our families bonded, too. My mom became friends with Chris's mom. My sister was Chris's sister. We were just a big family. You couldn't find closer friends than Chris and me growing up.

I mean, I spent Christmas at his grandparents' house sometimes. Chris and I used to sit around and talk about what our futures would be like. We were going to get married to girls from Dalton, have kids, and see them grow up in Dalton. I admired Chris. He was a type A personality. He was very focused on what he was doing. He was hard-core, and I wasn't. I was really shy as a kid, and Chris accepted that about me. He didn't care that I wasn't best friends with some of the other kids at school who had nice, fancy clothes and everything. Chris didn't give a care about any of that kind of stuff. We hunted together a lot growing up, and his dad was there to help teach us. As an ex-Marine, he was a pretty good shot; actually, he was the best shot I'd ever seen. I watched Jeff one day, sitting around the fire, and he spotted a deer and jumped up and grabbed his rifle. He tripped a bit over some of the firewood we had waiting, but he raised that weapon and shot a doe right between the eyes from 250 yards away. That was impressive.

Jeff also gave me my first deer rifle, a Remington pump-action 30–06 that had belonged to Chris's grandpa. It was a sweet little pump action. Jeff had been an officer in the Marines, and he took gun safety and operating a weapon really seriously. He was generally a pretty laid-back man, but when the guns came out, especially when he was teaching us, he got very serious. Looking back on it now, I can see that gun safety and hunting were the things that I took most seriously.

I was also into music. I had learned to play the drums and performed with the band. Country music was always my favorite, but playing in the band exposed me to other types and I learned to like lots of different kinds. Some buddies formed a band and asked me to play drums in it. I don't remember the name, but we never really did much except goof off. I was a decent student. I graduated with a 3.2 grade point average and went off to Dalton State College. I tried it but it just wasn't for me. I was in the General Studies Program and had no real idea of what I wanted to do with my life. I was considering being a teacher, but that meant being up in front of people, and I don't like to talk very much. I don't think teaching would have worked out very good for me.

Chris knew Joey from football, and they got pretty close because they were teammates. I wasn't a part of that, but Joey and I did have one thing in common—we were after the same girls. So, when Chris said that I should join him and Joey hanging out together, I said, "No. I don't like that guy. We don't need to talk to each other." I'd seen Joey in my neighborhood because he was dating the girl who lived next door to me. He was on the football team; she was a cheerleader. Same old story, right?

I wasn't part of any one particular group, especially not the ones at the top of charts. Chris was the same way, hanging out with people from all different groups. I figured Joey was one of those at the top and we'd have nothing in common. After meeting him a couple of times and spending time with him, though, I realized we did. So, eventually, if I wasn't with Chris, I was with Joey. Or it was all three of us together.

We had a bit of history to get over. There was some drama over a girl I liked. The timing couldn't have been worse. I was involved in a car wreck that injured my buddy and the same girl. I was pretty upset and feeling guilty because I was driving and wasn't hurt. Then, when she woke up, she said Joey's name. Of course, they called him to get him to come over and I was so mad I was determined to beat the crap out of him. Instead, we became inseparable.

★★★★★★★★★★★★★★★★★★★★★★★★★★★★★★★★★

I think Keith and I still "remember" some of our origin story a little differently, but that's part of our relationship. I really only had one girlfriend in high school, Meg, and I spent a decade convincing her to marry me, but before that I had dated, for a brief time, this girl Keith was dating later on. That night they got into a car wreck and as she woke up heavily sedated, she asked for me. Chris called me and I went to the emergency room because it felt like the right thing to do.

When I got there, I was greeted by Chris and Keith (with a row of stitches in the top of his head). Of course, Keith was mad. But not knowing what else to say, I looked at Keith and said, "Hey, man, you look like you need a cigarette." He paused for a second and said, "You're right."

The three of us walked to the back of the parking lot and shared a smoke, talked, and worked out a few years of animosity, and that turned into us becoming brothers.

The night we truly became friends was the night of that crash. Our personalities couldn't be more different, but when we stopped liking the same girls (at the same time) we realized we balanced each other out.

★★★

JOINING UP

I went to college mostly because I had promised my mom that I would. But joining the military had always been on my mind. I was probably high sitting in a math class when we found out about 9/11. That played some part in my decision to enlist, but more than anything it was Jeff. I thought so highly of him and my uncle for having been Marines. And Jeff was a successful man; he was a high school teacher and a coach and people liked and respected him. He had gone into the Marines as an enlisted man and then went through Officer Candidate School to become an officer and then was in reserves. I never considered any other branch of service and signed up. I was going to go to radio electronics. Everything seemed set, except I went out and partied the night before I was to show up. So the next day, I wasn't in the best shape for tests.

To be honest, I think that things worked out for the best with me joining the Army instead. The Army fit me better. At that point in my life, I didn't have the kind of discipline that it required. I had Chris setting a good example for me. He was in college and in the ROTC program, and he was making good on the plan that he had set up for himself. Joey and I had both enlisted in the Marines like we'd talked about, but I'd messed up that plan. I think that Joey kind of surprised Chris and me by joining. But it was exactly what he needed. Like me, he didn't have much of a focus for his life or a plan.

The three of us were all good friends by that time, but it didn't start out that way. It's funny that Joey and I were more like one another than Chris. We both just wanted to party. We were floating along and Chris was in a powerboat with a plan.

THE ONLY PEOPLE WHO "GOT IT"

Serving in the military separated us geographically, but we still kept in touch. Joey and I went off to basic training and boot camp. Chris was still in college for a while in the ROTC program. But the next spring Chris took a semester off college to join the Marine Corps reserves. He wasn't going to have his dad and two best friends in a fraternity without him in it, too. We continued to check in on one another. This was in the early days when Myspace and Facebook were starting, and depending on where we were stationed, we did or didn't have internet access. But we managed to check in every now and then. They'd give me a hard time about the going-away party we had before I went to basic training. Joey was legendary for hosting the best parties in high school, so even after that, he held this one at his house. We played a bunch of flag football and drank. We had a bonfire going, and I fell asleep by it and wound up melting the bottom of my shoes.

We also shared a bit about what we were experiencing. Nothing I experienced before in my life, including my military training, could fully prepare me for what it was like to be deployed for fifteen months in Iraq. In 2007, we started out in Baghdad but jumped around quite a bit. The funny thing was, Joey and Chris were also there serving in different units. We still tried to keep in touch, but it was hard, and there were long periods when we couldn't connect. We were all in high-tempo operational zones, and when we did get a chance to talk, we all expressed our concern for the other two and reassured the others that things were okay. We were fine. Don't worry about me.

The truth was that my Stryker Brigade was acting as a quick response squad. I was operating out of an eight-wheeled up-armored vehicle. One area of Baghdad was pretty bad. There was a Humvee unit there and it was getting beat up pretty bad, and we'd go in there in support of them. We'd clear the area out. We'd stay there for a month and then move on to another area where a Humvee unit was seeing a lot of troops in contact. It seemed like each place we were pivoted to was worse than the one before it. That went on for fifteen months.

The Army had done a good job of preparing us for the fact that things were going to suck. We were going to be uncomfortable. Going into battle and losing friends? Nothing can prepare you for that. I don't know if anybody . . . if there's any way to bear that. We lost twenty-six people out of our battalion in those fifteen months. It was an eventful deployment. Nobody in my squad was killed in action, thank God. But there were several in my company who were, including a guy I wrestled against who was part of the all-Army team.

Nothing brings you closer to the other guys than losing people.

Even if those who got killed weren't friends, weren't in the same squad, whatever, it doesn't matter. You still feel the loss.

But I only felt comfortable talking about things with Joey and Chris. During those fifteen months I was deployed in Iraq, we all made arrangements to spend our leave time together. I felt like I had changed, had become a completely different person after I joined the Army. Joey and Chris, they knew me from before, and during, and then after. They were the people I wanted to talk with about what I'd experienced, what they'd experienced, because we really knew each other. We would get together and drink a few beers and talk for hours. They're still the only ones who know what I saw and did and experienced. I still won't talk about those things with anyone else.

★★★★★★★★★★★★★★★★★★★★★★★★★★★★★★★★★★★★★

Keith's deployment was almost twice as long as mine or Chris's. I got to Iraq in 2007, around the same time Keith did. Chris had just left for Iraq in 2008 shortly before I ended my deployment and Keith came home for his mid-deployment break. Then Chris and Keith came home about the same time in late 2008. Of the three of us, all seeing combat on our respective deployments, Chris was affected most. We didn't see it at first. Keith was getting ready to get out of the Army and I was in EOD school looking at the rest of my career. We were still close, but Chris was always a little more intense, a little more detached. We just didn't realize what was driving that after his deployment. As the next few years passed, a lot changed in my life as Chris and Keith settled back in Dalton preparing for what would be their "after-military career." The year 2008 didn't just see the return of the three of us from war. It was also a year of economic recession, one that hit our one-industry town harder than most. Chris returned to school after his deployment and graduated with a teaching and coaching degree, but the downturned economy meant that by 2010 there were no teaching jobs to find in Dalton. So Chris settled in as a teacher's aide and coaching assistant, moonlighting as private security with Keith. While Chris struggled with the trauma of his deployment, he was also living the trauma of feeling like a failure in his professional life. He wanted to be a teacher and coach like his dad; he also wanted to go back and become an officer in the Marines like his dad was. But none of that seemed to be working out. Chris, an incredibly gifted young man, had two major flaws: he did everything at 110 percent, and he could not accept failure. Both were on high alert by the end of 2011.

★★

AFTEREFFECTS

It didn't take living with Chris to know that he wasn't doing well. He was diagnosed with PTSD and he was battling substance abuse issues. We had pushed him to get help. This went on for a while and in different cycles. Chris had opened up to me and shared stories of some of the traumatic things he experienced. Some of them were things that anybody would have trouble getting over. He chose some of the wrong ways to get over them. I can see now that, at the start and at other times, some of us, including me, were enablers. At other times, when that wasn't seeming to work, we thought the best course of action was to shut him out completely. We did that for short periods of time, too. Nothing seemed to work.

Finally, in the spring of 2012, Joey stepped in again and got us all together for an intervention. He figured that we needed to show a united front, to let Chris see that the bond we all shared together was so strong. We encouraged him to get into rehab for his substance abuse. He agreed, and we got him signed up for rehab. We all felt a bit of relief. We thought our efforts had worked. They hadn't.

On March 16, 2012, Chris took his own life.

I can never know what's completely in a man's heart and mind and what drives their choices. But I think that when Chris sobered up a bit and recognized what he'd done to his family and how far he had pushed everybody, he made that choice.

For a time, the bond between Jeff and I got stretched a bit. He had made the choice to practice tough love with Chris. I was trying to be supportive. That difference affected my relationship with Jeff. Afterward, of course, Jeff and I grew closer than ever. Jeff felt like he hadn't done enough. I felt like I didn't do enough. Both of us tried to blame ourselves.

But it was really rough on Jeff, as you would expect. Just as it was rough on Jeff's wife and Chris's mom, Paige. None of us, his sisters, everybody who tried to help Chris or who knew Chris, felt like they had done enough. All of that affects your relationships.

Jeff took Chris's place. He became one of my best friends. He lived about an hour from me, and I was up there visiting him as often as I could. It's almost been a year now since Jeff passed away. One of the strongest people I ever knew, and COVID got him. But at least the two of us got closer before that. Me and Jeff, when he passed away, were the closest of friends. I still haven't dealt with Jeff's passing. I've got too much other stuff going on to let that affect me right now.

I've got a wife and kids that I have to make sure are getting taken care of. Of course, I met my wife the same way I met all my other girlfriends before. Joey introduced me to Allana. She and Joey were friends on social media. I didn't do the social media thing back then other than to communicate with people I already knew, like Chris and Joey. This was back in 2010, and Joey was in the hospital recovering.

And of course, Joey being Joey, he was looking out for me while he was supposed to be healing up himself. I called him one day and he told me that he had met this girl, Allana, who he thought I would get along with very well. He had told her the same thing about me. He gave me her phone number so I could call her. It turned out that I already knew Allana. We met in elementary school. We lived behind each other for a little while. We went to high school together and talked sometimes, but there was nothing romantic. But now Joey wanted us to get reacquainted.

I listened to him, and Allana and I started talking, and it worked out. It worked out real well. Of course, when you're married or with somebody for a long time, not every day is great. I tease Joey and give him the credit for the bad days.

But I have had a lot fewer of those since I met and married Allana. I really connect with her. When we first met, I wasn't sleeping very well. I'd been diagnosed with PTSD and done some therapies. Mostly it was talking with a therapist, and I had a hard time with that and didn't keep up with it. So, when I met Allana, I was in bad shape. Joey and Chris both knew that. I think that Joey wanted me to get together with Allana as a way for me to heal. As I said, I had PTSD, and adjusting back to civilian life wasn't easy, either. So when I met Allana, I felt comfortable for the first time. It's funny that the Army prepares you to be uncomfortable, but it doesn't do a lot to help you get comfortable. But Allana did that. All of a sudden, I could relax. Even out in public. And I started sleeping better. With her I was calm.

It also helps that I don't have a lot of time to think about things. For about the last ten years, I've worked six to seven days a week. That's about the time since my son was born. I live in Chattanooga now and work at the Volkswagen assembly plant. I'm an equipment tech there. I handle basic maintenance, preventative maintenance on the robots, and recover the computer faults that come up. I also install and finish hardwood flooring with my uncle. I really like to work with my hands. My son is ten now and he's wrestling and I got to be his coach. I really enjoyed that, too. I want to be there for him.

That's what things were like with Chris, with Joey, with Jeff, and with Paige and Morgan and Brooke. They just show up. We go hang out.

I think about Jeff and Chris every day. Chris and I got into a bit there toward the end when I was trying to figure out how to help him. But, you know, I wouldn't go back and change much. Instead of changing things that happened, I'd want to add more moments like when Jeff and Chris and I would go up to the hunting land Jeff owned. I'd like to spend the weekend again in that little cabin that had no power. I'd like to have Jeff and Chris back together there. I don't know if that would change history, but it would be another good moment to have to hang on to.

CONCLUSION

— ★ ★ ★ —

While there are ten people named in the table of contents, throughout this book I've also mentioned many more. That's because these bonds are truly countless throughout our lives.

One of those bonds was with Jeff McDonald, who was a Marine, football coach, teacher, father, and friend. And at times he was all those things to Keith and me. In 2018, Jeff retired from our high school after thirty years of teaching and coaching, and in 2020, after I unexpectedly lost my dad the previous Thanksgiving, Jeff accompanied me on several hunting trips traversing the country for my Fox Nation Outdoors hunting show. Jeff and I spent a lot of time looking out the window of my truck recounting memories, proclaiming regrets, expressing gratitude, and logging miles. Jeff was a warrior to the day he died. Not because of the fight left in him, but for the love and care he kept for Keith and me as his adopted sons in war.

I love these men of war you've met in these pages. They remind me of what a man can do with strong hands, a determined mind, and a warrior's heart. They remind me of who I want to be, and perhaps on my best days, have been. War is ugly, unfair, and something to be avoided at all costs, but when fighting a war is necessary, I've learned you don't need much more than a few highly motivated good ol' boys and a damn good leader to accomplish a mission.

The bonds we share with one another, and with those we've served with along the way, define what it means to be not blood brothers, but brothers in blood. Our unbroken bonds, forged on many battlefields, are not the lingering resentment of wars but the resolute resilience of those who fight them. Now it's your turn. Find brothers and sisters in the tragedies and triumphs God and life throw your way. Lean in to those who choose to fight with you and let those who might be willing help you get back up when you're knocked down. Be there for them as well, as warriors are for one another. Find your unbroken bonds in the battle of life and tell stories of victory and defeat long into old age, as we hope to do.

ACKNOWLEDGMENTS

I want to recognize those who contributed to this book. Each chapter is the result of a lifelong friendship. These are some of my best friends, important mentors, and impactful colleagues. The tremendous courage each showed to pull back the curtain on their life of service, and sometimes tragedy, to give us all a deeper glimpse into what it means to forge a bond with another person through struggle and war should be honored. I'm so proud of them and likewise eternally grateful they trusted us to tell their stories. I love you all!

Pete Hegseth has always been more than a colleague. From the first time we met, he has embraced me as a brother and teammate. His generosity has opened doors for me in his wake, and his creativity and insight led to the creation of the "Modern Warriors" concept. Thanks to his work, dozens of men and women from our wars have had their voices heard in books and on television. I'm forever grateful he had the faith in me to write the next Modern Warriors story. Thanks, brother!

My family has been the rock upon which all things are built. My wife, Meg, deserves credit for any task I actually complete. She has been in my life in some way or another since the day we met, and I am most grateful for her patience and love. She inspires me to be a better man, even when I prove to her daily how much work I still need to do. My mother, Joyce, continues to remind me of God's grace, and her resilience through a sometimes difficult life is a constant reminder to keep pushing. My son, Joseph, saved my life, and my daughter, Margo, reminded me that life is truly a blessing. The rest of my family are necessary pieces of a full life. I'm forever grateful for the village on Bass Drive, which raised me to be the man I am today. Thank you, and I love you.

ABOUT THE AUTHOR

JOHNNY JOEY JONES provides military analysis across all FOX News media platforms, including FOX News Channel and FOX Business Network, also serving as a fill-in host for many of the most popular shows. Additionally, he hosts FOX Nation Outdoors on the network's digital streaming service, FOX Nation. A Marine Corps veteran who reached the rank of staff sergeant, Jones suffered a life-changing injury in Afghanistan, resulting in the loss of both of his legs above the knee. Since his recovery, he has dedicated himself to improving the lives of all veterans and their families.